Percy Bolingbroke St. John, James H. Graff

The Snow Ship

The Adventures of Canadian Emigrants

Percy Bolingbroke St. John, James H. Graff

The Snow Ship
The Adventures of Canadian Emigrants

ISBN/EAN: 9783337258665

Printed in Europe, USA, Canada, Australia, Japan

Cover: Foto ©ninafisch / pixelio.de

More available books at **www.hansebooks.com**

CAPT. MAYNE REID'S
CELEBRATED NOVELS.

James H. Graff,
Baltimore
No. 2123.

London: CHARLES H. CLARKE, 13, Paternoster Row.

Sold by all **BOOKSELLERS** and at all **RAILWAY STATIONS**.

THE MAYNE REID LIBRARY.

In Foolscap 8vo, handsomely printed on toned paper, cloth gilt, price 3s. 6d. per Volume, with numerous Illustrations by HARRISON WEIR, W HARVEY, HUARD, &c.

LOST LENORE;
Or, THE ADVENTURES OF A ROLLING STONE.

THE WILD HUNTRESS.

THE WHITE GAUNTLET.

THE MAROON;
Or, PLANTER LIFE IN JAMAICA.

THE TIGER HUNTER;
Or, A HERO IN SPITE OF HIMSELF.

THE SCALP HUNTERS;
Or, ROMANTIC ADVENTURES IN NORTHERN MEXICO.

THE RIFLE RANGERS;
Or, ADVENTURES IN SOUTHERN MEXICO.

THE HALF-BLOOD;
Or, OCEOLA, THE SEMINOLE.

THE WOOD RANGERS.

THE WHITE CHIEF:
A LEGEND OF NORTHERN MEXICO.

THE HUNTERS' FEAST;
Or, CONVERSATIONS AROUND THE CAMP FIRE.

THE CLIFF CLIMBERS;
Or, THE LONE HOME ON THE HIMALAYAS.

London: CHARLES H. CLARKE, 13, Paternoster Row.

Sold by all **BOOKSELLERS** and at all **RAILWAY STATIONS**.

THE SNOW SHIP;

OR.

The Adventures of Canadian Emigrants.

BY

PERCY B. ST. JOHN,

AUTHOR OF "THE SAILOR CRUSOE," "THE YOUNG BUCCANEER," "THE BACKWOOD RANGERS," &c., &c.

LONDON:
C. H. CLARKE, 13, PATERNOSTER ROW.

CONTENTS.

CHAPTER		PAGE
I.	Out West	1
II.	A Forest on Fire	15
III.	A Night Engagement	25
IV.	Travelling in the Snow	32
V.	The Lake of the Burning Plains	42
VI.	Summer Work	51
VII.	Lost in the Woods	57
VIII.	The Martin Trappers	64
IX.	Settling	70
X.	The Sleigh	78
XI.	The Boy Sentry	84
XII.	The Antoines	90
XIII.	The Caribous	94
XIV.	The Carcajou	99
XV	The Caribou Hunt	104
XVI.	The Moose Hunt	114
XVII.	Lost in the Snow	122
XVIII.	The Launch of the Snow Ship	131
XIX.	A Storm on the Lake	137
XX.	Frozen In	142
XXI.	Fever on Board	150
XXII.	An Unexpected Reunion	159
XXIII.	A Rencontre	164
XXIV.	The Snow Ship Deserted	171
XXV.	Under the Pines	177
XXVI.	A Discovery	181
XXVII.	Pete and Jack	285

CHAPTER		PAGE
XXVIII.	Perils and Dangers	192
XXIX.	The Snow Ship Again	197
XXX.	A Ride on an Ox	203
XXXI.	The Schooner Voyage	206
XXXII.	A Wedding	213
XXXIII.	Tree'd by Wolves	216
XXXIV.	An Unexpected Meeting	221
XXXV.	A Canadian Lake Hunt	226
XXXVI.	Jack's Cats	236
XXXVII.	The Bald Eagle. The Pigeon Cloud	243
XXXVIII.	The Conclusion	253

THE MERCHANT OF YAKOUTSK.

I.	The Young Widow	259
II.	The Yakouta Hunter	265
III.	Nijnei Kolimsk	273
IV.	The Frozen Sea	279
V.	On the Ice	288
VI.	Encounter with Tchouktchas	295
VII.	The Summer and Autumn	301
VIII.	The Voyage Home	306
	The Mammoth	316

THE SNOW SHIP.

CHAPTER I.

OUT WEST.

FAR AWAY! Far as the eye of man can reach, naught meets the view but forest, bush and water, with the arctic sun rising warm and genial over broad waves and mighty trees. Taking as a centre a small hill, destitute of any vegetation, save scanty grass and one stunted oak, millions of acres of wood clothe and conceal a soil richly fertile, but fresh as from the hands of the Creator, in all its wild, gloomy, and naked sublimity; while on the other hand, to the very roots of the trees, the waves of a mighty ocean come rolling in. And all is still. The voiceless wind, that harmony of time, scarce shakes the tree tops or their sighing boughs, while the glass-like surface of the water is all but unruffled. Flowers bloom beneath, and the air is balmy above. On what sea-shore, then, is this huge forest placed? On no sea-shore,—for the vast expanse of water is fresh as the bubbling streamlets, that run to it down the grassy hill sides.

Where are we then?

In the land of the grizzly bear and plodding beaver, of hungry musquitoes, and grey and clumsy moose deer, of peach-flavoured snow apples, and mighty lakes and noble forests; a land vast in extent, unsurpassed in riches, of admirable climate, whether during the summer heats when the sun shines warm, or during the winter when covered by its white mantle; a land of sleighs, snow shoes and snow ships—in the interior of Canada, that brightest jewel in the British crown, whether we consider its vast extent, its singular suitability to the Anglo-Saxon race, its mighty undeveloped resources, or its proximity to our own shores.

Of late the tide of emigration has flowed so rapidly towards this richly endowed land, that settling is comparatively easy, while roads, stage coaches, and steamers facilitate the progress of the adventurer, who seeks to exchange the hopeless toils of the old land for the bright prospects of the new. But forty years ago, the case was different, and whoso ventured beyond certain districts, had to endure perils and dangers and difficulties and disappointments, enough to turn any but a brave and undaunted man from the task.

Forty years ago, the spot to which we have alluded was an untravelled wilderness, hundreds of miles from any settlement, while not even a bridle path existed through the mighty forest of beech, elm, and bass wood, of sugar maple, hemlock, cherry, butternut, oak, and birch; but it was blessed with a salubrious climate and a fertile soil, watered by crystal springs and brooks, and bathed by a mighty inland sea, to the shores of which we will now descend.

Facing the hillock, to which we have already alluded, the forest left a narrow opening where the soil was probably too arid to admit of the growth of trees, and any one standing with his back to the eminence would have a good view of the vast lake, which, though wrapped in deceitful repose, could at times be lashed into fury, and exhibit storms that would have done little discredit to old ocean itself.

Many a time and oft, doubtless, the painted Indian had here launched his bark canoe, long ere the white man came to overthrow his empire; but now, for reasons which will appear in the course of our narrative, he seldom visited this part of his ancient dominions.

However, had a warrior been on the spot, his conceptions of solitude might have been somewhat disturbed, for, just as the sun burst warmly through some water clouds, the unmistakable echo of the human voice broke the stillness of the woods—which before had been, apparently, a virgin solitude.

"Pull her into deeper water, Harry," said a voice, "one might as well take pails and dip them out. It is awfully slow work."

"And therefore I like it," replied another voice, in a methodical tone; "it is quiet, easy, and profitable."

"I am rejoiced to hear you say so," laughed the other, "so land me. I may fly at higher game."

"Very well, my dear Ralph;—but why give yourself so much unnecessary trouble?"

"Trouble!—why it is the object of life to be ever doing. I can't bear your quiet fishing. There's a good fellow."

And as he spoke, a scow—the most primitive boat ever invented—came in sight, containing the two speakers. The craft was a long-shaped, flat-bottomed kind of punt, of the same width all along, but rising gently at each end, built of two-inch plank, very much resembling the rafts used to ferry horses and vehicles over rivers.

The craft contained two youths—the elder of whom, habited in the ordinary shooting dress of the British isles, leaned on his gun, while he gazed with a half-amused, half-contemptuous glance at his companion. He was tall, erect, with an open and manly countenance, somewhat tanned by exposure to the sun, but with an unmistakable air of refinement about him. His companion was shorter and stouter, wearing over the somewhat faded garb of the old country, the blouse and red cap of the Canadian habitant. This youth was about sixteen, and having impelled the scow towards the shore, he again threw his bait—a piece of brass about the shape and size of a tablespoon bowl, with a hook soldered to the narrow end—at which salmon, trout, and black bass caught eagerly, the troller quietly taking one about every five minutes.

The elder brother, for such was their relationship, having leaped ashore, the younger put out again, and once more casting his trolling line, he again paddled the heavy scow into deep water. The other, smiling, looked about him, and was preparing for a start towards the woods, when a sound fell on his ear which made his whole face become radiant with delight.

"Keep to the right, Harry, out of sight," he said, in a loud whisper, which was heard plainer on the placid waters than a cry.

"Ay, ay," said the phlegmatic Harry, but without hurrying himself to comply with the other's wishes.

Nothing more passed, for Ralph at once entered beneath the shelter of the forest, and stooping down, concealed himself in the deep hollow of a button-tree. What had startled Ralph was a sudden cry in the woods, or rather from the slope of a hill at some distance, a wild and unearthly din with which he was well acquainted.

A pack of hungry wolves were in full chase of a deer; and as he well knew that the animal would instinctively take to the water, and this open space showed signs of an old deer path, there was every chance not only of the fierce animals being baulked of their prey, but also of its becoming his prize. The young man's heart beat wildly. During the short space of time he had been in Canada, he had used his English practice to advantage, shooting ample stores of smaller game, but this was his first deer.

He had not long to wait. Soon he saw the head and horns of a large buck rising over the hill, and next moment it came dashing down the slope right for the water, followed by the ravenous wolves, which were close upon its heels. Ralph, though his heart was thumping against his breast with emotion, took steady aim, and fired at the fore shoulder just as the animal passed. The deer halted not a moment, but bounded even more rapidly on towards the placid waters. Not so the wolves, which halted, stood still, showed their white-pointed teeth, and seemed about to attack the young hunter. Hastily loading, he gave the pack both barrels, and then rushing towards them, fired a brace of horse pistols into their midst. This was too much for the cowardly animals, so they turned tail and fled.

Ralph now directed his attention towards the deer, which after seeking refuge from its four-footed enemies, in the deep waters of the lake, was slowly swimming ashore, the wavelets all around it tinged with eddies of blood. Fainter and fainter grew its efforts, until just as it reached the land it fell on its fore-knees, cast one look' as of reproach, at the young hunter, and lay dead.

With difficulty, Ralph drew his prize to a dry place, and then stood still to contemplate, with feelings which can scarcely be described, but may be understood, the first buck he had ever killed. On examination afterwards, it proved that a ball and five buck-shot had penetrated the body, one even entering the heart: but it is almost incredible the distance this animal will run after being mortally wounded.

"What a mighty heap of flesh," said the voice of his brother, awakening Ralph from a reverie which had lasted at least a quarter of an hour; "who's going to carry it?"

"We are, to be sure," laughed Ralph, recovering himself, "so lend a hand. It is lucky father made me take a few lessons in butchering, or else this would prove but sorry game. We can cut off a leg, and that, with some of your salmon-trout, will make a grand breakfast. The rest we can leave in the scow. Come, bear a hand, old fellow, or the wolves will be ready to eat us."

And hastily pulling a long bright knife from its sheath, he began to cut up the deer in quite a scientific manner, a task in which his phlegmatic brother assisted him with apparent reluctance.

While this duty is being performed, we shall take the opportunity to explain how two evidently well-educated youths found themselves thus on the very uttermost skirts of civilization; on a spot where never before had the foot of white man trodden, and which for ages had been the battle-ground of the painted and remorseless savage, as well as the retreat of the prowling panther and the bear.

Ralph and Henry were the sons of a gentleman farmer, the younger off-shoot of a noble house, too proud to see him work for his bread, too extravagant and selfish to assist him in the world. Early in life Mr. Hatfield had married the daughter of a neighbour, who was one of his uncle's tenants. This lady was remarkable as much for her good sense as for her beauty, and brought her husband as a dowry, her industry, cheerfulness, and gentle affection. From that moment his noble relations cut him off from the parent-tree, and. not content with this, commenced a secret persecution, in the hope of driving him from the county where he was known.

But Mr. Hatfield was brave, firm, and fortified by a sense of right, supported by deep religious principles, which had been instilled into him by his pious and devoted young wife. He therefore continued on his way utterly indifferent to all petty annoyances, and even to the painful voice of calumny. Three children were born to him, all sons. The eldest selected his father's occupation, unless, indeed, fortune should favour him enough to open the way to the army. His relatives would gladly have given him a commission, but he would owe nothing to them. Henry, the second son, of a somewhat slow nature, but shrewd and studious, passionately fond of books and angling, was placed in a solicitor's office, though with an ultimate view to the bar.

John was but a child of eight when the circumstances occurred to which we now refer.

Instead of dissipating his small patrimony when he came of age, Mr. Hatfield married a farmer's daughter and took the farm off his father-in-law's hands, thus becoming his uncle's tenant. Had he spent his money in fashionable riot, broken Susan's heart, and turned out a model rake, not a word would have been said against him. It was his prudent resort to labour which ruined him with his friends.

His uncle died suddenly, just as the lease expired, and Hatfield found himself at the mercy of a coarse, bloated, fox-hunting cousin, who hated him, all the more that in days gone by he had dared to look at Susan with a favourable eye. Hatfield's next neighbour was perhaps the most perfect specimen of a heavy agriculturist that the good old days could have ever produced. He had not an atom of intelligence beyond money-making; knew the value of wheat and oats and sheep to a penny, and made the corn laws his god. In everything else he was an ignorant stupid boor.

This man one day, in a most offensive manner, suddenly informed Hatfield, chuckling all the while, that he had taken his farm over his head, and that he gave him a week to move. Words ensued, the neighbour was grossly insulting, Hatfield dealt him one blow, followed by a sound drubbing, and then the stout and surly brute, falling on a stone, lay for a short time as if dead. The cousin now came on the scene. He knew Hatfield's sensitive dislike of publicity. The matter he said had better be hushed up, and the farm transferred to the neighbour; and that his cousin might remove with his family elsewhere, after taking the purchase-money, and a thousand pounds left by his uncle, of which Hatfield had not yet heard.

"Not in this country," he said, sternly, and he kept his word, becoming from that moment a most reserved man, to whom the sight of any but his own family was hateful.

Canada was then popular. Many retired officers in the army, with families, and too poor to live in England, had there found a happy home. True, it had its perils and its dangers, but none of these were likely to daunt Hatfield. Summoning his family around him, he called them all to his councils, and laid the whole state of the case before them.

Mrs. Hatfield soon saw that he had set his heart on going, and like a good and faithful wife, she at once gave her vote in favour of the project. Ralph, who had heard much of the variety and quantity of game in the promised land, was enthusiastic in furthering his father's views; while Henry, though heaving a sigh at his removal from his peculiar field of study, manfully plucked up his spirits at the sight of his father's troubles, and after a brief inward struggle agreed to go. No sooner had he made this resolve than a recollection of the wondrous abundance of fish in Canadian waters, almost reconciled him to this sudden change in his fortunes.

The family had always been so thoroughly united that no one thought of a separation.

Mr. Hatfield, in his leisure hours, had made the colony his special study. Under other circumstances, he would have hired or bought a lot near the settlements; but the conduct of his immediate neighbour had inflicted a blow from which he felt he should not soon recover. A kind of quiet but settled misanthropy had fixed upon his soul, not making him crabbed, disagreeable, or selfish, but creating a desire for solitude, except as regarded his own family.

Ever careful, the father transmitted the bulk of his money to a banker in Canada, retaining only enough to pay the family passage and provide such necessaries as were best procurable in England. This done, the exiles embarked on board a ship on a timber voyage to Quebec. It was late in the year, so that they experienced very rough weather, with snow and sleet; and by the shifting of the cargo a plank started, and the leak was only stopped when nearly every particle of food was destroyed. For four days and four nights their sufferings were fearful; but at length, the gale abating, they landed in Quebec, five as forlorn-looking wretches as ever emigration cast upon the hospitable shores of Canada.

But theirs were brave hearts, and nothing daunted by the sufferings they had endured, no sooner was the winter over than the whole party started towards the interior, with the intention of selecting a spot for a permanent residence, and preparing it to a certain extent ere they expended any money in stock. The first part of their journey was performed by water, but, when once landed, they were obliged to travel, first through partially cleared and occupied lands, then through the wild bush and dense forest. Hatfield, while staying in Quebec, had associated much with an old trapper, himself a wanderer and fond of solitude, and this man, discovering the Englishman to be made of congenial stuff, had pointed out a spot on the map where they would find grass, wood, and water, the three great requisites of an emigrant.

The whole store and outfit of our adventurers consisted of a narrow cart on two wheels, drawn by a stout and patient ox, some bags of biscuit, coffee, sugar, with a box of indispensable tools, some kitchen and other utensils; with these the cart was loaded, and upon it, when practicable, sat Mrs. Hatfield and her little boy. Each of the others carried a haversack, had a gun slung behind, while a huge axe rested on the shoulder ready for action. As long as they had not reached the confines of civilization, the way, though rude, was practicable. The roads and bridle paths, which we shall have ample opportunities of describing more minutely, enabled them to advance, though slowly, yet with certainty.

But the day came when they entered the pathless forest, with no guide but a pocket compass and the stars.

The order of march was now as follows. Mr. Hatfield, selecting as open a place between the trees as possible, would glance his eye at his compass, then picking out a tree as far off in as direct a line as possible, would walk straight to it, clearing obvious obstructions by the way with his axe, his two elder sons following close ahead of the ox to remove minor ones, and so on from early morn to dewy eve.

At times much progress was made in a day, while on others not a mile of ground was crossed. Courage and perseverance however prevailed, and at the end of two months from leaving Quebec, they reached the shores of the great fresh-water sea, wearied, exhausted, footsore, but full of hope, of thankfulness, of wonder, not unmixed with admiration at the vast sublimity of the scene which lay before them.

Mr. Hatfield was too experienced a man to rush at once to a conclusion. He knew that success depended on his selecting a good location, not too far from the water, where the land was rich, and oak, ash, elm, beech, bass wood, and sugar maple abounded. It was too late in the season to sow to any advantage. He decided, therefore, to erect a shanty, clear as much land as possible, ready for the plough, and then return to the settlements ere the winter set in. In the spring they would come up with their stores and finally settle.

The spot selected was a natural clearing or beaver meadow—a field of some twenty acres, left by these ingenious animals, whose dam, however, had long since been broken through and destroyed. To the north was a grove of pines, while round the whole clearing was a close belt of timber, growing thinner, however, outwards, until it was so sparsely treed as to be separated from the general forest.

The shanty was erected close to the pine grove. It is the rudest kind of dwelling known in the woods, and in this instance was composed simply of upright posts stuck into the ground and bound together with wooden spikes and withes, while the roof, slanting from the higher side, was hastily and rudely formed of poles, boughs, and prairie grass.

There was no help for it but to subsist on fish and game, sparing their biscuits and flour as much as possible; but as Hatfield and his two elder sons were expert fowlers and anglers, this was no great trouble. The next thing was to commence clearing. This, to a new-comer, was work far harder than they could possibly have conceived. Chopping down trees may sound very easy, but Mr. Hatfield and his sons soon discovered that it was an art in itself to wield the axe, while in the summer months the task was fearfully laborious, especially as during that season the musquitoes and black flies were a terrible nuisance.

Of the severity of this species of labour, no one unacquainted with the difficulty of clearing the bark can form any accurate conception. Felling the trees, however, forms the least part of it. When they are down, they of course cannot, with the scanty resources of the emigrant, be removed, but must be sawn and cut up into convenient blocks for removal or burning. This done, the hardest work has to follow. In such forests as these, the roots of the giant trees have been spreading underground for ages, forming a close and perfect network some eight or ten feet beneath the surface. To dig up the mass of interlaced roots would defy the strength and patience of ordinary men; and it is only the wonderful dexterity of the Canadian—and, indeed, of the American generally—in handling his axe, that enables him to enter upon, far less accomplish, so difficult a task. Their dexterity is indeed truly remarkable. Three men have been seen—one without a right arm—to fell a tree four feet in diameter in three quarters of an hour. This at first sight may appear no very formidable feat; but, after a few days' trial, the tremendous difficulties of such an undertaking will begin to loom upon the amateur backwoodsman. Not many years ago, an officer of Marines quartered in Canada, who thought himself, and who really was, no contemptible axeman, undertook for a wager to fell a certain tree, some three feet in diameter, in a week. He made certain of winning, and commenced work in the most sanguine spirits; but the end of three days found his hands blistered painfully, and the tree as upright, and almost uninjured, as before. At the expiration of the time agreed on, another week was given him, and still the monarch of the wood held his head erect. The story went abroad—this of course after the bet was lost—that he was found one night turning out some of his men to take a sly chop at the tree in the dark. Such is emigrants' work.

But our adventurers had come out to work, and at it they went with a will. At daybreak they were up, and every second morning two started in search of fish or game, which, being abundant, they never failed to capture in sufficient quantities. This dispensation of Providence makes Canada one of the safest resorts for the hardy and determined settler. Like all other colonies, it is no place for idlers or fine gentlemen. Men and women must both go prepared to work with great determination and energy.

At the back of the pine grove Mr. Hatfield had discovered a lot of about forty acres, which seemed to be suitable land. It was, it is true, densely covered by large trees; but this is the case in every good farm; the beaver meadow, with its high grass and bushes, being only fit for the ox to pasture on.

These three English-born emigrants, nurtured in comfort, and for whom labourers had done the heavy work of farming in England, now began their labour steadily, resolutely, and with a determination never to give up. They knew that the trees must come down, and when down, that they must be burnt. They were also well aware that the stumps must be endured for years, until they rotted, were gradually burned, or removed in other ways, that will be fully explained as we proceed.

Mr. Hatfield, Ralph, and Harry began, then, one July morning when the sun was hotter than in England at the same time. The task at once appeared to them in all its herculean magnitude. Ere the sun had half risen to its meridian, they were scarcely able to work from actual languor; but all persevered until mid-day, when, with a sigh of relief, they rushed beneath the shadow of the trees, to seek shelter and refreshment. For several days after, though continuing resolutely, they were stiff and in pain; this feeling, however, gradually wore off, though the work done was for a long time very indifferent.

Meanwhile, Mrs. Hatfield and John were not idle. As soon as a tree was down, and certain branches chopped off, the ox was harnessed to it, and the log drawn away towards a pile at the end of the clearing, which pile was, when the boughs were dried in the sun, fired and burned. What in other lands is a source of boundless wealth, is here destroyed as a thing without value—indeed, a nuisance.

Such was the state of things on the morning to which we have already referred in the opening part of our narrative.

CHAPTER II.

A FOREST ON FIRE.

No sooner had Ralph cut such a joint as seemed suitable to the wants of the family for the day, placed the rest in the scow, and sent it afloat in the lake, anchoring it by means of a heavy stone and a long rope, than he took up his gun, slung the venison on his back, and, followed by Harry with a load of fine fish, started on his way home, where their return, he knew, was impatiently expected. Their path was across the hillock already mentioned, and when its summit was reached Ralph again halted—he had done so dozens of times—to admire the beauty of the prospect before him.

To his left, slumbering in its might, was the silvery lake; while far as the eye could reach, north, east, south, waved the tall and varied tree-tops of that mighty forest, which, doubtless, had been growing up and dying away again to renew the vigour of the soil, since the days when the great earth was prepared for the residence of man.

At the distance of a little more than a mile could be seen the small clearing or beaver meadow, where the family shanty stood, marked by its spiral column of blue smoke, in striking contrast to the black vaporous cloud which rose from the stump clearing, where the huge half-green logs and boughs were smouldering away.

"This is the country for a man to live in," said Ralph, striking the butt-end of his gun upon the sward; "it is grand. No petty restrictions of hedges, ditches, or game laws. Here, in the sight of heaven, we are free to roam, to shoot, to fish, to live and carve out our fortunes, uncontrolled by man."

"It's very well and very fine," said Harry, quietly;

"but hedges and ditches are excellent boundaries of property, which otherwise might give us lawyers more occupation than it does now. Free shooting and fishing is all very well, but the day will come when that will be as impossible here as in England."

"Heaven forbid!" cried Ralph, drawing a long breath; "I am no misanthrope, but 'tis a glorious feeling to know that in these vast solitudes we are unrestrained by conventionalities and customs; that all we see before us we are free to use as we will—wood, water, game, the beasts of the field, and the fowls of the air."

"Until Government finds us out and makes us pay rent and taxes," added Harry, slily.

"That will be a long time hence, when, perhaps, old and sobered down, I may be glad to pay for its protection. But come on, Harry, I am getting fearfully hungry."

"Hist," cried Harry, who on an emergency would always show an amount of energy that astonished his more even-tempered brother; "look yonder!"

Before we record Ralph's reply, we may here mention that the season had been unusually dry, not a drop of rain having fallen for more than a month, so that the trees were far less moist than usual, while the grass was dry and inflammable as tinder; besides which, the broken underwood, vegetable substances, fallen branches, bark and withered trees, formed admirable conductors. The settlers, too, from want of experience, had not sufficiently isolated their log-heaps.

"The clearing is on fire!" cried Ralph, standing for a moment utterly helpless and dumb-founded.

No one in this country, even those who have witnessed some of the fearful conflagrations that sometimes desolate London streets, can form any idea of the fury and

A FOREST ON FIRE. 17

rapidity with which fires rage through the vast forests of America during a dry, hot season, when the carelessness of a settler, or the malicious recklessness of a camper-out, has once set a thicket in a blaze. In clearing land, much brushwood and lops of trees are cast about, and when the weather is hot and dry, with a brisk wind, the fire will run along the grass and dry leaves with inconceivable rapidity.

When Harry cried out and drew his brother's attention—which was, indeed, needless—he had been startled by an extraordinary roaring in the woods, something like the crashing, crackling detonation of distant and incessant thunder, followed by the uprising of a huge column of black and vaporous smoke, to which succeeded, in an instant, one vast blaze, the flames ascending straight to the sky, a hundred feet and more above the tops of the tallest trees.

They knew at once that the fire was upon their own clearing, and for a moment they felt not only no apprehension, but a belief that the devouring element would do their work for them. But next instant a faint breeze rose, the lake waters were rippled, the tall tree-tops waved majestically, and the lurid flames came rolling on towards the pine grove in red-hot billows, surmounted by a canopy of black, pitchy, sulphurous smoke that overshadowed the sky.

On! on! with a rapidity scarcely to be conceived, spread the fearful conflagration, fed at every step by fresh combustible auxiliaries in the shape of trees, whose trunks, bark, and leaves contained vast quantities of inflammable resin. Scarcely less quickly did the two youths, now seriously alarmed, cast away game, fish,—all save their arms and their hunting knives,—and rush with bounding steps that emulated the gait of aboriginal settlers.

The belt of timber that surrounded the clearing was, we have already remarked, itself surrounded by an open circle—this arising from a simple cause as yet wholly a secret to the inexperienced settlers—where, though the forest once had been, no trees now grew, save that from a mass of decaying vegetable matter young shoots began to spring up, giving promise of future maturity. Towards this space it was that the two bold and adventurous youths hurried, desolation already chilling their hearts, for now, like a flash of lightning, the conviction came to their minds that the shanty was too near the pine wood.

Hurrying on with all the agility of youth, and that speed which anxiety for others will lend to the human frame, they were soon close to the open belt, when, to their inexpressible horror and grief, they saw the clear, liquid, forked flames playing on the moss and bark of the timbered circle, next instant to rise with a rush and a roar upwards, until every leaf and bough was on fire.

Still the trunks were free from fire, and with undaunted hearts, the two brave boys rushed beneath the arches of burning branches, when, with a crackling roar as of desultory musket-shooting, and a rush as of a blast furnace, the underbrush caught, and drove them back blackened, breathless to the open ground. Defeated at this point, they at once hurried to another, but everywhere in vain—trees, grass, bushes, were all kindled, and the whole beaver prairie or meadow was encircled by a wall of fierce red fiery flame, charred stumps, and dense, black, choking smoke.

"To the stream!" cried Ralph, fiercely.

Harry made no reply. These sluggish natures, once roused, are terrible for good or evil. With him, all sign of sloth and indolence had vanished. He was now the undaunted soldier who would as readily have charged a battery of a hundred guns, as have leaped a dike. He knew what his brother meant, and wasted no time in words.

On the northern side of the beaver meadow was the stream which, previous to the destruction of the beaver dam by the redskins, had been the centre of their village. It had flashed across the mind of Ralph that they might fight their way up this watery path to the vicinity of the shanty, and thus discover what had become of their parents and younger brother.

The stream was neither very wide nor very deep, so that it was arched over not only by boughs, but by parasitical plants, which, just as they reached the vicinity of its mouth, were being caught by the curling flames. Nothing daunted, they placed their guns and powder in a safe place, and stooping low, began to ascend the stream, casting glances of deep anxiety overhead, where the yellow dancing flames were lapping up the vital sap of the trees, and showering every instant a whole volley of sparks on their devoted heads. Still on they went, though scorched by fire and choked by smoke, until, about a hundred feet from the mouth, the crashing fall of several withered trees just in front, warned them that they could penetrate no farther, but rather to beat a precipitate retreat, ere such an accident happening in their rear should consign them to certain death.

The feelings of the young men, cut off from all knowledge of the fate of their relatives, their minds full of mysterious dread and terror, alternately racked and harassed by doubt and elevated by hope, may now be said to have reached a pitch of intensity which could scarcely be surpassed. Not that they utterly despaired. They knew the calm courage and fertility of invention which characterized their father, while they entertained a faint hope in their inmost hearts as to the centre of the beaver meadow being a safe though unpleasant retreat. They resolved, then, not utterly to despond, but to be ready for any emergency that might occur.

Their first task was to make for the rear of the flames, to the clearing whence the conflagration had started, in the hope of following up the track of the fire; but they found that though the underbrush and limbs of the trees were all consumed, and the wood presented only a mass of blackened poles, they were still on fire, while the ground was red-hot and utterly impassable.

Nothing remained to them but to wait patiently. It was not clear that the flames would extend across the open circle, unless, indeed, the wind rose still higher, when whole sheaves of fire would be carried bodily through the air; and then such a disaster as once before occurred might again take place, when a conflagration raged until it had destroyed a region of forest one hundred and forty miles in extent and sixty miles in width.

Retracing their steps, and again shouldering their guns, the two young men, in moody silence, exhausted, wearied, and faint, strode from the sickening neighbourhood of the fire to the mound, where, nature asserting its rights, they cooked and ate that food which was so necessary to support their sinking frames, but from which, despite their hunger, their stomachs almost revolted, so powerful is the influence exercised by the mind over the body.

Then they sat upon the sward, their chins resting on their knees, around which their arms were clasped; watching the huge furnace, that seethed and blazed, and crackled and smoked at their feet, like the mouth of some mighty volcano, whose crater vomited forth fire and flame for the first time after ages of quiet and repose. Now it seemed to smoulder, as the wind abated; but the burning pile itself rarefying the atmosphere, kept up a breeze, which every now and then fanned the smouldering mass into fresh bursts of fire.

And thus the weary day passed, and night fell upon the scene, which now assumed an air perfectly hellish. The dreary night, the lurid, curling flames, the heavy clouds of white and black smoke, the sparks that flew upwards, the roaring of the fiery furnace, the hissing of the sap in the huge trunks, all presented to the senses of sight and hearing a scene and sounds never to be forgotten by the beholder.

All the afternoon the heat had been intense, irrespective of the fire, and both the boys had cast earnest and almost imploring glances at the sky, in the hope that the heavens would send forth a deluge, and thus assist in extinguishing the flames. But not a sign could they see of tears in that dry, arid, and sultry-looking sky, until just before night-fall some huge, double-headed thunder clouds showed themselves on the edge of the horizon, rising, as it were, out of the still waters of the lake in a north-westerly direction.

About an hour after sun-down, the distant and rumbling growl of the thunder itself warned them to seek some kind of shelter.

"Let us go to the scow," said Ralph, earnestly but hoarsely; "we can do no good here."

Harry followed with downcast looks. Neither dared venture an opinion as to the fate of those dear ones who, it was quite clear, were, dead or alive, within the awful circle of fire, which yet lay before them in all its horrors. The scow was hauled in, a tarpaulin sackcloth, which had served to cover their cart during the journey, was cast over a cross pole which rested on two short upright posts, and then preparations were made for the night.

Neither thought of sleeping; but, seated side by side, with arms entwined around waist and neck as in more boyish days, the two sad brothers awaited the coming storm and the next day. The scow was anchored stem and stern in a shallow pool behind a spit of land, so that, come what might, they were comparatively safe.

About twenty minutes passed, and then, with a rush that for a moment rocked the flat boat, a nor'-wester was upon them, accompanied by lightning, which soon became incessant. Clap after clap of thunder seemed to shake the zenith, while the huge sheets of lightning seemed to reveal the approach of advancing piles of mountains,—the dark clouds that carried the storm within their centre. Every moment the storm increased in grandeur, until at length its wild fury was perfectly awful.

And not one drop of rain.

Then suddenly an appalling and blinding flash was followed by a succession of fearful and deafening peals, that rolled off in tremulous shocks one after another into the distance, only to be taken up by fresh crashes of thunder overhead. Then came the blast howling along, and the heavy fall of huge monarchs of the forest soon proclaimed its power.

Then a lull, and along the waters the whispering patter, as of tiny feet on soft sand beach—a moment later, the sound of heavy rain drops, and then the sluices of heaven were opened, and rain, such as is known only where huge masses of water are surrounded by mighty forests, fell, driving the two lads to the extremity of the scow, where they cowered, helpless, cold, and utterly prostrate with anxiety and fatigue.

How long this lasted they never knew; for with the rain, the thunder, and the wind dying away, they fell into a deep sleep, from which they only awoke when the sun shone warmly from a blue and placid sky. But the lake was white with foam, kept up by a steady breeze—for that they cared not—their thoughts took in only one leading idea. The fire was nearly out, and nothing rose to the sky but columns of smoke from damp and smouldering piles.

Eagerly they rushed forward until they reached the confines of the fire; when, to their delight, they found that, though several trees still smoked and smouldered, the torrents of water which had fallen during the night had so cooled the ground, that they easily made their way through the blackened poles and over the piles of ashes and charcoal that strewed their path.

We have all felt a peculiar sensation on entering within the confines of a venerable church-yard, sacred to the dust of ages. The voice is hushed, the thoughts subdued, the very foot falls lightly on the soil beneath which moulder the bones of our ancestors. Some such feeling came over the two boys, as they entered within the blackened precincts of the clearing; which itself had evidently suffered the whole force of the devastating and remorseless fire.

Every blade of grass, every bush had been licked up by the cruel flames, while the shanty was a mere blackened ruin, of which only a few of the stouter poles remained. The brothers dared not exchange glances, their eyes would have said too much; dared not speak, their bosoms were too full for words; until at last, hand in hand, pale, ghastly, with a shiver that shot like an ice-bolt from crown to heel, they entered the ruined dwelling, glancing fearfully around. No sign.

"Father! mother! brother!" they shouted, by one common impulse, "if any be spared unto us—speak, in the name of mercy!"

A muffled sound, scarcely audible, made them both start, and then, with a cry of delight and wonder, rush towards the stream, whence at the same time rose first the haggard, blackened face of their boy brother, followed by those of their father and mother. In another instant they were all united, and for ten minutes, broken words, half sentences, cries of joy, embraces, precluded all explanations.

It was simple. They were surprised by the fire so rapidly that none could hope to retreat. Mr. Hatfield then at once looked out for a place of safety. Only one presented itself. Below where the beaver dam had been, the stream was narrow, with high banks. As this was their usual way to the clearing, Ralph and Harry had one day taken it into their heads to throw a bridge of solid logs across, at least ten feet wide. To enable the ox and cart the more easily to traverse it, they had laid a layer of twigs and then a thick crust of clay and earth, thus making an excellent road.

Beneath this shelter their father had rushed with his wife and child, and there had passed the weary hours until the presence of his elder sons assured him that danger was over.

Their sufferings had been great. The heat at times was intense, especially when burning brands fell on all sides into the water. They were, on several occasions nearly choked with steam and smoke; but, sometimes in the water, sometimes on a narrow ledge of land, they contrived to pass the weary hours, with no sustenance but a few biscuits, which Jack fortunately had in his pocket, and an occasional draught of water. Their first glimpse of hope was in the storm; while the reason of their not being afoot earlier, arose from the fact that while Jack had fallen asleep on his mother's lap she had done the same on her husband's shoulder, so utterly exhausted were they by their long and weary vigil.

"And now," cried the father, earnestly, "unto God let us return thanks for all his mercies. We are once more united, and have learned a lesson we shall never forget!"

Surrounded by so much desolation, and with a wife and children dependant on him, Mr. Hatfield's position was most trying.

CHAPTER III.

A NIGHT ENGAGEMENT.

ALL those pictures of emigrant life which depict the early career of a settler in roseate colours, are false and injurious. The establishment of a new home in a wild, savage land, teeming, it may be, with wealth, though still in a crude, amorphous state, must be difficult; while many who have undertaken the burden with neither bodies nor minds qualified for the task, have suffered utter failure. This was more true then than now, when roads, railways, and canals afford facilities of which the early colonists never dreamed.

Any one with less courage and perseverance would have given up all hope, and, as many have done before, would have turned his back on those blackened rafters and smouldering acres of forests, and abandoned the spot for ever. Such has too often been the hasty resolve of the over sanguine emigrant, who, having expected to succeed at once, and not doing so, has hastily returned to his former home.

Collecting together a few necessaries, carefully concealing the heavier tools, and, after some search discovering their ox, the patient animal was once more harnessed to the cart, and the return march entered upon. They had resolved to winter in Montreal, and early in the spring, to start with more experience and means, again to commence the battle of life.

"Father," said Harry, as they reached the outer edge of the conflagration, "I have several times reflected as to the causes of this strange circle which isolates us, as it were, from the rest of the wood. Can you explain it?"

"I do not believe, my son, that I can offer any explanation, but while examining it, I have several times thought of the sayings of travellers in these woods. One in particular, alluding to a fearful tornado, had observed with surprise that the fallen trees were twisted off at the stumps, and formed circular and wide roads in the forests. The explanation of these phenomena I leave to wiser heads than mine."

The sons listened attentively, unable themselves to comprehend that which is now no mystery, since it is proved that all wind storms move in a circular direction; and the nearer the centre, the more violent the wind.

The journey to Montreal, about three hundred miles, was safely accomplished; half by land, half by water. Their quarters were taken up in a cheap house, and their time was chiefly occupied in laying plans for the future, in studying the experiences of former settlers, and in preparations for the campaign; varied with an occasional sledge party, in which the young people took great delight, enhanced by the pleasant reflection that soon they would enjoy the luxury of travelling in these favourite vehicles on their own settlement.

It is well known that this peculiar mode of conveyance,

more than anything else, reconciles the Canadian farmer to what is called the rigour of the climate, which, however, if it has hard frosts and deep snow, has brilliant skies, without sleet, fog, or damp. Many, even now, regret the diminution of cold produced by felling the trees, and look back with a sigh to the old four months of snow, when every field, meadow, and plain was a kind of macadamized road.

Before the winter was quite over, the whole party was once more ready to enter upon the almost pathless wilderness; but this time better provided both for the journey and its termination. They had a waggon, which, in addition to a store of such furniture as was necessary for the requirements of an educated settler, who, if an Englishman, will have his comforts, had within its capacious canvas roof, seeds, stores, and agricultural instruments, as well as a sleeping place for Mrs. Hatfield and little Jack, the pet of the party.

The waggon was drawn by two pair of French Canadian horses, extremely rough-looking animals, with shaggy manes and tails, but plump, active, and strong. Behind these came a pair of oxen (their old friend had been left at a solitary farm-house, whence they had set out on their way down) harnessed in the local fashion, that is, with yoke and bows. The ox yoke is made of a piece of birch or soft maple wood, four feet in length, and nine inches wide in the centre, where a staple is fastened, from which hangs an iron ring, about a foot from the middle of the yoke each way. The yoke is hollowed out so as to fit the oxen's necks; on each side of this a hole is bored through it, into which the bow is passed and fastened with a wooden pin, the bow itself being of hickory, white or rock elm, about five feet and a half long, which, when heated by steam, had been bent to the shape of a horse-shoe, the upper or narrow ends being passed through the yoke.

This team was unfortunately driven by two young Irishmen, engaged by Mr. Hatfield as labourers to assist in the clearing of the farm; we say unfortunately, as no greater mistake can be made than to place much dependance on persons with the traditions of the old country still upon them. This was, however, too much the case with the whole family of our adventurers, and hence many and serious drawbacks to their success.

The father and his elder sons were clothed in rough shooting jackets with many pockets, strong corduroy trousers tied under the knees, after the fashion of modern English navigators. For wet, windy, and peculiarly cold days, there was a Hudson's Bay capot, a sort of blue frock-coat with a hood. They were further provided with coats and trousers of blue blanket for winter.

The labourers were warmly clothed, and carried both axe and whip. Their "duds," as they called them, were in a huge swinging basket under the waggon, in the body of which sat Mrs. Hatfield and Young Jack, half envious of his brother and father trudging through the snow, armed with rifle, and carrying axe and knife. The road from the settlement had been worn so hard and smooth by sledges, that the journey was quite practicable for the emigrants, too eager to await the thaw, with respect to which the smiling *habitans* threw out mysterious hints.

But though compelled to carry forage on a huge sledge behind the waggon, Mr. Hatfield, in his eagerness to press forward, was deaf to all advice; and as nothing occurred for some days to change his views, his spirits rose considerably, though both he, his sons, and labourers, found snow shoeing hard work.

As time was all-important, it was arranged that they

should not halt for meals, all eating from their hands whatever was provided; while Mrs. Hatfield kept a supply of hot coffee by means of a French earthenware stove, which consumed about a quart of charcoal a day. At night the whole party—Mrs. Hatfield and Jack excepted—selecting the skirt of a wood or thicket, scooped out a hole in the snow, about ten feet by seven; two trees were felled to within six feet of the ground, and from tree to tree a ridge-pole was laid, over which they cast a roof of boughs covered with green fir bushes. In the midst a fire was made of fir branches; and thus, wrapped in coats, capots, and blankets, they passed the night. Mrs. Hatfield and little Jack, closing the leathern front of the waggon, and wrapping themselves in huge buffalo skins, were scarcely as comfortable.

Next day they reached a spot where the road began to ascend a steep hill, covered with white pine, larch, and birch trees, which towered to a height varying from fifty to a hundred feet. The nature of the ground being flat and no underwood appearing, the head of the family would willingly have made a dash to the summit, but evening approached, the team seemed tired, the labourers and boys lagged, and he unwillingly therefore called a halt. A slight change of the wind, with a cessation of the intense cold, had made him uneasy.

The tent was however pitched, the animals were secured, the fire lit, and after a hearty meal all were seated round the embers, the Irishmen smoking, and the Hatfields chatting, their capots still on their backs, when there rose on the night air such a wild and unearthly din, such a fearful and diabolical chorus of yells, followed by the snorting of horses and lowing of cattle, as made all start to their feet in terror and amazement. A pack of hungry wolves was upon them.

Down the steep ascent, under the bare and naked pine trees, passing like shadows over the white and crisp surface of the snow, they came—their noses pointed forward, their ears erect, their teeth strong and sharp, their eyes fierce and sparkling—a drove of savage, hungry and voracious demons, that naught but blood could satiate, for though a more cowardly wretch in his solitary state is not to be found, in droves the wolf is formidable. Fortunately, the pack was not so large as usual, but made up for its want of force by hideous and frightful clamour. The struggles of the horses and oxen were fearful; but, as good luck would have it, they were so firmly fastened, that their efforts to free themselves were vain.

When within ten yards, the wolves, evidently aware of the vicinity of human beings, came to a stop, and seated themselves for a moment, as if in council; but finding no notice taken of their presence, they once more made a rush, only to be driven back by a volley from four guns fired into their midst, which sent them yelling, yelping, and limping away.

The scene now became one of terrible excitement and horror—the fierce animals raging around, the men firing steadily, but without seriously daunting the famished, ravenous beasts, which, if not so large or ferocious as the European tribe, are still no contemptible adversaries, especially in the dark, when their appalling cries rouse the forest echoes.

It was as much as the travellers could do, firing from sledge and waggon, to keep the brutes back, though after a while the death of some six or seven, and the disabling of twice as many, seemed to discourage their attacks, and the little band of adventurers began to beathe again, when a long, low, horrid howl over the crest of the hill, proclaimed the arrival of reinforcements.

"Fire as fast as you can, boys!" shouted the father; "spare no powder. If the packs join, we lose our cattle."

The waggon leather was now open, and the pale face of Mrs. Hatfield was visible, gazing with anxious eyes upon the fearful scene; whilst master Jack, the ten-year-older, clapped his hands with a delight which proclaimed him to be a true boy. Both were startled to see Mr. Hatfield leap to the ground, after bidding his wife load the duck gun and fasten it to the waggon. With this injunction he hurried forward to the hut, in which they had been about to camp, leaving his wife and son busily engaged putting powder and shot into the heavy gun, which was then lashed to the waggon. This had scarcely been done, when a loud cry burst from the agonized wife, as three huge beasts, which had approached under cover of the hut, attacked Mr. Hatfield as he emerged from the camp, and made him stand on the defensive—a burning brand his only weapon! On ordinary occasions this would have been enough, but the gnawing pains of hunger will give courage to a mouse. The father's position was therefore precarious enough; and the defenders of the sleigh were about to sally forth in his defence, when a loud report was heard, a fearful screech, and the raging animals fled to rejoin their companions.

It was Jack who had taken steady aim, and both cocked the duck gun and pulled the trigger in defence of his father. A loud shout rewarded the brave little lad, though no time for congratulations could be spared, for a dark stream of fresh and still more hungry brutes—the first had devoured their dead and wounded—were now pouring helter-skelter down the hill.

"Give it to them! they will have found their match," cried Mr. Hatfield, in an excited tone, and just when the junction was formed, he fired first Jack's redoubtable swivel, and then his own fowling-piece.

As he spoke, a bright light shot up through the roof of their camp. The dry fir, larch, and birch, were in flames, making a glorious bonfire, and driving back the wolves even more effectually than gunpowder. The adventurers now understood their father, and, leaping from the entrenchment, they soon kindled a wall of fire that effectually scared the disappointed brutes, which, however, sat patiently on the watch until driven away by the dawn.

CHAPTER IV

TRAVELLING IN THE SNOW.

NEVER was morning more gladly hailed than that which greeted the travellers, as the baulked brutes turned tail and fled. It was warm, too, and genial; and the head of the party determined on pushing forward with all speed. This he intimated to the weary combatants, who were only too glad to leave the scene of their night's encounter; and every one, after clamouring for breakfast, was about to prepare for departure, when again their animals began to snort and toss their heads, as their bodies sank in the snow.

"Hopple them," said Mr. Hatfield, setting the example.

In a moment horses and oxen had their fore legs fastened sufficiently close together to prevent them straying far, when the whole party, pushing the sledge close to the waggon, prepared to await whatever might happen.

The thaw had caught them in a hollow.

Soon, dark, bare patches on the hill sides began to show themselves, and as the sun rose, and a warm southeasterly breeze came murmuring over the hill tops, whole avalanches of snow glided down towards the devoted band of emigrants. In selecting their camp, they had been guided by the presence of trees, as well as by the circumstance that the ground where the waggon stood was perfectly flat. Behind them was an extensive plain, with, if anything, an inclination towards them.

Father and sons, standing on the footboard, gazed anxiously around, and now first marked the peculiar distribution of the trees in their immediate neighbourhood. They grew in a kind of winding meandering way, about forty feet apart, both to the northward and southward.

There could be no doubt of it, they were in the bed of a watercourse.

This was a fearful discovery, and one which would probably involve the loss of their waggon and stores, and consequently the relinquishment of their journey. But in this moment of alarming peril, the emigrants showed themselves worthy of their mission. A quiet hint was given to the Irishmen, who at once removed their boxes and parcels to the thicket, where they made them fast as best they could. Mr. Hatfield then searched for several coils of rope, and a chain, the uses of which were various, and lashing a double line to the shafts, tried, by means of two stout trees and the pulley, to draw the waggon more to the bank. The wheels were, however, too much embedded in the snow, which, at first soft, soon became slush, made so by the little rills and rivulets that came pouring from the mountain slopes. There was but one resource.

The trees to which the cords were attached formed part of a thicket, which, as the snow disappeared and the inequalities of the soil could be more plainly seen, proved to stand upon a knoll. This discovery once made, a hut was hastily erected, spacious enough for the whole family, within which Mr. Hatfield sent all save himself and Ralph, who watched by a huge fire outside.

There was no dread of wolves just then, but there was great fear lest the ark of their fortunes should be destroyed, and their hopes frustrated. Down the grassy slopes, over rocky precipices, along arid and stony inclines, poured the angry water, not pure and sparkling, but intermingled with leaves, twigs and dirt, that soiled and tainted its native beauty; and all came rushing to the bed of that stream near which they were encamped, until, just after nightfall, the placid, smooth, and once hard surface on which they had rested, was changed to a seething, boiling, raging torrent, that increased and widened every moment with a sullen roar;—in their situation singularly appalling.

About every five minutes, the anxious sentries felt the rope, fearing the tension would become greater, whilst their eyes tried in vain to pierce the gloom. The sky was cloudy, there was neither moon nor stars visible—all was left to the sense of hearing and feeling. Once Ralph started to walk alongside the rope to the waggon, but he had not gone three feet when his father heard him splashing in water, and called him back, remarking that nothing remained but to put their trust in Providence and await the morn. Ralph reluctantly yielded, made up the fire to a great size and heat, and then, taking example by his parent, lay down in his capote within the rude shanty; and "nature's sweet restorer" overcoming all sense of danger, he slept.

At dawn of day all were out with a rush, and the true position of affairs became evident. The adventurers, when making their halt at the foot of the hill, had selected a smooth drift of snow, covering a rocky ledge that ran from the wooded knoll to the very verge of the stream, which, now swollen by the melting snow, had so far overflowed its banks; and such was the volume of water already carried away, that the stream was receding to its natural bed. But for the timely intervention of the rope, the waggon must have been swept away, with all its valuable contents, for the hinder wheels hung half n, half out of the water.

Eager as the new settlers were to press forward and reach the scene of their future labours, they were compelled to halt for several days at this spot, not only until the snow cleared away and the ground became hard, but until the many watercourses they had to pass, had sufficiently diminished in volume to permit of their being forded.

One advantage was derived from the halt, namely, the good condition in which the cattle were found at the end of a week, after feeding upon young grasses, with a proper supply of fodder at night. On the second Sabbath all looked fair for a start; but Mr. Hatfield, despite his impatience, resolved to keep that day holy, and accordingly the final "leg up" was made on the following Monday morning, soon after daybreak.

The oxen were put to, the horses harnessed, and under the united guidance of the whole party the journey recommenced. Now it was that the real difficulties of a new country showed themselves. There was no road except what might have been a bridle path, to which each passing emigrant had done a little, such as lopping a branch here, cutting down a tree there, and filling up a hole or two with wood, stones, and rubbish. The waggon laboured terribly; and before the first half day was over, such was the fearful nature of the jolts, jerks, and threatened spills, that both Mrs. Hatfield and Jack resolved to walk.

They were still within the bounds of scattered settlements, and here and there they found roads that had been turnpiked, that is ploughed on each side, and the earth so raised, thrown upon the centre by means of a road scraper, or turnpike shovel, worked either by horses or oxen. They were approaching by the rude zig-zag way which they had themselves, with pocket compass in hand, cut through the forest, an undertaking impossible to have been carried out had they not taken advantage of every accidental opening, glade, or burn, thus increasing their journey by at least fifty miles.

As their waggon was a very different sort of thing from the one-ox cart of the previous year, the road often required widening; and in order to save delay, Mr. Hatfield hit upon a very ingenious device for ascertaining whether it could pass, long before the lumbering vehicle itself came up. He cut a pole twelve inches longer than the width of the widest part of the waggon, so that, wherever this pole, held in a horizontal position, could pass, there, of course, the waggon also could pass.

When the ground was even, and no extraneous assistance was required, the horses and oxen being docile, they were given into the charge of Jack and his mother, while the Irishmen, with axes and bill-hooks, followed Mr. Hatfield; the young men being, whenever they could be spared, out as a sort of flying column in search of game or fish to add to the evening meal, which, rely upon it, no one ever knows how to really enjoy who has not earned it in some such way.

As the obstacles in the shape of trees and shrubs were generally small, the Irish labourers were mostly able to overcome them; but when the difficulty presenting itself was a hole, all hands were called, and sometimes it was as much as the cattle could do, to drag the heavy vehicle onward, though the whole party assisted to raise it by means of handspikes, crowbars, rollers, and other contrivances. It will now be easily understood why they sometimes travelled only one mile in a day; never more than twelve; on the average, six.

In general, unless recalled by their father's loud-tongued horn, the elder brothers were at the intended night camp first, their experience indicating a fit distance. The camping ground once fixed upon, they collected wood, made a fire, found water, cut logs for the night, collected fir and hemlock boughs to sleep on, beneath a rude tent which generally made its appearance from the recesses of the waggon. Then, when the wearied voyagers came up, they would prepare dampers, boil a kettle, or do any other useful cooking work, while Mrs. Hatfield and her husband looked on approvingly. A damper, be it known, is a cake of dough rolled out to the size of a plate, and from one to two inches thick, and either baked in the wood ashes of the fire, or fried in the pan with bacon fat.

All these details may appear very prosaic, but we are describing real downright life, the ups and downs of a settler; and if any of our readers in after life should shoulder the axe and the rifle, and take to the canoe and the saddle, they will thank us for these particulars. Our emigrants met with adventures exciting and wonderful enough before settling down; but to them personally, these early days of travel were both trying and interesting.

All hands retired early, as the word was, start at sunrise, no other breakfast being allowed than what remained from over night, the first real meal being taken between eleven and twelve, so as to break the day for the horses and cattle. In this way, with a few accidents, with many hardships, after trials which in the old country would appear both ludicrous and impossible, the whole party reached the favoured spot which was to be, as it were, the nucleus of their future home; although Mr. Hatfield had already decided on making a careful search for better land ere he finally committed himself.

It was the beginning of May. They had arrived just in time to see to their spring crops, before engaging in any other duty. The emigrants now found their Irish labourers useful. The object was to plough about six acres to bring forth spring crops, such as potatoes and Indian corn. The Irishmen stared with open mouths and wondering eyes at the clearing, with its charred stumps, and ground already beginning to be overrun with wild raspberries and Canadian thistles, and still more at the odd way of ridding themselves of them.

Despite their experience of fire as an enemy, they now used it as a friend, and thus destroyed the noxious weeds, preparatory to ploughing. For this purpose they used the docile and easily-managed oxen, as among the green stumps and roots—the plough being continually checked by roots and stems—the horses would have been restive. As soon as about six acres had been prepared, the Indian corn was planted with a hoe, in rows three feet apart and thirty inches in a row, while between every other one a pumpkin seed was thrown in.

Potatoes, that made the worthy Irishmen grin from ear to ear, were also planted with a hoe, in drills, and about five thousand to the acre. A hole was made, into which four or five sets were dropped; the earth being then heaped over them in the form of a moderate molehill. The usual yield to an acre was from two hundred to five hundred bushels. A few swedes and turnips were added; and then, as nothing more could be done until autumn, the more serious business commenced. Mrs. Hatfield having in the meantime produced from a mysterious coop in the waggon, a strutting cock and lively brood of hens, that promised wonders to the infant colony.

All emigrants in those days were content with a log-house, which, when the settlement came within reach of civilization, was replaced by a substantial stone, brick, or frame house. Our adventurers were no exception to the rule, and accordingly, before entering upon the manifold undertakings which make the first years of a settler's work exceedingly hard labour, they resolved to erect a house, outhouses, stables, pigsties—Ralph undertaking a winter's sleigh voyage of discovery in search of pigs—so that, whatever their arduous labours might be, they would at least be sure of a comfortable home.

There was, however, one more day's work before they started in life as builders. The six acres of crops had to be fenced. In one or two places, the stones of various sorts and sizes, which all but the ploughmen had been engaged in clearing away, being piled up between stumps, made a good wall, but the rest was encircled in the usual way. Bass trees of a straight growth—and straight also in the grain—were cut into twelve-feet lengths, and split into rails as near four inches square as possible; these were laid in a zigzag direction, crossing each other about a foot from the end, making an angle of about six feet. Seven rails in height, crowned by a stake and a rider, completed the fence.

The Americans—as a rule, push and go-a-head people—generally begin with a frame-house. Now, as this latter has to be put together "judgmatically," it requires time, so that a log-hut is wanted in the meanwhile. The consequence is, that, as no emigrant has much time to spare, little of the frame-house is erected but the uprights and cross-beams, which rot away, a dreary skeleton of home, while the pioneer and his family burrow in the warm mud and wooden structure.

But Mr. Hatfield and his family were more methodical; and no sooner had the future been tolerably provided for in the way alluded to, than operations were commenced with a view to erect suitable buildings for masters, men, and cattle. In the meantime, those who did not belong to the tent, lived in slab-houses; and this was all the party, save Mr. and Mrs. Hatfield, and Jack.

The slab-huts were simple enough. A level spot was selected, with two trees behind, which were twelve feet apart; from one to the other a pole was firmly lashed; parallel with this, a huge black oak was felled, and from the pole to the log a row of split slabs was laid, while the ends were stuffed with hemlock brush, to keep out wind and rain, the blankets and coats already alluded to forming the bed. On the open side was a roaring fire—which served the huts of the two youths and the two labourers.

Mr. Hatfield and his companions had read about erecting log-huts and frame-houses, but they little understood the difficulty to the uninitiated. It is an art in itself, and those who make such buildings without the supervision of an experienced hand, must always make a bungling job of it,—forgetting, probably, a door, a window, or a chimney. In the first place, after selecting a suitable spot, they discovered that no wood of the right sort grew near at hand, so that they had to cut down trees, shape them into logs, planks, and shingles, and then haul them, by means of their oxen and horses, to the right spot.

But these were hardships easily overcome. The two stumbling-blocks were, how to build a "log," and how to fell the proper trees for beams, for planks, for shingles, of which important fact none were informed. We have already alluded to chopping, to which arduous work the whole party betook themselves, except Mrs. Hatfield and Jack, who mounted their old and faithful ox; Jack guiding him, as he drew along the logs, while his mother used the goad or whip to urge him on.

The Irishmen worked with a will for a day or two, though the toil was so utterly new to them, that not only were their hands blistered, but their backs bent double, and they were heard at night moaning and groaning in their sleep. This was not so much their fault as Mr. Hatfield's, none but emigrants of some years' standing knowing the true art of chopping, logging, or fencing. One good man will do the work of six new hands. But the worthy fellows continued cutting, sweating, and cursing in their own tongue, until Saturday night, when, after retiring to their slab-hut, they were no more seen; they had, in fact, "skedaddled," but they took nothing except their own "duds," not having waited even for their wages.

This unlooked-for desertion did not dishearten the settlers, it being more disastrous in the future than for the present; on the contrary, it roused them to new exertions, which were never relaxed one moment, though water poured down their bodies like rain, though every muscle was strained, and every bone seemed sore as if beaten by cudgels.

Little progress was made. Mr. Hatfield, a man of considerable ingenuity, *recollected* much about the building of a log-hut, but *knew* nothing. A great deal of what was done, therefore, was by guess work. Still all persevered, and one morning, with the sun shining brightly overhead, the scene was not without its picturesque point of view. Mr. Hatfield, with saw, hammer, and nails at hand, was busy upon some minor details; Ralph and Henry, the latter sighing a little now and then, were shaping a log with their axes; Jack, with his mother by his side, was urging the ox forward, with a large log at his heels, when a loud, ringing, merry laugh startled them all.

"Ha! ha! Monsieur Jone Bool—make one log-hut—one frame maison—ha! ha! vel, bon jour, how you do?—ver humble sairvant, madam."

And the speaker—a tall French Canadian, with sallow complexion, high cheek bones, a turban-shaped fur cap, a blouse over a leather jerkin, high boots, his powerful and elastic frame supporting a huge rifle, heavy axe, and all the usual accoutrements—stepped into the clearing; a genial, though slightly mocking smile upon his hard, weather-beaten features. Mrs. Hatfield stared, Jack and Harry looked indignant, but both Ralph and his father welcomed the stranger heartily, the latter shaking him by the hand; while Ralph, reddening up to his ears, unseen by any one, placed his fingers on his lips, and received an almost imperceptible nod in return.

Now this involves a mystery, which must be solved.

CHAPTER V

THE LAKE OF THE BURNING PLAINS.

RALPH HATFIELD had been unanimously elected huntsman to the party; and, as a very large store of provisions was consumed by the hard-working emigrants, his expeditions were proportionably numerous. His brothers were half inclined to envy him when they saw him start, prancing on his shaggy steed, with his bright face illumined with smiles; but Harry, at all events, was generally compensated by the circumstance that he returned nearly always footsore and weary, his horse laden with "plunder," as the produce of the chase is usually denominated in America.

But in the case of the young man himself, these expeditions were productive of unmitigated pleasure; though such was his genial nature, that he would gladly have been accompanied by one of the party, if they could have been spared. It certainly did not detract from the excitement attendant on these journeys, to know that they sometimes brought him within less than a hundred miles of the territory of the Six Nations; this spice of danger, indeed, added to the zest with which he trod the woods.

On one occasion, Ralph secretly resolved to make a longer journey than usual, as nearly in a northerly direction as possible, until he fell in with sufficient game to load his horse. Armed with rifle and fowling-piece, he waved his cap as he rode forth from the clearing, mounted on the best horse that could be found. He had intimated his intention to camp out for one night; and, as he invariably brought back interesting reports to his father after every expedition, this was rather approved of than otherwise. One reason why he had selected this route was, that during his wanderings he had hit upon an old Indian trail, which had so excited his imagination, that he could not rest until he explored it.

Under the greenwood trees then, where the tops waved gracefully in the wind, Ralph rode onward, neither tempted to the right nor to the left by sight of deer tracks, nor lured by the cluck of the wild turkey, until, two or three hours before sunset, his constancy was rewarded, after a dangerous journey through mighty forests, deep ravines, and up steep hills, by suddenly emerging upon what are now known as The Plains. Beyond these lay, glittering in the golden light of the setting sun, the mirror-like surface of The Lake of the Burning Plains, dotted here and there with gem-like islands, wooded to their summits with sugar maple, that towered terrace on terrace, ledge upon ledge, until they concealed even the cone-like tops.

It was a sight well worth all the labour he had endured; and he felt, as he rode along, that there it was they should have located, amid that park-like scenery, amid those flowery knolls, deep ravines, and oak-crowned hills, admitting at every step a view of the blue waters of the lake; and he made a vow, that if ever he should set up housekeeping for himself, there his home should be. The trail now led him through a somewhat gloomy but well-wooded ravine, winding round the base of lofty hills crowned with oak, until, after nearly a mile of sharp descent, the whole lake lake lay before him in all its calm and placid beauty.

But why does the young man start—why do his eyes dilate as he reins in his horse? The secret wish of his heart is realized—he is in the presence of a link, at all events, in that chain of mystery which so strikingly attaches itself to the Indian race. On a small plateau close to the water was a redskin village, small in extent, but still a redskin village. There were not more than eight or nine large wigwams, and all appeared deserted, Ralph riding into the midst of them without even the cry of a child, or the yelping bark of a pack of dogs being heard. The village was deserted, and, as was subsequently discovered, it was the winter quarters of a small branch of the Chippewas, known as the Mississauga Indians. Dismounting, and giving his horse a long lariat to graze by, the young man examined these dwellings of the aboriginal inhabitants, with a mixture of that curiosity and interest which is always aroused in us in connection with savage tribes.

The poles of these huts were planted about a foot apart at the bottom, meeting together at the top, while they were closely and securely covered with birch-bark. The diameter of the huts was about twelve feet; with a fire-place in the centre, and opposite each end of the fire a small doorway, which, when the hut was inhabited, was covered with a blanket.

Pleased and gratified by this discovery, the young man resolved to use one of them for the night; though, as he was quite alone, he determined on fastening the doorways more securely. This decided on, he turned towards the lake, not unmindful of the task he had in hand. To his no little surprise, and much to his delight, he could see, slowly sailing towards him with the wind, some hundreds of wood-ducks, which he knew by reputation to be delicious and beautiful birds, appearing always in spring. The head and part of the neck are green; while from the head a long crest depends, richly variegated with green, white, and dark purple feathers. The lower part of the throat and the breast are cinnamon, speckled with white; but under the wings, and the sides towards the tail, grey speckled, and fringed with black; the back of the wings, dark blue and black feathers.

Ralph gazed around. He knew very well that, were he in possession of a canoe, he might easily approach them; but nothing of the kind was to be expected in that vicinity. The wood-ducks were near the shore, feeding on the wild rice with which the lake abounds;

while hundreds upon hundreds were bobbing up the closely-wooded streams and little bays, or were seated on old logs or limbs of trees that had fallen into the water.

This put an idea into our young sportsman's head. Of a keen and quickly observant character, Ralph saw, nearly afloat, a large tree, the bushy part of which, from the shape of the trunk, rose at a sharp angle upwards. A few strokes with the axe at the roots, and a shove or two with a hastily cut pole, set the ponderous mass fairly out into the scarcely-rippling waters. Ralph was delighted, as, the wood-ducks being at no great distance, he was soon able to get within five-and-twenty yards of the birds, utterly unnoticed. Then he began to work; and being not only a keen, but a careful and cautious sportsman, he contrived, before sundown, to kill fourteen brace; with these he returned to the shore, made fast his weighty raft, and took up his quarters in the red-skin wigwam, where soon a bright blaze, and the odour from the cooking, proclaimed the presence of civilized man.

Ralph was tired, but he was now a practised traveller; so out he went, took off his horse's harness, hoppled him, gave him a handful of beans, and let him loose. Then a goodly supply of fuel was thrown within the hut, the two doors were closely barred, and Ralph—his two guns loaded, and his pistols to his hand—composed himself to sleep. Not a quarter of an hour later, just as he had dozed, he had to thank his good fortune, as well as to test the stability of his redskin wigwam; for there came a roll of thunder, with vivid flashes of lightning, followed by torrents of rain, which, after continuing an hour, left him as dry as ever.

Replenishing his fire, and fervently thanking God for

the goodly shelter he enjoyed, Ralph was soon once more in a sound sleep, which lasted for many hours, when a violent shaking at the door of his hut startled him. With a caution which spoke well for his future career as a hunter in the wilds, Ralph drew back from the fire, clutched his pistols, and listened. See, he could not; for though there were interstices between the bars, there was no moon, and the glow of the embers within the wigwam made all dark without. Still Ralph could make out a tall figure, two eyes shining like coals, and a heavy breathing, as the assailant strove noiselessly to push in the doorway. Satisfied no band of marauders would take such precautions, Ralph now levelled both pistols and fired, by no means afraid to tackle one or more ruffians. No words, not a cry, succeeded the sharp report; but when the smoke cleared away, the doorway was vacant, and the pale, sickly light of a star or two poured into the wigwam.

But Ralph had no further desire for sleep. He could not understand what had happened. Assaults by armed bands of Indians, as well as outrages by a single savage, were conducted according to rule; and one of those rules was to make the attack just before daybreak, and if foiled, to retire until a more favourable opportunity. This Ralph knew, and found himself, with all his romantic notions about the aborigines, wondering with something of anxiety and disgust, to which tribe of the Six Nations he was indebted for a visit.

Half dozing, but never quite sleeping, he was surprised by dawn, and at once went forth, rifle in hand. But all was still; the surface of the lake was unrippled, the forest tree-tops scarcely moved, the grass waved its feathery tips slowly and mutely—while of man, his tricks and malefices, there was no sign. Taking heart of grace, in the keen morning air, Ralph bathed, his rifle close to him, and then having breakfasted, he moved slowly along the bank of the lake, in search of some larger game than wood-ducks.

The small-birds, fat and delicious as they were, to a hungry party of emigrants working in the open air, would prove but tit-bits. Something more solid was required to appease their ravenous appetites. A couple of fat wild turkeys soon paid the penalty of early rising, and were hung high on the branch of a tree, while Ralph pursued his way, which he did until at length he reached a close cedar swamp, along which it was his intention to walk until he could make for the shores of the lake, where, doubtless, he would find some deer tracks as they went to water.

The scene was now novel to Ralph. To his left lay the cedar swamp, while to his right was a clump of American *arbor vitæ*, its full juicy verdure sweeping to the ground, a marked relief to the monotony of the stark stems of the fir forest.

The trail now plunged into thickets impenetrable but for its aid. Where ancient trunks had fallen, there they lay; some had become green mossy mounds, the long grave of prostrate giants, so carefully draped in their velvety covering, that all sense of ruin was gone; some, more freshly fallen, showed still their purple bark deepening in hue, and dotted with tufts of moss.

Suddenly Ralph, who carried his fowling-piece in his hand, his rifle on his back, stood still, as a low growl fell upon his ears, and from behind some fallen logs and brush, up popped an enormous bear, at once bringing our sportsman to a stop, and explaining the aggression of the previous night. Now, a bear is no contemptible animal at the best of times; while to attack and kill a grisly bear is one of those daring deeds which immortalize a local reputation. I know that many persons have ridiculed the idea of any one man coping with the huge monarch of the Rocky Mountains; but though many have paid the penalty of their rashness, in a contest where courage and skill have to compete with fearful brute force, and where the snapping of a lock or cap, the miss of an inch in hitting the spot on his breast where the hair grows in a sort of round, or the want of time to reload, have been the occasion of fearful mishaps; yet have there been many renowned white men and Indians, who have, single-handed, killed their half-dozen grislies, and worn the claw-collars; while many have escaped by climbing trees, a feat which this powerful but ponderous animal cannot perform.

But it was no wonder that Ralph hesitated. Still he did not move, but dropping his fowling-piece, he unslung his rifle. The bear all this time had been standing on his hind legs, and staring wildly about him, as if in doubt whether to fight or run away; presently, however, he began shuffling off at a great pace, which so carried Ralph beyond the bounds of prudence, as to make him take aim and fire.

With a savage growl, the bear turned round, clawed at the wound, and stood still, irresolute; while Ralph, whose blood was now up, proceeded to load with as much rapidity as possible. Again, while the bear was examining his wound, the young man fired, and this time hit Bruin on the head, which had the effect of rendering him so mad with rage, that he charged Ralph with a velocity which made escape impossible; indeed, with a mounted hunter it is often a question which shall gain the day in a fair race.

Ralph, though fully prepared for a fearful contest, retained his coolness, the result of that admirable physical and moral training which he had received in a school purposely selected by his father. With the eye of an eagle on the wing, he caught sight of a fallen log, behind which he placed himself with a fearful leap, not forgetting to take with him both guns.

Not an instant of time was to be lost. The bear was close at hand, and must be met by the knife or axe, though the more he was weakened the less he was to be feared in a hand-to-hand encounter. With this view, Ralph gave him both barrels of the fowling-piece, which, though it did nearly blind him, made him doubly ferocious. With a terrible growl, that might have chilled the stoutest heart, he dashed at the log, received the contents of the rifle hastily poured forth, and then, before Ralph could step back, he had his left arm and shoulder in the claws of Bruin, who used all his remaining strength in an effort to drag the young man to his own side of the log. Ralph, despite the excruciating pain, dashed his long, sharp, glittering knife into the bear's neck, who though now bleeding at every pore, did not relax his grip; but, growling horribly all the time, and his almost sightless and bloody orbs rolling spasmodically, he tried to snap at the knife with his teeth. The fearfully rapid blows which the young hunter struck, so exasperated the already infuriated bear, that for a moment he relaxed his hold, only to give a final hug, in which both rolled over the log, Bruin uppermost, and Ralph only faintly striking with his knife at the thick hide of the animal.

At this moment the low croaking of a buffalo calf was heard; the bear paused in its fury to listen, and Ralph, making one mighty effort, struck home to the bleeding animal's heart, and then fainted.

When he recovered, Pete, the Canadian hunter and trapper who had recommended to Mr. Hatfield the particular location on which they had settled, and whose imitation of a buffalo calf had so opportunely distracted the bear's attention, was leaning over him, dressing his wounds. They were superficial but weakening, and forced Ralph to camp another day and night on the Lake of the Burning Plains, during which time Pete hunted for him; and finally, having restored him to health, he sent him home loaded, not only with venison and ducks, but with bear-hams. This adventure with the bear had never been mentioned to Ralph's mother, lest she might object to future expeditions; and so Ralph blushed when the old *habitant* unexpectedly visited them some time afterwards.

Pete was called old, as is the fashion in America, though much under forty; and if we were to judge from his exploits, he was deserving of the epithet. There was scarcely a spot of any note on the North American continent, he had not visited—he had fished with the Esquimaux, dwelt a winter in their tents, had scoured every lake that divides Canada from the States, had drunk palque with Mexicans, rum with the king of Klalams, had fought with Yankee redskins, hunted and trapped on a hundred streams, and now he had strolled three hundred miles through morass, forest, and over parched prairies, to see what progress had been made by a family of raw emigrants from the old country.

CHAPTER VI.

SUMMER WORK.

THERE is no every-day life in an emigrant's career. All is fresh, unexpected, and varied. The work of one twelve hours does not indicate what will be the occupation of the next. But for the arrival of Batiste, the emigrants might have gone on labouring at log-hut building and chopping, without much permanent advantage to themselves, for, with all their good-will and devotion to work, nothing could compensate for want of experience.

"Vell, my vere goot frens," said the *habitant*, as soon as he was seated at the emigrants' hospitable table, "so *vous* findé the *location*—hein!—ver goot lant, ver good vatère, vere fine *arbres*, vat you call de number," and he held up three fingers. "Oui! oui! I dis remembare *tree*." And he laughed heartily.

"I have found it all exactly as you promised me. The spot is magnificently chosen; and we want but the knack of clearing the forest and making roads to the water-side, to be independent of the world."

"Vant house, too—hein!" continued Batiste, with a grin.

"Yes, Batiste; and I tell you what," said Mr. Hatfield, "if you would only stop with us, I should be very glad to pay you anything in reason."

"*Ma foi*, de idea is not so vere bad—not at all. I chop for you, if you wish—so ve come to terms."

This was not difficult, as the Canadian was honest and practical, while Mr. Hatfield was thoroughly aware of the immense advantage to be derived from the co-operation of a man who knew the country so intimately as Batiste. In the present day, the usual price for clearing land and fencing it, fit for sowing, is, for hard wood, from eleven to twelve dollars per acre; for evergreen, such as pine, hemlock, cedar, and where that kind of timber predominates, from twelve to fourteen dollars per acre, while for swamp there is no fixed price.

To clear an acre of land, a thorough good chopper, after the land is underbrushed, will, in eight days, on an average, fell the trees, and cut them up into fifteen or sixteen-foot lengths, and pile the branches into heaps. As soon as the bark and tops of the trees are burned up, a yoke of oxen and four men will log, or roll up into heaps, an acre a day.

At the time of which we speak, labour was cheaper than it is now; and the Canadian readily agreed to do the work at ten dollars an acre, which delighted Mr. Hatfield, who had calculated on paying nearly thirty dollars per acre, which he must have done had he continued to employ the Irish emigrants, who, however, when once seasoned to the country, make some of the very best and most successful settlers.

The first job undertaken, with the assistance and under the supervision of Batiste, was to complete the house, which took some little time—chinking between the logs, plastering up crevices, cutting out a place for a doorway and window, casing them, and then making a door and shutters, and hanging them on wooden hinges, assisted by leather supports. By way of ensuring some comfort, they also made a rough table and some stools, which, though not much better fashioned than those of our old friend Robinson Crusoe, at all events answered the purpose for which they were intended.

They then, guided by their factotum, who was already a great favourite with everybody, sought out and found four slabs of limestone, which, placed upright in one corner of the shanty, with clay well packed behind them, to keep the fire off the logs, served admirably the purpose of a chimney, with a rude plank flue, and a hole cut in the roof to carry off the smoke.

Then some ironwood poles were cut, and from these a rude bedstead was manufactured, by stretching strips of elm bark across, which were strongly plaited together, to support a bed of hemlock boughs. This was for the parents; the younger members of the family sleeping in an outer room—they made two at night by means of a partition—until such time as they erected a larger house. Batiste slept in a small shanty of his own, erected in the woods, where Ralph often joined him when a hunting expedition was contemplated.

Batiste was perfectly independent. He worked when he pleased, and rested when he pleased; which suited the settlers admirably, for his "rests," as he called them, were genuine pieces of hard work. He would hunt, fish, or superintend agricultural occupations. Mrs. Hatfield found him admirable in inventions, his ingenuity producing various pieces of furniture; Mr. Hatfield did nothing without asking his advice, which he would give, seated on a stump, with his black pipe in his mouth. Through him, Ralph had many a glorious day's shooting; Harry swore by him as an angler; while little Jack believed there was not such another man on earth, especially since he had made him a real bow and arrows, like those formerly used by the Indians.

The bow was made from a young hickory, strengthened at the back by sinews of deer glued on; and the arrowheads were made from flints picked up on the shores of the lake; the feathers were plucked from the woodpecker; while a quiver of doe-skin completed the whole array.

But what finally attached Jack to Batiste, was an adventure which happened a full month after the arrival of the Canadian, like a good genius, in the new settlement.

The hunter had no sooner taken up his abode with the family of the Hatfields, than he inspired them all with his ardent love of the chase. No Nimrod celebrated in history, or immortalized in fiction, ever indulged with more ardour in every kind of sport than Batiste. After supper, while mending his mocassins, or doing some such useful household work as making baskets for Mrs. Hatfield, or teaching the others to do so, he would at intervals, when the father neither read nor spoke, indulge in such tales of bear-fights, deer-hunts, Caribou-stalking, or relate such exciting narratives, as fairly roused in all a passion for hunting.

Now Mr. Hatfield had every desire to see his farm progress; but, as both the Canadian and Ralph were to visit Montreal in the autumn, he had no objection to his sons spending a good deal of time upon an occupation which was useful in procuring food, and profitable when skins were brought in. The brave Canadian, who had an eye to business, and was saving of powder, readily instructed his pupils in the art of trapping, which occupation he had followed so many years with rare success. Even Harry liked this, though fishing was his favourite sport. In the first instance, Batiste accompanied them to teach what was necessary, but the young men were sharp adepts, and at last ventured out alone one day, to trap and hunt a new district.

With a wry face Jack saw them depart. He had several times asked to accompany them, but his mother was fearful for her pet boy, at which the juvenile aspirant for the honours of woodcraft was vastly indignant, being like many others at his age, in his own opinion at all events, quite a man. So Master Jack took refuge in sulks—which of course was very wrong—and going to the back of the house, he sat for some time in moody silence.

By dint of incessant practice he had become very dextrous in the use of his bow, so that he firmly believed he could shoot a deer as well as any of them. This idea once in his head, like a very thoughtless boy that he was, he determined to make the experiment at any price. Not having been able to obtain permission, he resolved to take it—that is, to do what many a youth has sadly repented all his life—run away.

Sauntering into the house, which was empty, Jack, as he had full permission to do, took his dinner from some cold deer's meat and corn cakes, provided himself with his bow and arrows, with a small knife and wooden cup, and then believing himself amply protected against all accidents, he entered the clearing and took his way towards the woods, which lay at the back of the location.

Now, not only did Jack do a very wrong thing, in acting in direct violation of parental commands, but a very foolish thing for himself. He should have remembered that there were in the woods other animals besides those which supplied food—such as bears, panthers, wolverines or carcajous, which he would have been very sorry to meet, even had he been armed with more telling weapons than a bow and arrow.

But Jack, though rather headstrong, was a brave boy, as we shall have many occasions to indicate, and thought no more of the savage denizens of the woods, than he did of the howling Indians he might have also met with.

Be this as it may, his strolls round about the plantation being common, he was not missed until night, when, to the surprise of father and mother, and the annoyance of the Canadian, all three sons were absent. At first, Mr. and Mrs. Hatfield thought Jack might have gone with his elder brothers, but Batiste shook his head, and said that he had seen the boy, full two hours after their departure, going in another direction.

The mother's fears were at once excited, and sinking

into a chair, she clasped her hands in speechless agony.

"Me find him," said Batiste quietly, "de boy be lost in de voods."

And snatching up his rifle, he hurried out of the hut, and taking the direction where Jack had been sauntering, he soon disappeared beneath the leafy arches of the forest.

CHAPTER VII.

LOST IN THE WOODS.

JACK no more knew where to look for the deer, than he did to kill it when found. This was partly the fault of his education. Had he been born in the same station of life in the United States or Canada, he would, by the time he was eight years old, have had a light fowling-piece of his own, and now at twelve, he would, in all probability, have been a pretty good shot, from practice at ducks, quails, pheasants, and squirrels. But he had been brought up in England, where such precociousness is not so much encouraged.

But Jack believed that he could easily come across some deer, which he thought, from the many successful expeditions of Batiste and Ralph, were to be found in every forest glade. With this idea in his head, he made directly for the hills, and soon began ascending the wooded slope, and this for hours; but not a trace of deer or any other game did he see, though every now and then he heard strange noises in the forest, which indicated that he was not alone.

After some time, while in a valley, he became tired, and stopping beside a small stream, he ate his dinner; which, after his long walk, he enjoyed very much. Rising from the green sward, he continued on his way, utterly forgetful that time was passing, while his mind was keenly alive to the sense of mortification which would overcome him, if, after running away, he returned utterly empty-handed to the camp. This thought roused the lion within him, and he struggled on manfully beneath hugh pine and hemlock trees, through cedar swamps, and over ridges, until the lengthening shadows and the approach of darkness suddenly brought him to a stand-still.

Many boys would have been frightened, but Jack was not. A night in the forest glades, under the greenwood tree, did not seem to him, as it might to stay-at-homes, so very dreadful, though he did feel a deep pang of remorse at the thought, that his disobedience would cause sorrow and alarm to his parents. But at his age, the sunny side of the future is ever uppermost, and Jack was already in fancy clasped in the arms of his fond, forgiving, and weeping mother. We are sadly afraid, that Mamma's weakness of heart, has often much to answer for.

The first thought of the lad was, to find a place to shelter himself from the weather, which looked threatening, and soon his eye fell upon a dry smooth spot beneath some spreading cedars, whither he carried, as long as a glimpse of daylight lasted, such fuel as he was able to collect, in the form of dry brambles, fallen boughs, and pieces of rotting logs. He had his flint, steel, and punk—a substance, obtained from the sugar maple, like German tinder—and with these, and some dry cedar-bark, he soon had a genial blaze, that cheered while it warmed him.

A boy's eyes are in general larger than his appetite. Jack, fortunately for himself, had provided twice as much dinner as he could eat, so that he had still a hearty supper left—which was more than he deserved. The meat and cake were sweet indeed, while even the muddy water from a neighbouring swamp was not to be disdained, with a little of the fruit of the papaw.

Jack's knife was again brought into requisition after supper, to cut a quantity of hemlock brush for his bed, while with larger limbs broken from the evergreens, which grew in abundance on that spot, he made a wall on the side whence the wind came. He contrived, it will be seen, to be very comfortable, though, in his heart, he would gladly have given up all this romance, to have seen the mild eyes of his mother beaming in his face.

We have said that he was not frightened; but still he was uneasy and uncomfortable. It was quite possible that he might be attacked by wild beasts, while at home he knew how sorrowful must be all the faces around the supper table. These thoughts kept him awake some time, during which the wind increased to a gale, and made things very uncomfortable, while its howling in the woods was indeed rough music for a lullaby. Jack said his prayers more solemnly than ever he had done on any previous occasion, vowing never to run away any more, though at the very instant an undercurrent of thought was telling him how much he enjoyed the excitement. At last he slept, nor woke except for a minute or two now and then, when he put on fresh fuel.

With the first upward leap of the sun he was on foot, and, to his great joy, the morning was bright. His conviction was, that he could without much trouble retrace his steps, though he had heard it was easy to lose one's self in the wood; and so it is until you get familiar with the creeks and ridges. He breakfasted on a crust, some papaw fruit, and water that left a sediment of mud in his cup. By this time the sun was obscured, so that Jack had no guide, save his memory. But in forests, trees are so much alike, that without compass or sun, it is all but impossible to find one's way, except you are an experienced woodman. This the Canadian afterwards explained fully to the boy, giving him a well-known direction, which, if ever you emigrate, you will do well not to forget.

If lost in the woods, the great secret is to move always in one direction, and this you may do by observing the moss on the trees. If you are in a forest of deciduous or hard wood—the moss grows in much greater abundance on the north side of the trees. It will not avail the anxious traveller to examine one trunk, which may mislead, but the general aspect of the wood. On the northern side they will be of a light and cheerful tint; but on the southern, dark and spotted. Then again, in pine woods, the usual inclination of the timber is *to* the southeast, while ridges run mostly north-east and south-west.

But these signs, by reading which in the open book of Nature the redskins become so expert, were as a sealed book to Master Jack, who, however, fearlessly struck out, as he thought, for home, despite the gloom of the overcast sky, and heedless of the falling rain. For some time he was satisfied that he was going in the right direction, nor was he frightened when he came to a thick cedar swamp, which he skirted for some time, until he found what he thought was a suitable passage. In another moment he was in a dense thicket of cedar, where every tree was like the last, and nothing could be seen in the way of a landmark. Presently, however, he saw the forest before him, and rejoicing at having crossed the swamp, he pressed forward until he met with occasional marks of his own footsteps coming from the opposite direction.

He was satisfied that he had come upon his own trail

of the previous day. His spirits revived wonderfully, though he was nigh fainting with hunger, not an eatable root or fruit that he knew of presenting itself. But soon he would be home, and then his sinking frame would be revived by proper food. Scarcely had he made this remark in his own mind, when above the trees rose a small wreath of curling smoke, and he felt that he was near his friends. They had doubtless been searching for him, and were now halting for rest and refreshment. On he hurried with a wildly beating heart, with a contrite speech ready prepared, dashing, despite his fatigue, over every impediment, to find himself in the presence of the smouldering fire which he had left in his camp of the night before.

Jack sank on the ground in the agony of his spirit, for a moment utterly heart-broken. He had gone round in a circle all day, the common fate of the man or boy who is lost in the woods,—a circumstance explained by the Indians, who assert that men and animals on the prairies and in the woods always bear to the left. But of this at a future time. Hunger now pressed him to rise; and eagerly searching the woods, he found some roots and beech mast, which he soon devoured, and night again coming on, he prepared once more to pass the weary hours, but in a very different mood to that which sustained him on the previous evening.

He was half-starved, while a vivid imagination painted to him the terrible suspense, the exquisite terror his friends must now be experiencing, and he vowed, if spared this time, never again to disobey his affectionate and loving parents. This resolution come to, he said his prayers, and making up a huge fire, he lay down once more beneath that leafy arch, to seek much-needed rest and slumber. It was not so easily obtained as on the night before. His ears were sensitively sharp, and keenly alive to every sound, so that at one moment he heard in the far-off distance the howling of wolves, and even fancied he detected the growling of savage bears. He knew that his best protection was fire, so he rose and kindled a fresh one on the other side of him.

Then once more he laid himself down to rest. Close to his head were the bow and arrows, his pride in which, and his own dexterity, had first led him astray. His eyes now became heavy, and his head fell upon the bosom of Mother Earth. Despite a fancy that overcame him that there was danger, sleep asserted its irresistible power, and all the world, its trials and its sorrows, became a blank.

About an hour before dawn he awoke with a sensation of chilliness, and rising, he found that his fires were burning low. This want was speedily supplied, as there was plenty of fuel about, and soon the huge furnace-like piles glowed with heat, the green hemlock boughs and other damp wood, spitting and emitting sparks and volumes of smoke.

His body in a glow, as much from exercise as from the warmth of the renovated piles, Jack, though very hungry and sad, once more stretched himself upon his leafy bed. Scarcely had he done so, when his quick ear caught the sound of something like the light cautious tread of a panther, or a redskin on some dry twigs higher up in the valley. Again it was repeated, and he knew that some powerful animal was stealthily approaching him.

Then all the terrible stories which the Canadian had told him of bears and panthers, carcajous and catamounts, flashed upon his excited brain, and he felt that his last hour was come. With a sad and bitter thought of those he should never see again, the brave boy placed his knife close to his hand, and clutching his feeble weapons, he resolved to sell his life dearly, and to yield only when overcome by superior force.

He had no time for any but a hasty prayer, for the cautious and stealthy footsteps sounded close at hand. Drawing his arrow to the very flint-head, his little manly heart beating with excitement more than fear, he waited. There was a slight dizziness about the eyes for a moment, caused by a rush of blood, and then, the boughs parting, he saw the honest face of Batiste Lanfry peering through the darkness ;—he had approached quietly with his mocassins, for fear of waking the slumbering lost one.

With a wild cry, the arrow was launched into the air, and then he was clasped to the honest hunter's heart, whose bronzed cheeks were moist with emotion and joy.

"De brave boy—he shoot: he no see me—he stand like one hero—no 'fraid in him!" said Batiste when telling the story, which he did with pride and delight ever afterwards.

A glass of brandy, a biscuit, and a slice of meat, soon restored Jack, who at once started for home, from which he had never before been distant eight miles. The Canadian had taken a wrong direction at first, but just at sundown the night before, while on a distant hill, he had observed a column of smoke, which he knew must arise from the camp of the boy hunter.

We need not add that Jack was freely forgiven by his delighted parents, and never again repeated his folly, which, however, did not keep him from undergoing many more startling trials afterwards. Scarcely had the excitement of his return subsided, when he found that he was not the only one who had had an adventure.

CHAPTER VIII.

THE MARTEN TRAPPERS.

THE Marten (*Mustela vison*) somewhat resembles a common weasel in form, though it is larger, being from eighteen to twenty inches from muzzle to tail; the tail itself ten inches, and the whole weighing about five pounds. The ears are short, broad, and round: the tail covered with long hair; the colour varying from a chestnut or dark brown, tinged with dirty yellow. It inhabits the Northern States of America and the British possessions, lives in the forest, and climbs trees in pursuit of its prey. The female has from three to six young ones. The flesh is eaten, but not esteemed. The fur is soft and valuable. In New England and other places it is called the Sable, while the Indians give it the name of Wappanaugh.

Furs have been always assiduously collected by man, and both Ralph and Harry, the latter especially, enjoyed a sport which was likely to be as lucrative as it was amusing. It will be necessary, to the full comprehension of our narrative, to describe minutely the process of marten trapping, an occupation which, in those days, was much followed. The traps are placed on a line of about three or four miles of forest and bush, which is blazed, that no one of the hunters may lose his way; that is to say, large slices are cut out of the trees on one side every now and then; one being always cut before the previous mark is lost sight of.

This part of the task is carried out by one man, while another sets the trap (which is called a dead fall) in the following manner:—Two lines are drawn on the ground, about a foot apart, into which short sticks are driven, one end only of the enclosure being left open; and this entrance being artistically covered by brushwood. The trapper then takes a piece of wood from two to three feet long, which he beds in the ground in summer, or in the snow in winter; on this a falling pole is supported by three pieces of stick notched together in the form of a figure 4; the centre piece being made long and sharp at the point, to which the bait is fastened, and projects well into the miniature house. The marten inserts its snout, to steal the bait, snatches at it, springs the trap, and the pole falling across its neck, the animal is killed at a single blow.

This is not only a sure but inexpensive way of procuring furs, and was therefore followed with ardour by the new settlers. Ralph would have enjoyed a shooting expedition better; but he was a reasonable young man, and knew the value both of powder saved and of furs gained. Harry, whose pride made him devote some of his time to woodcraft, not unwillingly accompanied him on the morning in question, to examine the traps, secure any prizes, or restore baits to those falls which had been disturbed.

There was a trail leading to the spot, which Ralph knew well, having followed it three times; so that about eleven they reached the middle of the line, which was four miles long, and there they parted, Ralph going to the left, and Harry to the right, each agreeing to return the same way as soon as their relative tasks were completed. Harry was delighted. The air was serene and balmy, the sky above, a mottled blue, while all around were lovely prairies, with their interminable carpet of green; or thick woods, through which, however, the youth made his way easily by means of the blazed trees. On his way he secured three martens, which he hung on trees; and having reset the traps, he continued his journey.

The end of the line once reached, Harry seated himself with his back against a log, took out his dinner and sedately began eating it. When this agreeable task was completed, and the solids washed down with some spruce beer, he leaned his head against the fallen tree, and admiring the prospect, or thinking of something, or nothing, he fell fast asleep, nor did he awake for perhaps an hour, when in a half doze he heard a strange noise—a kind of vibratory sound like the distant roll of a drum.

Now, if Harry was somewhat slow in his actions, he was quick in his thoughts, and at the same time curious. Taking up his gun, therefore, he hurried ahead, dashed through a thicket, gradually decreasing his pace until he was creeping with due huntsman care, when he came upon a scene which well rewarded him for his journey. The drumming noise which he had heard was from a covey of Canadian partridges or grouse, the male of which, in the season of courtship, perches himself on the top of a hollow log, or fallen tree, and with his wings makes the drumming, which, in still weather, can be heard in the woods at the distance of a mile.

Determined not to be behindhand, Harry fired at the covey, killed three birds, and then loading, started in pursuit, nor took any note of time until he had secured six brace. Then, and only then, he began to look about him, with a view to returning. One glance at the country somewhat startled him, though he entertained no fear about finding his way back to the line.

He was on a summit, or ridge, and all around were gloomy woods, and thickets of grey pine, hemlock, and red cedar, while at no great distance were deep ravines, precipitous rocks, and one or two small lakes, which, in the excitement of the chase, he had not noticed. Now, Harry, without having Ralph's experience, had all his confidence, so he set out upon his return journey without a fear of the result, and rather proud of his achievement than otherwise. Twelve fat partridges were things by no means to be despised. Trudging along the plain, forcing his way through tangled ravines, climbing up steep rocks, Harry pushed on for some time without losing any of his confidence of being right; but by degrees his elongated face showed the rising doubt, and when he sat down on the summit of the rock, under a huge white pine, towering more than a hundred feet into the air, the solemn conviction forced itself upon him, that he had lost his way.

Two brothers lost on the same day! But in Canada such matters are of daily occurrence; and many a good-natured neighbour who has turned out in search of a missing one, has lost himself, while rarely does the wanderer stray to any great distance, being generally found within a radius of a few miles.

When Harry came to this conclusion, he at once fired off both barrels, as a signal to Ralph, and waited, but no responsive shot coming to cheer him, he looked up into the sky, and keeping his eye fixed upon the sun for a moment, he took the bearings of another mighty pine at a considerable distance, and made straight for it. This for a few minutes was easy enough, but as he neared it he found that this one tree got muddled up with the others, and his land-mark was again lost.

What puzzled Harry most was, that he still kept on a rocky ridge which seemed strange to him; so, after a moment's reflection, he resolved to try once more the effect of a signal. Looking keenly round, he selected a large, ancient, and hollow cedar that stood apart from any other trees, and around this and in the hollow of it he piled brush and brambles and pitch-pine knots, with other combustibles, to which he then set fire, the whole taking light with a crackling and a roar that sounded through the woods like a dropping fire of musketry.

Then Harry leaned on his gun and waited.

It was in vain. Ralph had either not seen the signal, or was too far off to respond to it; so Harry in desperation began to pluck a partridge preparatory to roasting it. But as yet it was impossible to reach the raging pile, the trunk of the cedar having taken fire inside, and burning with the loud roar of a blast-furnace, sending flames and sparks flying in all directions from a yawning opening about twelve feet from the ground. As the twilight came, and the dark mantle of night fell upon the earth, the blazing tree presented quite a grand appearance, and beside it Harry felt no alarm from the wild beasts. Presently the bark, after shrivelling and curling, caught fire, and then the whole body of the tree was in flames, the cedar boughs crackling and hissing with a sound that might have been heard many miles.

Harry was a philosopher, and took things mighty easily, so, after eating a partridge and some biscuit, he slept soundly, and as soon as morning came he once more took his way through the forest in a north-westerly direction, as far as he could judge by the sun, leaving the cedar to smoulder and smoke until reduced to ashes.

By moving very slowly, guided by the sun, and taking large trees as landmarks, Harry contrived to get over a good bit of ground; and at noon, after floundering about in a zigzag and winding direction, he came suddenly upon a blazed tree.

Next instant he saw a fresh marten trap, and in a transport of joy he gave a loud shout, which was speedily followed by another; and before he had time to survey the ground, Ralph came in sight. The meeting was hearty indeed, though the elder brother had felt no alarm, in his own mind believing that Harry, having missed him, had gone home, whereupon, it being late, he had resolved to camp out and visit the marten traps a second time. The sight of the partridges delighted him, and leading his brother to where he had camped, he heard the other's story over a substantial breakfast.

Both laughed heartily, and, their morning's survey over, they returned rapidly to the settlement, their horse heavily laden with deer's meat, grouse, and martens; they heard that their brother Jack was lost in the woods, and that Batiste had gone after him. We need not now pain our readers by a description of the suffering endured by the parents and elder brothers; it suffices to say that the re-union was a happy one, and that the occurrences of the two previous days gave an additional zest to some stories told by the Canadian.

He had known people die within half-a-dozen miles of their own door, after moving round in a circle day after day; but this was generally in winter, with snow on the ground and on the heavily-laden trees, and falling so rapidly as to obliterate the trail, and render it impossible to recognize a road from an open glen of the forest. Then, if the traveller, without means to make a fire, yields to the terrible inclination for sleep which comes over him, he will never wake more, but be found frozen to death; or only a few bones, picked clean by wolves, will remain to tell his fate.

He knew an old woman and her grandson, who, journeying from house to house, in sight of one another, lost the track while the child was plucking flowers, and were not found for eight days, and then thirteen miles east from the starting point. They were alive, but had suffered much from exposure and privation. In every instance, the shrewd hunter declared that the sufferers had turned to the left, to which men and animals "always bear their course." This assertion was as thoroughly believed in by Batiste as it was by Catlin and other hunters, and resulted in his giving the same advice as that wonderful hunter did.

"When a deer does run," he would say, "if it is on a plain, don't run after him, but turn to the left, when you will meet him. He runs in a curve, and when he stops he is always watching his back track."

CHAPTER IX.

SETTLING.

IN the intervals of these and many minor adventures, which, if narrated, would swell our book to an inordinate size, the farm labours were not neglected. While the chopping was going on, care was taken to put aside such logs as would, when well seasoned, serve to set up a more complete house the following year, settlers in this respect resembling the aboriginal inhabitants, who use skins, grass, dirt, mud, bark, and timber in the erection of their houses, but never stones.

One of the most important works to be undertaken was to prepare for the plough as much land as possible previous to the frosts, as these pulverize the ground, so that in the spring it only requires harrowing. But before the plough could be driven over any large space of ground, it was necessary to clear it as much as possible; and this was done in a variety of ways.

It must be remembered by the home farmer, and by all my boy readers, that when the trees are cut down, about two or three feet from the ground—much depending on the height of the axe-man—there remain the stumps and the roots, which the ruder kind of settlers generally, and squatters always, allow to rot away; oak, ash, beech, and maple take about ten or twelve years, and the evergreens, such as pine, hemlock, and cedar, a much longer period.

Now, nothing can be more unsightly than the presence of these stumps in a field, while they interfere with agricultural operations in a way that needs no explanation. Mr. Hatfield, who, in a permanent residence, had an eye to beauty as well as utility, desired that such fields as would be seen from his front windows, in the future, should be as free as possible from eye-sores; so all set to work to endeavour to eradicate them.

With this view the logging chain, to which allusion has already been made, was fastened round the top of the stumps, and then, according to the size or tenacity of the root, a part, or all the team of oxen and horses were fastened to it, and made to start off with a quick and sudden jerk, which in most instances sufficed to pull it up. Others, however, were much larger and more tenacious, being firmly fixed in the ground; and in these instances a huge lever, twenty feet long and more than twelve inches thick, was chained at one end to the stump, and to the other the oxen were fastened and driven in a circular direction, which, in most cases, sufficed to break up the obstruction. But whenever the roots had not rotted at all, they were left for another season.

Batiste hit upon an ingenious plan with regard to the cedar stumps, which afforded considerable amusement to the young people. The weather had been unusually hot so that all timber was very dry. One evening, therefore, Batiste proposed to clear a few acres of cedar stumps in a novel kind of way. As they had been busy during the day, the operation was left until evening, when Mr. Hatfield usually indulged in the pleasures of a pipe before his log shanty, which all settlers find very grateful after the labours of the day have been completed.

The Canadian and the boys had selected the ground, and when all care had been taken to avoid any danger, a large fire was lit just before sundown, which, during the evening meal, was reduced to embers. Then the actors in the scene took each a quantity of hot coals, which were shaken on the crown of the cedar stump, and which, after smouldering for some time, were fanned into flame by the evening breeze. Tree after tree in this way presented the appearance of gigantic torches blazing about two or three feet from the ground, until at last from two to three hundred, flaring in the night air, presented one of those grandiose and impressive spectacles which can scarcely be realized in the old country.

This operation performed, and the roots being burnt to some little distance below the surface, the land was ploughed, crossed, and harrowed; it was then rolled twice previous to the final ploughing and ridging, which takes place in August. Soon after this, fall wheat is sown; for the earlier the seed is in the ground the stronger the plant will be, and hence better able to withstand the frost. All this was hard work; and when we consider that over forty acres had also to be fenced in the way already described, we have some idea of the early labours of a settler.

One very important requisite to emigrants is fodder; the want of it is found by farmers to be among the greatest inconveniences they have to endure for the first three or four years after their arrival in the land of adoption.

During the whole of this period he has to depend on the bush for pasturage for his cows and oxen,—at all events during six or seven months of the year. It must not be supposed that there is any want of food; it is only too abundant in the woods, on the beaver meadows, and on the margin of lakes and streams, where, if cattle be turned out towards the autumn, they will become excessively fat and in good condition. The difficulty you have to suffer from, is that of not being able to find them when you want them, which, both with cows and oxen, is a very serious one. Many a wearisome and anxious day, sometimes a week, is spent in hunting up your cattle; and you may not only consider yourself lucky to find them, but esteem yourself fortunate if you do not lose yourself.

Mr. Hatfield was naturally anxious to provide against this, and therefore hurried on as fast as possible the clearance of land suitable to be sown with timothy grass and clover mixed, or the former alone, which in Canada is considered the best for hay. Timothy is a solid grass, with a bulbous root. All worked with a will, especially Ralph, who was looking forward to a glorious winter with an impatience and ardour which, perhaps, some of my boy readers may understand, when I give a slight programme of their designs.

The Canadian and Ralph were to start on horseback to Montreal, making arrangements as they went for the purchase of cows and pigs to be delivered in the spring. At Montreal they were to sell their furs and skins, and then lay in a stock of necessaries, such as coffee, tea, and sugar, after which they were to purchase a sleigh and return home as rapidly as possible.

Batiste bade them not trouble about domestics, as he would find efficient ones himself before the arrival of the cattle, and before the enlarged and extended operations of the following year made labourers necessary.

Mr. and Mrs. Hatfield had agreed that on their return, and as soon as they had taken a moderate rest, all the boys, Jack included, were, under the special surveillance and guardianship of Batiste, to start on an expedition to certain mountainous lakes for the purpose of caribou hunting. For this purpose Jack was to have a gun, while all the long evenings were spent by the mother in preparing clothes and blankets for their snow campaign.

From early morning until night, the ploughs and harrows were at work, after which the seed was sown broadcast, at the rate of six quarts of grass-seed and two pounds of clover to the acre—on virgin soil, be it noted. On old, cleared farms double the amount would have been needed. This done, the thought of the hay-making next June intruded itself, and made them think of raising barns; but this was a serious undertaking, which was deferred to next summer, as a cow-house, pigsties, and storehouse were far more pressing matters.

These were made from logs and shingle, which is a word so often occurring in these and other pages as to need some explanation. Shingles are of pine or cedar, the former being preferred, as less liable to gutter and make an uneven roof. Nothing is more necessary to a backwoods-man than to be a good shingler—that is, to know how to select the right tree and how to cut it. Many, after cutting down a four-foot diameter tree, and sawing a block of eighteen inches out of the centre, find either that it will not split fair, or that the wood eats, by which is meant that the grain, though straight lengthways, makes sharp deep curves which render it bad to split, and causes holes in the shingle when shaved.

Now, the grain of most trees naturally inclines towards the sun, or the same way round the tree as the sun's course. It may, therefore, happen that a tree may be quite straight in the grain, where you chop it down, yet ten feet higher it winds so much as to be useless.

The Canadian, whose knowledge of the woods was marvellous, taught them to obviate this difficulty; and under his guidance they chose trees—the largest possible—clear of knots for sixty or more feet, with luxuriant head and drooping boughs; this done, the bark was peeled off as high as possible, and the grain examined. If it was in the least inclined *towards* the sun, it was rejected; while, if its curves were ever so slight the other way, or *against* the sun, it was further tried by cutting out a piece a foot long and three or four inches deep. This was split until it was reduced to the thickness of two shingles, when it was split again, and if the timber were fit and good, the pieces flew apart with a sudden snap, and were perfectly even in the grain; while, on the other hand, one grain would cut into the other, or run off the whole length without splitting clear. The blocks for use were cut eighteen inches long and split into quarters, and the sap wood dressed off.

Then, in addition to these duties, there was laying in a stock of provisions for the winter. In such a plentiful, rich, and favoured country as Canada, they had no fear of a supply both of fresh pork and game, during the snows and frosts; but it was necessary to provide for those days when the weather or other circumstances prevented hunting and fishing. With this view, boxes and rude barrels were made, to hold dry and salt fish and venison, after which large quantities were procured.

Salmon-fishing was the greatest sport, and this was indulged in by all the males, Mrs. Hatfield watching them from the bank. It necessitated the making of a canoe, the scow being too heavy; and this of itself was a delightful amusement to the boys. Over the bow of this, an iron grate or jack, as Batiste called it, was suspended—the said grate being a small cradle composed of iron bars three or four inches apart. This cradle is allowed to swing in a frame, as it is thus kept on a level, otherwise the swell would pitch the pine knots out. The fire is made of light wood and fat pine, which throw a clear bright light for several yards round the bow of the canoe, and enable the fisherman to discern his prey many feet beneath the water.

Each canoe holds two, the striker and the paddler—the latter seated, the former kneeling. Ralph was content to steer and row this autumn, allowing the Canadian to use the spear, which he did with marvellous success, throwing ashore whole piles of fish, then so abundant that one day Harry and Jack, after driving a shoal up a stream, caught seventy with a pitchfork. They took also sturgeon, pike, mullets, eels and trout, the latter with worm and fly; while Mr. Hatfield amused himself by trolling for muske-longe, or black bass, with an imitation mouse of musk-rat fur, a red and white rag, or a green frog. About this time they first saw passenger pigeons in incredible numbers, but as they had no regular *battue* until the next year, we reserve our description.

And now that pleasant harbinger of winter was upon them, the Indian summer, when the air is unusually mild and temperate, when a haze, like distant smoke, pervades the atmosphere, at times, however, so thick as even to obscure the sun, or, if it remains visible, changing it to a blood-red colour. Batiste knew that this was a sign not to be mistaken, so the departure for Montreal was hurried; the horses saddled, the furs packed, and for five weeks Batiste and Ralph were absent.

Just as their absence began to excite uneasiness, up they dashed with the loveliest sleigh, as Jack thought, he had ever seen.

The vehicle was what is called a family sleigh, to hold six, with a high seat in front for two, and room for four behind, or for luggage in considerable quantities. The horses were harnessed tandem fashion. There are many which hold ten persons, and others two, called cutters; while now all farmers have lumber sleighs for general purposes—it being well known that far larger loads can be conveyed on runners in winter than can be drawn on wheels in summer, even over a good road.

It is worth while to make a voyage to Canada, if only to enjoy the supreme luxury of sleighing, which, with skating, is the favourite amusement of both sexes during the winter months; though it is some time ere the former can be perfectly enjoyed, as it takes several falls of snow to fill up and level all the inequalities, when alone sleighing can be good.

Then with a good whip, warm furs, with winter-shod horses, with bells upon the horses' necks, away you go at a pace which is perfectly delicious, but which makes the blood tingle, the heart beat, the eyes flash, and the whole being become pervaded by a glow of general happiness and excitement incomparable, which only the practised sleigher can understand. But our sleigh has a long and adventurous voyage before it—so we must defer it.

CHAPTER X.

THE SLEIGH.

October was the great fishing month; and about November, the ice was strong enough to bear a man upon it; while, by degrees, the ground became whitened with snow. Nothing could be more wild and yet more picturesque than to gaze out from the shanty upon the narrow expanse which, while the snow fell, remained within the circle of their vision, and to note the evergreens changing their upper boughs for a snowy hue, while under this silver layer shone in dark relief the native colour of the tree; to remark the heavy clods, as it were, of congealed water filling up holes, carried in drifts, and at last making one vast sheet of lovely white.

But the falls are not continuous until Christmas, before which time sleighing seldom begins in earnest; and it has to be left off in January during a temporary thaw, which, though periodical, is not every year of the same duration. It is often attended by strong gales of wind from the southward, with heavy thunder and lightning, which our adventurers discovered to their cost; but we must not anticipate. However, we may mention here, for the information of our readers and intending emigrants, that February is the coldest month. A great authority makes the following statement:—" I have frequently known the thermometer range from 16 to 20° below zero for a week together. On one winter's day it was as low as 35°. The coldest day was in 1833. The quicksilver in Fahrenheit's thermometer was frozen in the ball, which marks 39° below zero. The day was clear; not a cloud was above the horizon. The sun was of a dull copper colour; and the horizon, towards the north-west, was tinged with the same hue. I was only a quarter of an hour out, but I felt the cold severely. We sat round the fire at dinner, with plates on our knees."

The excessive cold is of short duration, while the snow and the extreme dryness of the atmosphere make the cold less felt than in England. It was resolved on all hands that the caribou expedition should commence two days after Christmas Day, and no time, therefore, was lost in making preparations for a journey which was not without its dangers and perils, and which certainly could not be completed without many trials.

The long wished-for morning came, and there stood the sleigh before the door, the horses harnessed, and to all appearance impatient for a start. The seat in front was to contain the Canadian and Ralph, while Harry and Jack were to be perched amid a confused heap of guns, spears, blankets, buffalo rugs, snow-shoes, mocassins, a couple of hounds, and other necessaries—not forgetting a good store of coffee, sugar, and bread, with a small supply of meat.

The worthy Batiste was grave and solemn, as behoved the leader of a party. Ralph strove to emulate his calmness while he stood holding the bridle of the leading horse. Harry never allowed excitement to overcome his discretion; but little Jack was in such a state of excitement as is, perhaps, only known to a boy when about to start for the first time on such an expedition as that which now marked an era in his life. No warrior going into the battle for the first time, no actor appearing on his maiden board, no speaker rising for the first time on a public platform, had ever felt his heart beat more wildly than did Jack Hatfield.

No word-picture can do justice to the appearance of

that morning. The day, for the 27th of December, was magnificent. Only a few clouds, resplendent with reflected light from the mass of snow which covered Mother Earth, floated in an ocean of the brightest blue, while there was a singularly novel glittering in the atmosphere, that appeared full of shining particles, moving like dust atoms in a sunbeam.

There had been rain on Christmas Day, which circumstance added much to the beauty of the landscape. Wherever on cedar, pine, or maple, the rain had half melted the snow, the sudden frost had caught and frozen it afresh into myriads of strange shapes; which, whether coaters of ice or dependent icicles, whether projecting lumps or drifts in corners, displayed their silver frontings under a sun that turned them to every colour of the rainbow.

There was no good road to the lake, but the hunters had taken care, during the summer, to remove all such obstacles as would stand in the way of a sleigh. This was the more necessary as, from peculiar circumstances, they had to start at headlong speed. The rain, succeeded by a sharp and sudden frost, had turned the snow into one solid mass of ice, over which a tandem sleigh must be guided with the most consummate skill, to prevent the leading horse finding "his head where his tail should be," by the mere gliding or slueing of the sleigh. This an experienced charioteer will prevent by keeping a tight rein on the side which shows a tendency to slue, and at the same time launching the steeds at full gallop, the body of the horse counteracting the sidelong movement of the sleigh. On such a road any attempt to pull up a horse will result in the sleigh turning round rapidly, as on a pivot, and inevitably throwing the animals.

Mr. Hatfield was rather grave, but confident in the skill and devotion of the Canadian. He felt quite proud of his sons; though he was somewhat startled when, with a loud halloo and a sudden cracking of the whip, the sturdy and well-fed horses were launched down the road at a pace that appeared, to an unpractised eye, literally fearful.

Before it was out of sight, the sleigh was going at the rate of at least twenty miles an hour, which compelled Harry and Jack to lie down, and Ralph to hold his breath, and glance inquiringly at Batiste to know if the animals had not run away. Any one passing through the frosty air at that fearful pace, and seeing the trees glide swiftly by, would have been somewhat alarmed in those days of slow locomotion, though much greater speed is often attained now.

Over the glass-like ice, away through snow-drifts, now shaving a huge trunk, now jostling a charred and frosted stump, now rushing down hill, and then as suddenly up, never halting, never stopping, the horses sending forth volumes of smoke-like vapour from their nostrils; while, ere many miles were traversed, flakes of foam fell upon their harness, and upon the front of the sledge. Batiste slashing his long whip, and holding his reins firm, Ralph burying his head, all but his eyes, in his furry robe, Harry and Jack watching with flashing eyes the woods and forests, that seemed to flit by, the hounds growling as they were loosed above,—out came the sleigh upon the vast lake, which was one single sheet of snow, unspotted as far as the eye could reach,—a white and glittering plain.

The snow being more suited to sleighing, Batiste gradually compelled his foaming, panting, snorting steeds to slacken their pace, until they were whirling along at about ten miles an hour, when out sprang the hounds, while Harry and Jack stood up holding on to the back of the driver's seat, to gaze at the scene around, which was still sufficiently panoramic to be exciting. They were rushing up the lake in a northerly direction, and could gaze beneath the tall pines and hemlocks, with here and there a beech or chestnut, until all was dark at the extremity of the forest vista, of which only a glimpse was caught.

"Ha! ha!" said Batiste, flourishing his whip, "ah, ah, my frens—how you like de *traineau* voyage—de 'slay,' as you say him? Fine, *hein!* monstros fine."

"Prime," replied Jack.

"Ha! ha! dis is noting—noting at all—vate a beet—you vill see vat you shall see."

"And what is that?" asked Ralph, looking inquiringly at Batiste.

"Something—vere fine," grinned the French Canadian. "A leetle vay up de lake—some two honree—mile you fine—my frend Antoine—and all de leetle Antoines, and den—you vill see vat you shall see."

And despite their curiosity, the Canadian would say no more, but that, when they reached the head-waters of the lake, they would be made acquainted with an old trapper, who had lived for years with his family upon a certain spot, the centre of the finest hunting country in the world, abounding in bears, black and brown, in racoons, in all furry animals, as well as caribou, moose, red deer, and wapiti, and who would be the means of giving them rare sport.

As mid-day came on, the faint sun of that high latitude was at its greatest height; the horses were gradually brought to a standstill, close to a steep bank, under the shelter of which a fire was made, first with fuel from the sleigh, and then with boughs, cut, thawed, and dried, and then again with wood from a huge tree felled by the stalwart Canadian.

The horses were hoppled, and some hay, carried in closely-pressed parcels, was given to them;—then some scanty grass from where the huge fire thawed the bank, was cut for them. The masters, having seen to their beasts, ate a hearty meal, after which the sleigh was again brought into requisition until an hour before sundown, when the Canadian ran ashore upon a small plain, sheltered and isolated, which he appeared to know well.

All being guided by Batiste, the youths fastened on their snow-shoes, and then taking the horses from the sleigh, they rubbed them down with extreme care, and put upon them a complete suit of cloths, after which they were placed beneath some trees, entirely sheltered from the wind, while loose, easily-cut shrubs or boughs were so piled up around them, as not only to afford shelter from wolves, but to keep them warm.

Then the camp of the young hunters was made, almost precisely as the one which they had formerly erected from description, but which they did now under the guidance of Batiste, who was out on the water otherwise engaged, though shouting to them when he thought they needed his advice. The snow was shovelled away, until they came to the hard frozen ground. Then the frame of the camp, made at home from poles cut the requisite length, was set up. It was about six feet high, and sloped off to the ground; over this was placed a thick layer of fir and hemlock boughs, upon the top of which was shovelled as much snow as it could well bear, leaving only a small opening, in front of which the fire was placed, so as to allow none but warm air to enter. Hemlock boughs and buffalo robes covered the ground.

This done, just as the fire was completed, a shot was heard; and hurrying towards Batiste, they found that he had been even better engaged than themselves. With something shod with iron, like an Alpine climber, he had dug a hole in the ice, and had got up two leather pails of water. These were carried towards the fire, after which, returning to his post, the Canadian threw in some hooks baited with pork; and as fish gladly rush to air-holes, he soon had a nice dish of various sorts. These he was about to take to the camp, when some ruffed grouse attracted his attention, and then fell at his discharge.

CHAPTER XI.

THE BOY SENTRY.

This, the first night out, must be described with more minuteness than we shall often be able to give to the occurrences of any other ten or twelve hours. The Canadian was anxious to indoctrinate the boys with his own experience and knowledge in woodcraft. The hearty trapper had taken quite as much a fancy to them as they had to him, and it was his firm determination that his pupils should do him credit.

The fire was by this time blazing so fiercely as to melt the snow for some space around, which was no inconvenience, as the tent was placed above. To keep the fire up the whole of the night, was absolutely necessary; so, leaving the young people to cook the fish and grouse and make the coffee, Batiste moved aside to where some huge-limbed trees stood erect, and using his giant strength, he soon laid them prostrate. They were then cut into suitable lengths and dragged to within a proper distance of the camp.

By the time this had been accomplished, the supper was ready, the hunters sitting down to their meal with a hunger and relish which is unknown to the pale dweller in towns. The grouse were pronounced delicious, the fish was voted excellent, a damper fried with fat pork very good, and the coffee superb—and superb it was, for the cunning trapper had taught them how to make it, which is a secret worth knowing; for no matter how good the raw material, the manufacturer can easily spoil it.

It was now (by Jack's watch, without which he never moved) about six o'clock; and it having been settled that, as a rule, eight was to be the hour for turning in, all proceeded to undertake some employment which might, with laughter, songs, stories, and adventures, while away the time. Their guns were carefully examined and cleaned, mocassins overhauled, snow-shoes repaired, and many little things made ready which are necessary on an occasion like this.

But Batiste it was who kept them chiefly alive. He had hundreds of stories at his tongue's end—stories of bears, stories of Indians, stories of trappers, and of animals, which were an endless fund of amusement to the boys, who watched his animated face, as, with his everlasting black pipe stuck in his mouth, he gave forth his narratives in a language which, it is quite certain, none but those who had been accustomed to him for some time would ever have understood.

About eight the word was "Turn in;" upon which three of the party laid themselves down, wrapped in blankets and buffalo-rugs, while one "turned out" to act as sentry, and keep the fire to a proper state, both with a view to warmth and as a protection against wild animals, all of which have a great dislike to fire. Jack was first sentry on this occasion, and went forth into the open air with a pride and satisfaction that of itself warmed and cheered his heart, making him feel, at length, a man.

Warmly shod, with ample clothes, the boy shouldered his gun, and selecting, by Batiste's directions, a shaded walk along a beaten path that took him from the fire to the horses, and from the horses to the fire, began his task with more than a due sense of its importance. The night was clouded and dark, but the reflection of the snow made it quite clear enough for him to see, while the fire he was careful to keep up made a cheery and pleasant blaze, which, with the crackling of the green wood, and the spitting, sputtering noise of the resin, was of itself company.

At first the dogs, as if in duty bound, came forth to join him; but Jack pitilessly drove them into the tent, knowing that they had quite enough to do to keep up with the sledge in the day, and anxious also to do his duty himself. It was the first time that he had had any responsibility cast upon his youthful shoulders, and he was anxious to fulfil it properly.

The walk which the boy sentry tramped upon was long enough not to be too monotonous; it passed under a row of pines that sheltered him from the prevalent wind, and gave him a free view of the huge expanse of white lake that lay outstretched to the very shores of the United States of America. At first Jack met with no greater interruption to his meditations than the creaking of the huge trees, and the moaning sough of the wind; but presently, as the evening advanced, he heard the hounds growl in their sleep, as there came sweeping down from the hills the most dismal music conceivable, when heard in the stillness and the dead of night.

It was the howling of approaching wolves, which would certainly have drawn forth the dogs, but Batiste swore at them in French—a very energetic proceeding—upon which they nestled at their master's feet, and sought no more to move. Jack half-cocked his gun, determined to pepper the assailants if they came too near, and then resumed his walk, listening all the while to the approaching enemy, which, avoiding the tremendous fire that now blazed up, were soon heard to rush past, next moment appearing in great force upon the lake.

There they sat, evidently scenting men, horses, and the offal cast from fish and grouse, but, for the present, not venturing to approach. Their tactics were peculiar. The whole party could be seen in bold relief upon the white background, seated in a semicircle. One savage lanky brute at one end would begin barking, followed in an instant by another, until the whole ravenous and ferocious pack had let loose their tongues, when the snappish bark turned to a howling chorus that, once heard, is rarely if ever forgotten — and this continued without ceasing.

Jack felt his bold little heart beat wildly, though not with fear, as he halted and stood gazing at the gaunt, horrid, and hungry-mawed pack, which, if they had only had but courage, might have torn him to pieces ere any defence could have been offered. Now this halt was dangerous. The Canadian had laid strict injunctions on Jack never to stand still, but rather to stamp and trudge quickly over the beaten path; as to fall asleep in the night air in the snow, is fatal. But Jack was so excited by the presence of the wolves, that he entirely forgot this part of the sentry's orders, and found himself standing erect in a statue-like attitude, watching the greedy brood. His chin rested on his gun, and it struck him that he should particularly like to have a crack at the savage brutes.

Then they all mysteriously disappeared; a strange sensation came over his frame, and next instant he was as sound asleep as those he watched over—a sleep that might have proved eternal, but that, slipping from his grasp, the gun fell to the ground, and he went sprawling over it. Jumping up, Jack shook himself violently, and looked hurriedly at the wolves, which were still upon the borders of the frozen inland sea.

The boy sentry shouldered his gun, and was eagerly about to resume his walk, when a new and unexpected interruption made him bound a couple of yards, turn, level his gun, and speak:

"Who goes there? Answer, or I fire!"

As he had risen to his feet, close to one of the tall and waving pines, his ears had been assailed by a frightful peal of such fiendish laughter as made him not only feel a little alarmed, but roused in him a sense of anger, that any one should thus treat his very slight dereliction from duty.

"Who goes there?" he repeated for the second time.

Again the laughter was repeated, this time with a kind of echo, that convinced Jack they were surrounded by secret foes, who, if the camp were not roused, would overcome them in the silent watches of the night. At the same moment, his sense of vision was struck, while his heart was nearly chilled by the sight of two glowing orbs that peered at him over the bough of a cypress in front. Without a thought of the consequences, acting only on the sudden influence of surprise, he took steady aim and fired. A strange wild yell followed, and then a heavy body fell at his feet, as Batiste and his two brothers rushed forth to the rescue.

"*Eh! mon garçon*," cried Batiste, "vat is de mataire?"

Jack looked about him, unable for a moment to reply, and then he said, in a low tone,—

"I thought I saw an Indian glaring from yonder bush."

"An' no vondaire," shouted the Canadian, as he picked up something from the ground; "it is von horned—vat you say?—*hibou*—howl."

"It is a great horned owl," added Harry, laughing. "Bravo, Jack! we'll take him home and stuff him as Jack's first game."

Jack took the monstrous specimen in his hand, and looked at it with some awe. The horned owl (*Stux Virginiana*) was indeed both large and ugly enough to terrify a boy Its wings had a spread of quite five feet.

"Now, my boys," said Batiste, "'fore we *allons coucher*, let's peppare dem debils on de lake. Take one pine torch."

The Canadian, trailing his gun on the ground with his left hand, seized a brand, and approached the howling crew which still was drawn up on the brink of the lake in battle array. Then at a signal from the trapper, all being similarly provided, the brands were hurled high in the air, and falling among the wolves, sent them scattering over the lake, but not before some half-dozen were killed and wounded.

This done, all returned to the camp, and two hours having passed, Ralph took Jack's place, to be relieved by Harry at twelve, and by the hunter at two.

CHAPTER XII.

THE ANTOINES.

At early dawn the horses were brought out and put to, so that after a hearty but hasty breakfast, they were able once more to start the sleigh, now further loaded by the presence of the horned owl, which Jack was determined to take home in token of his first watch. He didn't say much about it, but it struck him that, perhaps, but for the sudden arrival of the huge bird, it might have been his last watch. The weather was still very fine, to the great delight of all, who every hour more and more appreciated the delights of coursing along the crisp and lovely mantle in which the earth was wrapped.

There were stoppages, too, when Batiste shot some ruffed grouse, to which, at the hour of the midday meal, he added a couple of hares. Then again the journey was continued, nor was any further halt declared until evening, when the camp was again constructed. The night passed on this occasion without any accident worthy of record.

Again they are on the wing, away up the great waters, day after day, until at last they are skirting what the Canadian stated to be islands, thickly wooded and hilly, but not mountainous. They were now at no great distance from the spot where the boys were to be introduced into all the mysteries of caribou-hunting, and all became equally excited. The old trapper smiled grimly—not a sneering smile, but one of pleased remembrance of his own sensations in early youth.

About eleven one morning, he himself began to look a little flushed. The country was now composed of a mixture of wooded hills, rolling prairies, and dense belts of forest, while in front of them was a projecting spur of land, round which the Canadian whirled with unusual rapidity and skill, drawing up his steaming horses in front of what was evidently a white man's settlement.

There was a large frame-house, also stables, out-houses, a small block-house two stories high, ploughed fields and clearings with stumps, now all frosted with silvery coating; but what made the youths glance at the Canadian with a keen and inquisitive eye, was the absence of any smoke curling from the chimneys, in token of welcome.

"Vell!" said the trapper, "de ole vagbone out, he and all de leetle vuns—nevare mind."

And without any further observation the Canadian alighted from the sleigh, and led the horses up a slight acclivity to the door of a large barn-like edifice, into which he drove, vehicle and all. The animals were then unharnessed, the goods unpacked and carried into the house, which was well built and admirably secured against the weather, and in every way a most pleasant and cheering sight, after ten days of outlying in woods and snow, despite the look of cold discomfort which in winter there always is about an empty fireplace.

The Canadian, whose trick of opening the door showed his familiarity with the place, began at once to light up fires in the principal room, which served for both kitchen and parlour, all the while explaining to the delighted boys the history of this settler, who had selected as a residence, a spot so utterly beyond the pale of civilization.

Monsieur Antoine was, like our friend Batiste, a great hunter. Together they had scoured every acre of ground from the borders of Esquimaux to Texas; but Antoine, who was slightly older than our Canadian friend, married early in life, and married a woman who had great influence over him. She was better off, more refined, and more polished by far than the hunter, but equally fond of the glorious freedom of the wilds, though still sufficiently a woman to desire a permanent home.

It was a matter of indifference to her where it was. It might be in the deep solitudes of the Andes, on the slopes of the Rocky Mountains, or beside the magnificent Amazon, but home she would have; and M. Antoine found her one on the borders of that mighty inland sea, where no landlord owned sway, where no tax-gatherer ever came, and where, for their lives, and the lives of their children's children, there would be game enough, and fish enough, and land enough too, to make them, in all that man requires, rich as kings.

The trapper, for the sake of his wife and children, two little girls of twelve and fourteen, and a boy of eight, had buried the hatchet with the Indians who lorded over that portion of the soil, and who were its genuine owners. It is all very well for us to argue in favour of the wants of advancing civilization and the requirements of over-population; but the Indian is none the less to be pitied when dispossessed of his hunting-fields. The rich and civilized Roman used the same arguments to explain his raids and forays on the naked savages who lived in wigwams on the borders of old Father Thames, and were the rightful owners of the soil. The change we know must come, but it is a pity it cannot be realized in a less awful way; while to hold up the Indian to execration for defending his possessions, is simply wicked.

Old Antoine had very little love for the redskins; but he liked a wild life, and loved his wife and children, and so he thought it best to live in amity with the Indians, to hunt with them, purchase their peltries, supply them with goods, and thus add to his own fortunes, while securing his scalp. In this way he remained unmolested, though, with the extra caution of his nature, he had built a block-house in case any unlucky accident should happen.

. And this was the family of whose residence the young Hatfields had taken such unceremonious possession, and in whose kitchen they were making a fire, unpacking their goods, hunting down pots and pans, and treating the place just as if it had been their own. The Canadian bade them be of good cheer, laughing all the time, and encouraging them to pile on wood and warm the old deserted place, from which the family was evidently away on a great hunt, to which it was always their habit to take the children, leaving their home to the honesty and mercy of the wayfarer.

And so by the time the shadows had fallen, and the fire burnt clear, the huge hearth glowed, while bacon, venison (taken from the stores in the pantry), fish, grouse, fizzed and stewed on and around the fire, near which, too, bubbled a large pot of coffee that sent forth an aromatic odour which overpowered all others.

Everything was ready to a turn, and the Canadian, with a hungry expression, had bidden them all fall to, when a confused noise was heard outside, the hounds set up a fearful barking, the door burst open, and in rushed a motley group of two grown people, three more youthful personages, four tremendous hounds—all the human members of the party laughing heartily as they cast down heavy burdens of game.

It was the Antoines.

CHAPTER XIII.

THE CARIBOUS.

The meeting was a most uproarious one for a few minutes, and then, after some mutual shakings of hands, introductions, and hearty welcomes, the whole party sat down to a meal which was as welcome to the new arrivals as it was to those who had taken their house by storm. For some little time, indeed, nothing was heard but the clatter of pewter plates, spoons, and knives, the growling of dogs over the bones cast to them, and other noises incident to a heartily-enjoyed meal.

The rage of hunger, being, however, appeased, the hospitable hunter brought out a jar of tobacco and a demijohn of whisky, which Mrs. Antoine began to brew into very strong punch. Teetotallers were not heard of then, nor were they, probably, wanted—people not, perhaps, abusing the good things of this earth so much as to make earnest, well-meaning men find no other remedy than a prohibition against the use of nature's choicest gift to man—the red rosy wine, that always cheers, and never should inebriate.

The two hunters, with a delight which could be seen in their tanned and sunburnt faces, raised their first glass to each other's health, really and truly happy at once more meeting. Antoine then told the Canadian that he, his wife, and children, had been caribou-hunting for three days, and had that day, about an hour previously, halted some distance off, to pass the night, when the lad saw a column of smoke rise from the direction of their home. From the huge volumes of black smoke which ascended to the heavens, it was clear that green wood was being used, without any efforts at concealment ; and partly suspecting what had really occurred, the family had "lifted leg," loaded their *tarbogins*, and hurried home.

There were plenty of caribous in the hills, the hunter said, with grouse and hares, and if they were inclined to prolong their hunt, who knows, he added, but what they might fall in with some mooses and elks ? The Canadian nodded approvingly, and replied that his young friends were out for their first great cruise, and would not be particular to a day or so. His good hosts, however, must not consider them greenhorns, as Monsieur Ralph had killed his bear, and Monsieur Jacques his horned owl, at which they laughed, looking, however, at the eldest brother with great respect.

The young people got on wonderfully. The young girls had not for many years had any other guests save the Canadian, and some red Indians, to whom the daughters of Antoine were bound to be civil, whilst disliking them with all the keen prejudice of the wilds. To them the two English youths were something so entirely new as to be charming, while Jack and little Pete were sworn friends in half-an-hour.

The girls, whose dress was Indian—deer-skin tunics, leggings, mocassins, with close caps of furred skin for the open air—had a hundred merry stories to tell of their life in the woods, which were charming to both Ralph and Harry, coming from such bright, rosy-cheeked, unsophisticated children of nature. They had been accustomed to the wilds from their birth, and looked upon bear-hunting, still-shooting (deer-stalking), moose and caribou chasing, as every-day occurrences. Their narratives were told with a *naïveté* which made the sons of civilization laugh heartily.

It was ultimately arranged that the next day should

be an off-day, during which preparations were to be made for a grand cruise, in which the whole party were to join. The elders elected to stay at the house, making needful preparations, but all the juveniles secretly agreed on a scamper round the neighbourhood, with no particular object in view, but just to see what might turn up. This settled, preparations were made for bed. The sleeping accommodation of the house was unusually great, three doors at one end of the kitchen opening into as many small rooms; one for the husband and wife, one for the girls, and the other for young Pete. This was now to be shared by Jack, while the Canadian and his young friends spread their horse-blankets and buffalo-robes on the ground in front of the fire.

With a "Hey chevey, high chevey!" Pete and Jack burst into the room as soon as a faint streak of daylight illumined the eastern sky, rousing the sleepers and making other uproarious demonstrations, until in self-defence they rose, cleared away all signs of bedding, went into the stable to wash in water taken from beside the fire, which they then heaped up until it roared again. By this time, Bertha and Lotty were afoot; and, active and lively as they were pretty, simple, and artless, they busied themselves preparing a breakfast of hot coffee, corn dodgers, and venison.

We have said that their mother was a very superior woman, and so she was, educating these wild young colts as thoroughly as if they had been brought up in a plain boarding-school; so that, if they could shoot, ride, fish, skate, and drive a sledge, they could also sew, read, and remember what they read—a greatly different thing—from a select box of books from which the English-bred girl never parted. She was a good, a noble, and virtuous woman, and how she came to be the wife of a rude trapper, is a story which we hope we may yet live to tell.

Breakfast being over, the arrangements of the night were adhered to, the elders taking their abode at home, while the others, armed with gun and rifle, burst forth upon the bright white upper crust that concealed the earth, supported thereon by their snow-shoes. The way the young guides, Bertha and Lotty, took them, was across the fields, by a pine thicket, up a hill, and then down a slope towards a small lake, which in summer was celebrated for its fish, and in winter, from its sheltered position, was often frequented by caribou. There was a terrible story connected with it, said Bertha. One winter's night an old Indian squaw had begged for shelter, and at dawn of day had hurried off to overtake her tribe; but two days after, Antoine, the hunter, found a few bones and bits of rag, a broken tomahawk, and three monstrous wolves, lying gaunt and stark, proving that the old woman had made a desperate defence before being devoured.

"What is that yonder on the edge of the lake?" said Ralph, in a low tone.

"Hist—down!" said Bertha, eagerly; "caribou!"

Without another word, the whole party ranged themselves in Indian file, Bertha leading the way, Ralph following, then Lotty, Harry, and the two boys. They had seen a small herd of reindeer feeding on the skirt of the forest, browsing on the shrubs and boughs, and hoped to still-hunt them, thus surprising the elders, who of course never thought it possible they could do so unassisted.

Their way was down a declivity, beneath trees that wholly concealed the lake from view; but the girls knew their way, and conducted the young hunters with unerring accuracy to where the reindeer were collected—a splendid buck, a doe, and two young ones. They were about three hundred yards off, close to the shore, their pretty bodies boldly relieved against the snow, and overshadowed by the dark evergreens. To approach them from the lake was impossible, so all continued, with intense caution, treading one for all, steadily, cautiously, on the crisp, crackling snow, until Bertha declared they were within easy shot, and all levelling their guns, the caribou trotted off deliberately, their sharp hoofs cutting the ice like a winter-shod horse.

At the same instant Bertha, who was much taller and slighter than Lotty, stooped, untied her snow-shoes, put on the skates hanging from her belt, and springing out upon the lake with a joyous shout, she rushed in pursuit of the deer at a pace which distanced the others instantly, though they made frantic efforts to keep up with her. The caribous had gone off at a hard gallop to the right, making a curve, however, immediately afterwards, to the left, *as is the custom of all game;* while Bertha, as if aware of this fact, had launched out in a straight line. Away she went with railroad speed, winging her way, one foot in the air an instant, then the other, her rifle waived in triumph over her head, until she came rushing to meet the astonished deer at a pace that for an instant checked their headlong career, and gave the girl, as she whirled wildly past, the opportunity to take aim, when down went one of the deer,—the stately buck,—and Bertha, slackening her velocity, halted, took off her skates, and rushed to secure the prize.

The astonished and admiring young Englishmen soon came rushing up, to launch out into rapturous praise of her lightness, dexterity, and courage, at which Bertha blushed and smiled, really much gratified, while Lotty, with a sly laugh, bade them remember that they did not know her sister yet. She could do much cleverer things than that. But where were Jack and Pete?

CHAPTER XIV.

THE CARCAJOU.

JACK would have followed the deer chase, had not Master Pete checked him; but the boy Pete, who was a huge chap for his age, was too much accustomed to his sister's freaks to take much interest in any such expedition. He therefore contented himself with watching the scene from a distance, telling Jack that it would be "jolly good fun" to scour the woods themselves in search of game. Pete was a rare hunter. Everything to him was fair game, from buffalo to squirrels, so that he walked about, a perfect armoury. Not satisfied with a gun, he had pistols, a knife, and round his waist a long lasso, with, at its other extremity, the formidable bolas.

The lasso had one leaden ball to propel it in the desired direction, while the bolas had three extremities armed with leaden balls, which, if thrown dexterously amid the horns of deer, or against any animal, was sure either to kill or capture. Jack had his gun and a knife, and readily agreed to follow an old trail in search of game. He was bold, venturesome, and as plucky as the other was stout and strong, so that, unless they fell in with a bear, there was little danger, even wolves shunning men in the daytime, unless on terrible emergencies.

Pete led the way, this not being the last, nor by any means the most serious adventure into which the headstrong boy led our gallant little Jack. The fact is, that while Pete was in his sisters' company, he was nobody. Their superior dexterity, experience, and wit overwhelmed him; and as Master Pete, like a good many others of his age and sex, didn't think much about "nonsensical girls," he preferred to act upon his " own hook," when, if he did anything, he received full credit for what he did.

The trail led them along the lake for some little while, to where the trees were scattered and thin, when suddenly Jack, with eyes like saucers, and a cry that astounded Pete, who was a little to his right, seized his gun and was about to fire, when the young Nimrod of the forest came up and checked him.

"What's the row?" he said.

Jack pointed to a tree, and explained that the minute before he had seen a queer-looking animal rush from the bush and make for a tree, on which it was now lodged.

"Whar?"

"There," said Jack, pointing; "let's shoot him before he gets away."

"It's a carcajou," cried Pete, with a shout of delight. "Don't shoot un. I tells you what, Jack—if you'll jist look sharp, we'll have un alive."

"I'll do what's right," said Jack, manfully, " but I do not think it is possible."

"Oh, *mon ami!* " continued the excited hunter-boy, his face crimson, his eyes flashing, " you jist see. If the coward turns tail, shoot—if he don't, leave un to me."

Pete said no more, but began casting off all superfluous burdens. His rifle, pouch, haversack, all were thrown upon the snow, until his only weapons, offensive and defensive, were his lasso and knife. But before the audacious boy attempts his dangerous task, a word on the animal will not be out of place. The wolverine (*Ursus luscus*, Linn.), which is known in Canada by the name of

Carcajou, and the beaver-eater, is a beast of clumsy appearance, about a foot and a half in length, with a bushy tail six or seven inches long, short legs, large long paws, and hind feet plantigrade. It is of a brown chestnut colour on the upper part of the body and sides, its flanks marked with a band, the belly dark, the back and tail darker still, and the head a sallow grey.

It was first described by Edwards among birds. Shaw considered it a variety of the glutton (*Ursus gulo*), a rufous brown bear of the northern parts. The one seen by Linnæus had lost an eye, and, with the true carelessness of naturalists, he called it *luscus* from this accidental circumstance. It is found in all the uncultivated parts of the United States and Canada, where, from its thievish and predatory habits, it is better known than liked. It shows the greatest cunning and ingenuity in finding out the hordes of the Indians and the cachés of the trappers, as well as in stealing the beaver from the trap of the hunter. When deer and other animals retire to the shade of rocks and trees, it leaps on their necks, and destroys them by tearing open the jugular vein. When the Redskins are abroad on their hunting parties, it will enter the villages, devastating and plundering their wigwams.

This fierce animal, which often commits nocturnal depredations in the sheepfields and yards of Canadian farmers, is more noxious than a fox, while its only value is its skin, used for ornamenting sleigh robes, each fur fetching from five to eight shillings.

Now Pete knew this; and all the proceeds of the chase secured by him being his own, and saved up by his careful mother, he was anxious to capture the wolverine without making any hole in his skin. He knew full well that the animal was dangerous, but he was more than brave, he was fool-hardy and headstrong. Besides, he knew that at the worst they could resort to firearms if his own audacious plan did not succeed. He had often been told that not even a man should attack a wolverine except when well armed; but he had an idea in his head, and carry it out he would, no matter at what peril to himself.

He had taken off the ball from the **lasso-end** of the coiled rope, and substituted a slip-knot in its place. With this and his knife he ventured, single-handed, to approach and attempt the capture of the animal. The wolverine lay in the fork of the tree, showing as little of his body as possible, though his small red eyes were fixed keenly on the sportsmen. There were very few branches below the fork, so that Pete had to put himself almost within reach of the savage beast before he commenced his attack, which he did in a very methodical, cool, collected, but fool-hardy manner.

When, after a severe trial, he clutched the lower branch, and then hoisted himself, out of breath, upon the bough, he was only seven feet from the savage animal, which glared, and gave forth its strange and startling cry in vain. Pete, though he did not take his eye off the carcajou, never flinched a moment, but prepared his slip-knot. He had often thrown the lasso and the bolas with success, so that it appeared to him the easiest thing in the world to noose the wolverine.

Still watching the animal, Pete again ascended until he stood on a level with his enemy—thus, as he walked erect on the bough, commanding him. He rose, fastened his rope once or twice round a strong branch overhead, and then, collecting the extremity in his hand, he threw the noose right at the crouching, cowering foe. The feat had seemed to him easy enough, but it had no other effect than to rouse the wolverine to fury, which was shown by its again emitting its savage cry, and lashing the bough with its tail.

"It'll spring," said Jack, in a tremulous voice. "Shall I fire?"

"No," replied Pete, coolly, "cut me a long hickory stick—look alive, old hoss."

Jack put down his gun with alacrity, and hastened to cut the stick and hand it to Pete, who took it in his left hand behind, all the while watching the movements of the cruel animal, which, had he turned his head, would have had him by the throat in an instant. Once the stick in his hand, Pete, with all the calm phlegmatic manner of an old hunter, put the noose on the end of the stick.

The wolverine, with a singular cry, rose just as Pete dropped the noose over its neck. Regardless of this, and urged only by its own savage instinct, the beast gave a loud and fearful yell, leaping, as it did so, full at the boy's throat. The attack was so rapid, the spring so unexpected, that Pete could have no chance of escaping; and Jack, not daring to fire, could not repress a wild cry of despair and horror, as he closed his eyes to shut out the fearful tragedy.

A series of shrieks of a most horrible nature made him quickly unclose them, and there at one end of the lasso rope hung the wolverine by the neck, while at the other dangled Pete, kicking his heels, shouting, clapping his hands, and shrieking with delight, at his unexpected and unlooked-for victory.

The explanation of this change was simple. When Pete threw the lasso over the boughs above, he had not loosened the bolas-end from his waist. The wolverine's attack had been so sudden, that Pete was fairly startled into letting go his hold, when he fell from the tree, just as the angry brute grazed his breast. Had the rope not been fastened above, or had it been longer, the savage beast would have grappled him; as it was, he was brought up with a round jerk, that sent him flying back; and there hung hunter and victim, one by the neck, the other by the waist.

CHAPTER XV.

THE CARIBOU HUNT.

WHEN Jack saw that all danger was over, he sat down upon a log of wood, and burst into one of the most inordinate fits of laughter that had excited his merry nerves for many a long day. The wolverine and Pete were about six feet apart, hanging from different boughs, not more than ten feet from the ground, the first still quivering in the agonies of death, the latter twirling round,—first one way, then another,—like a teetotum, in a fashion that was supremely ridiculous.

"I say, stranger," growled Pete, "when you've done larfin' like a horned owl, p'rapp you'll come and let a fellow down."

"D—d—d—directly," said Jack, trying in vain to stop his laughter, "b—b—but you do look s—so f—funny."

"I dar say," continued Pete, grinning in spite of himself, "but I've no notion to swing yar all day like a 'possum play'n tricks. Make tracks, or them gals 'll be here—and I nivir shall—hear the last—"

A shout of woman's laughter from several throats soon proclaimed that it was too late to conceal his catastrophe; and in about ten minutes Pete was on the ground, answering the eager inquiries of Ralph, Harry, and the girls; who no longer laughed, but looked very grave indeed, when they took down his enemy.

"Always shoot them, Pete, dear," said Bertha, shaking her little head, "father says they are dreadful spiteful, and very dangerous."

"An' spile their skin," growled Pete, examining his prize with pride and admiration.

"Better spoil the skin, Pete, you naughty boy," said Lotty, "than have it spoil yours. But never mind, you are a brave boy, and won't do it again. Bring it along—we're going back to dinner. Won't father be proud?"

And his father was proud, and his mother too, though they extracted a solemn promise from him, that he would never again run so terrible a risk; which promise Pete gave, and kept too, or he would, in all probability, never have been the great world-renowned hunter he now is.

The rest of the day was spent in preparing for the great caribou hunt, to which all looked forward with enthusiasm: even those who were used to such matters every day, taking delight in the eagerness and anxiety of the others, who had never seen any such chase, except in so far as the little incident which had happened to Bertha could be called so.

It is true that Ralph was impatient for the caribou hunt to be over, having unwittingly overheard a slight passage between the two old hunters, during which they had spoken of some wondrous surprise to be given to the strangers, but which the Canadian had begged might be kept a profound secret until their return. Ralph had some vague and peculiar suspicions as to what the surprise was, but he was too honourable to pump the young people, so he restrained his impatience, even when his quick and subtle ear had caught the magic words—"Snow Ship."

But the sun must rise and set many times ere his wish could be realized, so the secret rested within his own bosom, as he sedulously joined in the preparations for a long and arduous hunt. The first thing was to load the tarbogins with provisions, such as hard biscuit, flour, split peas, rice, onions, tea, coffee, brandy, and pork, also with buffalo robes. These tarbogins, or tabougins, as they are indifferently called, are small sleighs drawn by hand over the snow. Of these the party took three,—one was given in charge to Ralph, another to Harry, while the third was entrusted to Jack and Pete, who were already inseparable. Each person carried his own ammunition, so that the only other load for the sleighs was composed of a coffee-pot, saucepan, frying-pan, gridiron and tent-poles.

The horses and the cows and pigs were supplied with abundant food; for though animals may over feed one day, they will not keep it up very long, while, if their stay proved longer, nothing was simpler than for one of the party to run home and put things to rights. This being settled, and everything being ready for a start, the whole party sat down to supper; after this the hunter brought out his fiddle, which he played well, and with wonderful execution and liveliness, though his stock of tunes was limited. It turned out that the girls were in the humour for a frolic. They could dance; so that Ralph and Harry, whose education had not been neglected in this particular, were suddenly astonished to find themselves dashing through country dances, reels, and French fours, in great style. The Canadian sat smoking his pipe and sipping whisky punch, which Mrs. Antoine made for them, giving the young people as much spruce beer as they required, and, considering the action they went through, this was not a little; but at last the French part of the hunter's nature overcame him, up he leaped, took Mrs. Antoine round the waist, and dashed into some whirling *danse du pays*, and next minute, amid a furious hubbub, roars of laughter, and not a little dust, the whole party, fiddler and all, were turning and heeling it to their hearts' content; nor did this really jolly evening end until the unconscionable hour of eleven.

No one was behind-hand in the morning, the young people especially being eager to show that the frolic had not unfitted them for the day's work. Everything had been prepared over-night, so that in an hour after rising all were ready.

Fortunately the day was fine, the snow dry and crisp, or the journey would have been laborious indeed, as snow-shoes are very fatiguing over damp and loose snow, especially with tarbogins to draw. The order of march was simple. The Canadian and the husband and wife marched in Indian file, stepping firmly, so as to leave a marked and hardened trail for the hand-sleighs, which slipped over the snow with ease, Ralph and Harry finding the way lightened considerably by the merry talk of the girl hunters who hovered on the flank of their line of march.

In this way the hill was ascended, two lakes skirted, a rough ridge crossed, and then there lay before them a long expanse of table-land, smooth, white, and silvery in its hue, except where here and there the Canadian pointed out to his allies the fresh tracks, not only of caribous, but moose, which had evidently passed that way within a few hours. But Antoine took no notice of them, making in a direct line for a distant dark row of tall pines, where a halt was declared for the mid-day repast;

after which the whole troop hurried on again, this time down hill and through a dense forest, which brought them ere nightfall to a chain of lakes, said by these two experienced men to be the best hunting-ground in the whole province, and known only to themselves and a few Indians, who, in all probability, would join them ere many hours were over.

The tent erected for the night, and which was to remain in one spot during the hunt, only differed from that already described, in being singularly commodious, much larger, and supported not far from the middle by three uprights, on which they hung a double blanket when slumber was finally decided upon. By this means they cut off a little more than a third from the tent, and set it apart for the ladies, the door being towards the larger one occupied by the males. The fire was outside, which, with so many persons within the tent, made the atmosphere sufficiently warm.

The day had been a somewhat trying one, and the erection of the tent—for which a considerable space of ground had been cleared—had so fatigued the whole party as to render sleep pleasant, and it was, therefore, at a very early hour that the fire was made up, the dogs placed near the door, and the silence of night reigned within the arched roof of this wood and snow wigwam.

Only the men and boys started the next day, the female part of the establishment being content to remain in charge of the camp, preparing the meals and looking out for any birds or other game which might chance to come that way; while the lords of creation knew what sport was to be obtained by much harder work. Most persons make unto themselves a very terrible picture of a Canadian winter; but experienced travellers assert, that the chill is felt less than in England, the sharp cold of the colony being really invigorating; and warm, thick clothing protecting the person from the effects of the climate, while nothing can guard the frame from the damp we continually breathe in England.

This must be particularly borne in mind in every record of winter adventure.

Antoine was the leader on the present occasion, the whole party forming in Indian file, and following in his footsteps. The morning was bright and cold, with about three inches of newly fallen snow on the ground, which gave the whole scene a sparkling freshness that was very pleasant. The young English hunters were becoming daily more and more accustomed to the snow-shoes, which have a certain awkwardness at first; but now they trudged after the old guide with an alacrity that called forth great praise from the Canadian.

Presently the leader halted, and the whole group, standing a little behind him, saw the caribou trail which he pointed out, and declared to be very recent. This made every eye sparkle, though Antoine commanded the most perfect silence to be observed, as with cautious steps he began following in the animals' tracks, which led along a hard wood ridge where the snow had, in a measure, been blown away by the wind, so that not only were there boughs and brush for the animal to feed on, but frozen grass.

Presently they came to where the deer had lain in the snow all night, and where the trail struck clear and defined, so that they were likely to fall upon a herd at any moment. The Canadian whispered all to be ready, allowing Antoine to keep a little ahead, while every hunter now advanced separately, skulking behind one tree, and then another, as if they had been in the heart of an enemy's country, and displaying a perfect knowledge of the most approved arts of bush-fighting.

Suddenly Antoine halted again, waved his hand to the hunters, and put his gun at half-cock, tightened his belt, took off his snow-shoes, which he cast on his back, and began his journey once more, treading now in the tracks of the caribou. All did the same, with the precision of veteran soldiers, though they found the task very arduous and trying, as in many instances the holes were quite three feet apart, which was no joke of a stride. Indeed, Jack and Pete gave it up, and floundered along as best they could.

Every moment the marks grew fresher, so that in a few minutes the young hunters were directed to put on their snow-shoes again, and take up their posts behind trees, and wait while the old and experienced trappers headed the Caribou and drove them back on the trail, when all parties could try a shot. Each person now selected his hiding-place, screening himself as much as possible by bushes, not only from the wind, but the expected prey; so that, when the guides made off with quick and noiseless strides, each watcher remained, to all appearance, alone in the heart of the wilderness, hundreds of miles away from civilization, and with a temperature below zero.

Upon all, Ralph and Harry especially, fell that sense of awful loneliness which is inseparable from the stillness of a North American forest in winter, and which tyros, wholly dependant on others for guidance, feel more than any one. Nothing is so easily obliterated as a snow-shoe trail—a breath of wind, a ten minutes' fall of snow, and it is gone. The solitude, therefore, after a time becomes all but insupportable; and the lonely one will hail with delight even the whispering of the chill north wind in the pine trees, or welcome with a glad shout the loud report of some monarch of the forest, split by the wind, or the boom of the ice cracking on some neighbouring lake.

A sharp crack, that of a rifle, put all the hunters on the alert, and next minute a crashing of underwood announced the approach of heavy animals; and a large caribou, followed by several others, came ploughing through the snow at a tremendous pace, raising such a dense cloud about them as almost obscured their forms from view. Four sharp cracks followed, and then every hunter darted forward in pursuit of his wounded prey.

"Be careful," shouted Ralph, "they are dangerous!"

There was no time for other words, as each hunter dashed eagerly in pursuit. The eldest brother had leaped forward as he fired, and put a ball through the reindeer's left shoulder, after receiving which he made a few plunges, and pitched heavily forward in the snow, never to rise again. The ball had passed clean through his body, and he was quite dead. Harry had not been quite so successful; but the animal was in a few minutes brought to bay by the dogs, when a second shot settled his struggles.

Then the whole party, reinforced by Antoine and the Canadian, rushed to a thicket whence rose wild and shrill cries. Not a moment was to be lost, as the caribou, when wounded, is very dangerous to be approached, having a vast deal of pluck and resolution, making a most sturdy and resolute defence, not with his horns, but with his legs, with which he strikes out in every direction, so that all are glad to wait until loss of blood weakens him. One blow with his sharp hoof would knock a man's brains out, while if it struck a limb, it would surely crush the bone. Even the boldest hound will stand back, barking at a respectful distance.

The boys had both aimed at the same animal; and, though neither was able to say which had been the immediate victor, both pursued the wounded beast until it turned at bay. There it was, with a broken hind-leg, and a wound in its flank, sprawling on the snow, and kicking violently when any one endeavoured to approach him. Jack was reloading his gun, while Pete had the bolas whirling round his head, as they came up; and next instant it flew forward, and struck the animal round the neck, nearly strangling it.

Quick as lightning, Jack was on its back, and one well-directed blow with his knife put the animal out of its misery. The two old trappers, who had sacrificed themselves to the pleasures of the youthful party, had only one caribou to show, so that in all there were four, captured by the whole band of hunters.

The next thing was to cut them up, then to feed, and return to the camp. It was already late, and the trees cast lengthy shadows; but, the excitement somewhat allayed, all were hungry and tired. Still, no rest could be obtained at once; for, while the elders proceeded to do the butcher's work, the juveniles shovelled away the snow, cut down and collected wood, made a huge fire, and then erected a wall of brush to windward—a few poles being stuck in the ground, and large boughs cast against these.

Then, and only then, all seated themselves between the wall and the fire, from which soon arose the aroma of coffee; while a few minutes later all were enjoying, with eager and sharpened appetites, the deliciously tender caribou steak, than which nothing is more agreeable, pleasant, and satisfactory. All ate with the air of hungry men, the elders winding up with brandy and a pipe, the juveniles with coffee, after which preparations were made for a march. All would have gladly camped where they were: even the dogs, that had fed to repletion, rising with a lazy and dissatisfied mien; but to march was imperative, as the ladies would be seriously alarmed at their prolonged absence.

The four caribous cut up, the offal thrown away, the bones as much as possible extracted, were still a serious load; and for the purpose of carrying them, the usual backwood contrivance was resorted to. They were divided into six loads, proportioned to the strength of the bearers; a rope about six or eight feet long was twisted out of the swamp ash, which makes admirable cordage; and this being tied round the game, the whole load was swung over the left shoulder.

It was now nearly night, with a long walk before them, so everybody provided himself with a good pine-torch, the old hunter, with his torch blazing on high, leading the van. It was a weird and strange procession that now walked beneath the whirring pines and hemlock, six men and boys armed to the teeth, and loaded with game, while flaming sputtering fire branches and knots startled the owls and bats, disturbing even the squirrel from its warm nest. From a distance the scene must have been strange indeed; and any warlike party of Indians would have thought them fools, as they watched their *ignis fatuus* lights. Indeed, their flickering, flaring illumination would have been the height of folly, had not Antoine been in amity with the Indians, and confident of safety, though, alas! we shall see that this confidence had fatal results.

Waving their torches, purposely provided by way of lightening, as well as lighting the way, the young people plunged through the snow,—now singing, now laughing, but all footsore and weary; so much so, that when the camp was reached, they cast down their burdens, and lay alongside of them for some time near the fire. This did not prevent them, an hour later, from eating, late as it was, another and heartier meal, nor from fighting the battles of the day over again, bolstered up with buffalo rugs; nor from winding up with some thrilling stories of Indian peril and fights, which the Canadian told with rare gusto.

Such, at that period, was every-day winter life in the wilds of Canada. How do you like it, boys?

CHAPTER XVI.

THE MOOSE HUNT.

THE summer life of a settler is all work,— at least, for some years; while, to many minds, such scenes as those we have passed through are all play. Now, I am often asked by "big boys" here at home, if I think they could get a living by hunting and trapping out West, on the outskirts of civilization, on the carpet-like prairie, or in the Rocky Mountains. My answer is, certainly not. Where is the home-bred boy who could *alone* endure what we have already described, much more earn an existence, provide himself with powder and other necessaries, winter and summer, contending with cold in the one, heat in the other, inexperience in both, to say nothing of Indians, whom some of my querists seem afraid will die out ere they can get a sight of them?

No. If you emigrate with a family to the very *ultima thule* of civilization, and meet with a good-natured hunter or trapper, you may enjoy much sport, but get your living, never! until you have served a rude apprenticeship, and found, before that is over, that, however exciting, romantic, and delightful hunting may be, to pursue it for a living is hard work, and nothing else.

Next day the ladies were to be of the party, and Jack and Pete were to keep house. This was a matter of little regret to these juveniles, as their walk home the night before was very tiring, while both felt their feet sufficiently sore to be glad of a moderate rest. Another source of gratification was that they had ample provender, and were required to do nothing but keep up a glorious fire, have coffee and caribou soup—made with tit-bits, marrow-bones, brains and shins, with rice and split peas, cooked in a cauldron suspended from three sticks—ready by sundown.

They could then run, slide, make snowballs, loll in the hut, just as they liked; and you may be quite sure that, as Jack and Pete stood near their wigwam, watching the others disappear, they felt themselves mighty big men indeed.

The object of the day's journey undertaken by the adventurers, was a visit to a charming lake at some distance, which Bertha and Lotty declared to be, in summer, the most delightful spot on the face of the earth, being wholly surrounded by trees, that grew in most places right into the water, whence rose wooded swells and slopes to a considerable height. The girls had here a boat-house and canoe, spending a portion of their time there during the summer heats, which they could easily afford to do, as their father depended for his living more on fishing and the chase than upon agriculture.

A moose-yard had been seen in this direction by Antoine, and as he was anxious to give his young friends a taste of this amusement, much as it resembled caribou hunting, he had resolved on taking them in this direction, even if they camped all night, and sent the long-legged Canadian back to keep company with the boys. The journey was joyous in the extreme. One tarbogin had been taken along to carry lunch and to load with game; but this was no hindrance to the movements of the young people, as Mrs. Antoine willingly took charge of it, whenever they wanted to rush forward, or scamper and flounder over the snow.

The juveniles contrived to bag quite a considerable load of grouse and hares, also some grey squirrels, upon which a merciless war was made in those days. This animal (the ash-coloured squirrel—*sciurus cinereus*) is a native of the whole northern continent. It is an elegant animal, with a long feathered tail, which it often raises in the form of a curve, so that the tip touches the head. The body of the largest is about twelve inches. They were once so numerous in Pennsylvania, and held to be so destructive to the grain, that the Legislature offered a reward of threepence a head for their destruction. In 1849 this premium amounted to *eight thousand pounds* currency, and was so exhaustive to the treasury that it was reduced to one-half.

In winter they live in decayed trees, where they lay up a store of nuts and acorns, and bring forth their young. In summer they construct a nest of sticks and leaves, near the top of the branches. They migrate with the change of the seasons; and in crossing rivers and streams they are said to show a most wonderful sagacity, by placing themselves on a piece of the bark of a tree, and shaping their course by means of the tail, which serves both for ornament and rudder. If a strong wind springs up, all their skill is of no avail, and many perish in the waters.

It was somewhat past mid-day when the fairy lake was reached; and both Ralph and Harry saw at once what a charming place it must be in the summer months, though now it was one white sheet of snow and ice, while every tree and shrub glistened with a frosted coating. The summer-house of the Antoine family was only a slanting roof, supported by poles; but it would have required very little to make it fit for a winter residence. The boat-house was behind, and now wholly hidden by snow.

The programme of the day's hunting was to discover the moose-yard; and then, letting loose the hounds, to course the deer—a most exciting style of sport, and which gives the animals more fair play, or "law," as the hunter says, than is usually allowed them. For this purpose it was necessary to go round the lake until they hit upon their feeding-ground, when the dogs would drive them to the ice, and all could join in the exciting work.

The moose, which many confound with the elk, is very different from that animal. It is a large, clumsy-shaped beast, in some things like the elk, it is true, but essentially different in others, particularly in the shape of the horns, which are palmated and spreading. It has a most powerful leg. There are two kinds;—one of a black colour, said to grow to the height of eight or nine feet; and the other greyish, which seldom exceeds the size of a common horse. Both have the head large, and out of all proportion to the body, small eyes, long ears, large nostrils, the upper lip furrowed, and much larger than the under; the neck short, with a thick and erect mane; the hinder part of the body large and broad, legs long, and more slender than those of the common horse; the fore legs longer than the hind ones, the hoof deeply divided. The horns, without antlers, spread out four or five feet from the base, so that the distance between the extreme branches is from five to six feet; on the outer side they are armed with sharp points.

They shed their horns in December and January, and they have been found to weigh forty pounds. The female has none. The animal weighs sometimes 1600 pounds. It moves in a heavy trot; and, though it lifts its feet high, it goes with great speed. The male is inoffensive and harmless, except when wounded, or when its sultanas are interfered with. He will then turn fiercely, and attack with horns and feet. In summer they feed, like the elk, in families, on the pasturage of the plains; in winter, on the tender branches of trees, particularly those of the willow and poplar; but, in such northern regions as those we speak of, with the snow deep, they beat it down with their hoofs until they come to the shoots and bark of trees.

The animals had been at work at a large moose-yard upon the extremity of the lake, and towards this the band of hunters took their way, holding in the dogs, and leaving the ladies by the fire under the shelter of the summer-house. They used extreme caution, as these and all animals of the same tribe are easily alarmed; and if you approach them with the wind they will dash off at a rate impossible to be kept up with. The lake was surrounded by a belt of dense foliage, while a little way from the skirt the trees were more sparse and scattered. Peering beneath the overhanging boughs, the youths presently saw a whole herd of moose, and next instant the dogs were after them at full bay, while the eager and panting riflemen were rushing to the frozen lake to head the game.

There they went, tearing along in their ungainly way,

scattered like scared sheep over the snow, already out of gun-shot, and nearly across the narrow expanse of water, when ping! ping! a crack of a gun, a wreath of smoke, and the heavy brutes return upon their trail, to meet a circle of foes who give them no rest. The enemy on the banks being less numerous than those advancing to meet them, they again reversed their flight, one huge buck alone moving slowly, as if severely wounded. Towards this one at the same instant rushes, with a joyous shout, Bertha, the skater, delivering a second shot as she neared the animal, which, furious, turns against the girl, and, regardless of its sufferings, rushes full tilt at her. But she, prepared for this, launches at her fullest speed along the glazed surface of the lake, describing now graceful curves that madden the unwieldy brute, now straight lines that defy even its great speed.

Back she looks triumphant, with sparkling eyes, and then up go her arms in the air, a wild shriek escapes her, and she is seen no more. A cry of anguish and despair from the mother and sister, a wild shout of horror from men and boys, and then, dashing from him as he ran, gun, hatchet, and every useless incumbrance, Ralph is a dozen yards before the others, floundering in the snow; now he is thirty, now fifty, and now he halts as he gazes with staring eyes at the round space of broken ice where Bertha had disappeared.

But his halt was only for an instant, to loosen his snow-shoes; and then, just as the whole party come up, shrieking and crying to the undaunted youth to stop, he took one header, and disappeared beneath the closing waters. A rush of air, a thousand bubbles, and all was still.

"*Comme ça!*" shouted the Canadian, in a voice of thunder, and he began wildly striking the ice in an unbroken place.

The air-hole where Bertha and Ralph had plunged was about five yards across each way, with edges that would never have borne any weight; but, wielding his ponderous axe, in less than a minute Batiste had cut out a piece of the hard ice, which he was about to enlarge with another fearful blow, when the head of the brave young hunter appeared suddenly above the water, and, all hands grasping at him, he was hauled on to the snow, with the insensible body of Bertha in his arms, while, as he sank by her side, to him also the world became as a blank. Bidding the younger ones go meet the frantic mother, and tell her and Lotty all was well, the Canadian laid the girl nearly on her face, with her head resting upon her arms, when at once the water flowed freely from her mouth, and a sigh clearly indicated that she had not reached the borders of that drear abode, from which many a drowning person seems to have been violently drawn.

A somewhat free administration of brandy to both followed; and, just as Mrs. Antoine came up, both Ralph and Bertha were seated on the snow, staring with wondering and bewildered eyes at each other. After the first wild congratulations were over, it turned out that Bertha had no account whatever to give of her mishap, having lost all sensation at once; but Ralph, who was a splendid swimmer, had never lost consciousness. No sooner had he taken the plunge than he was at the bottom of the lake, where he saw Bertha, who was convulsively clutching some weeds that grew there. With a calm self-possession which was the mainspring of Ralph's character, he cut away the weeds with his knife just in time, for Nature was asserting its rights; and next instant they rose together, almost equally lost and helpless.

Bertha gave her hand to Ralph as she rose; and, dashing away a tear, asked him to run a race to the fire, which they did, none following too closely upon the tracks of that strange pair, who had been so nearly made one in death. Indeed, Mrs. Antoine and Lotty themselves needed the aid of their friends, though Antoine himself was so wild with happiness, so loud in his expressions of delight, so warm in his demonstrative gratitude, that his actions were little better than those of a lunatic.

"My life, my life!" he cried, as he shook hands with Ralph beside the blazing fire, "whenever you asks it, young mister. And now let's feed and liquor, for this child don't hunt no more tu day."

A regular feast it was, the moose defraying the chief part of the expenses; though the backwoodsman, in his exuberance of animal spirits, made them all drink more grog than had ever fallen to the lot of the juveniles at any one time during the term of their natural lives; nor was he ever wearied of shaking hands with Ralph, and swearing eternal friendship. Mrs. Antoine, though less demonstrative, was even more deeply grateful; and her eyes wandered with a softened and motherly look to the handsome face of him, but for whose noble courage she must have lost her eldest child.

CHAPTER XVII.

LOST IN THE SNOW.

That moose-hunt was never forgotten as long as any of those present lived; but no one was very anxious to resume the chase that day; so, throwing aside the offal, the game was piled on the tarbogin, and all set forth on their way home. Ralph and Bertha, who were now bound together by a tie almost stronger than that of brother and sister, walked in front, even their arms piled on the sleigh, which Antoine would have carried in his stalwart arms rather than they should have touched it.

The run from the air-hole, a walk for a quarter of an hour round a huge fire, a very stiff glass of hot steaming brandy and water, had guarded against the evil effects which so disagreeable a ducking might have inflicted, but a quick walk would further prevent any danger; so all hurried forward with eager steps, and, about half an hour after nightfall, they came in sight of the camp-fire, which blazed on high until it was seen far and wide in the forest. A loud shout announced the arrival of the return hunters, who pressed on eagerly, expecting a response; but none came, only the dismal howl of a drove of wolves, that sat in a circle at some distance from the fire, waiting patiently for it to glow less fiercely ere they attacked the boiling caribou soup which scented the circumambient air.

"Boys, boys!" shouted Antoine, almost angrily; "none of this!"

And levelling his two barrels at the wolves, which scoured away at the shouting and firing, he rushed to the camp, searched the wigwam—but no sign of the boys could be seen.

Every member of the hunt now took the alarm, though the women were forced to remain in camp, and the whole male party dispersed themselves in search of the truants, holloaing, shouting, and rousing everywhere the sleeping echoes of the forest. Torches were eagerly lit, and then everybody, taking the fire as centre, dispersed to search around with something more of adherence to method than had as yet been adopted.

Everywhere in the snow could be found marks of their footsteps, where they had run races, where they had slided, where they had piled up a huge snowball, where they had chopped up and dragged wood to the camp,— but no marks seemed to serve as a guide to what had become of them.

That they had not been long gone, was quite evident, as the fire had been recently made up, while no one suspected them of having run from the wolves. The elders looked about with keen eyes for signs of Indians, but there were none. The first conclusion all had come to was, that the boys were hiding; but this supposition was immediately discarded, after the Canadian had shouted forth their names from his stentorian lungs.

Something had happened to the boys, but what, all the ingenuity of the experienced woodsman failed to suggest. Lost they were not, as, with a view to have their beacon seen, it was piled to a huge height, which, from where they were camped, must be seen for miles. The dogs ran about for some time in circles, but at length came in; as if giving the whole affair up as a bad job, and, after two hours of arduous search, the hunters were compelled to do the same, and leave to the morrow the solution of what appeared a terrible mystery.

Silent and sad the dwellers in the camp sat eating their caribou soup, from sheer necessity, but not enjoying it, as all had expected to do. Everybody was moody; and no sooner did all declare that he or she had had enough, than Antoine abruptly announced his intention to seek rest, upon which the buffalo robe that separated the sexes was rolled down, and all relapsed into silence. The youths, tortured in mind as they were, yet respected the father's sorrow too much to make any remark; but, feigning sleep, in reality watched the two elders, who, leaning each against a corner of the wigwam, smoked in silence, their faces once now and then lit up by the glowing tobacco bowl.

The boys saw, or fancied they saw, that each watched the other intently, until, at last, Antoine spoke in a hoarse whisper, and asked if the other was ever going to close his eyes, which, glaring at him in that way, were by no means agreeable.

"*Non! mon ami*," replied the Canadian, in a *very* low whisper; "I wait—ven you ready, me ready."

Antoine made no reply, except by a kind of grunt, and next minute glided from the wigwam into the open air, followed by the Canadian, after he had whispered to Ralph and Harry to talk awhile, that the anxious "womankind" might not suspect they had started on a night search.

When the two grave and solemn hunters stood erect upon the snow, they peered cautiously round, listened to every token of the night, examined the atmosphere, and then each unburdened his own private thoughts to his companion. Both feared the same. Round about the hill upon which they were camped there were many deep valleys, where the snow had collected in drifts, in some places twenty feet deep, into which the boys might have been tumbled by a slip, and perished miserably.

It was to explore these valleys that each hunter had lain awake, at first intending to go alone, but mutually delighted with companionship. With huge strides, Antoine now led the way towards the nearest valley, through which meandered a small stream, skirted on its upper banks by trees.

The crest was soon reached, and then each hunter turned, clutched the other's hand, and looked inquiringly into his face. They both had evidently found some sign.

But we have left Jack and Pete too long alone. Let us record their day's adventures.

They were not many. They had shot a few birds, peered about for squirrels, made a snowball, ate a hearty dinner, slided on the smooth surface of the snow, collected wood, and, finally, they had seen to the supper for the hungry hunters. This done, they resolved to start, and go part of the way to meet them. To do this they followed the morning trail some little way, until they came to a spot where the snow lay white, virgin, and untouched, on the surface of a slope, without a tree, root, or projection of any kind for some hundred feet, where a row of trees and underbrush proclaimed the commencement of a thicket.

"Ain't it ripping?" said Pete; "let's have a hog-slide."

And, without another word, he seated himself on the snow, having, fortunately, leathern continuations. Jack did the same. The fun was, to descend the slope as rapidly as possible, racing one against the other, without overbalancing themselves or losing all command, as many descending a snow mountain in the Alps have had their clothes burnt off and their flesh carbonised, from the extreme velocity causing undue friction. But the hillside by a Canadian lake was not Mont Blanc, and there was little fear of any such catastrophe here.

Away, away! start these joyous boys, their heels in the air, their hands waving, as they madly glide down the slope, at a rate which, if not particularly dangerous, is sufficiently rapid to be exciting in the extreme. On, on! they speed, still almost side by side, giving themselves an occasional push forward with their hands, until, half way down, where they were neck and neck, Pete gets foremost, wildly shouting and screaming, to the manifest astonishment of two squirrels that hopped upon the boughs of an evergreen, to see what was the matter.

Jack is after him, both now rushing downward with a velocity which is not to be checked, though, as they near the trees and bushes, they would fain do so. But Pete has selected what he calls " a soft place to fall." It is under the shadow of some bending pines—the bushes are thick and close together, and will break the blow.

"Come along, ole hoss!" he shouts, and disappears from the sight of Jack, who, next instant, finds that he is rushing headlong into a terrible void!

With a wild, despairing cry—with a shriek of such mortal agony as passes the lips but once in this life, he caught with desperate hands at the passing boughs— in vain!

Next instant he was hurled against some hard substance, and became insensible.

How long he lay thus he could not say; but there came at last a glimmering of sensation, accompanied by great pain, amidst which he opened his eyes to encounter the most complete black darkness. Involuntarily a groan of excessive anguish burst from him, which found an echo at no great distance.

"Are that you, Jack?" moaned Pete; "are yer alive?"

"Yes," gasped Jack, "but every bone's broke. Where are we?"

"Don't know nothin'; feel kinder sore everywhar, particular 'bout my head and the rear of my pants. I say, Jack!"

"Yes."

"Ain't this a precious pickle? Wonder where we is?"

Jack sat up, and, feeling about, discovered that he had his flint and steel, with which he soon struck a light. When they started to meet the hunters, they had provided pine-torches, with which to light the way after dark, and one of them was soon ignited and held on high, when the whole horror of the scene was disclosed to them. They had fallen into a deep hole, of which they could neither see all the sides nor the top, though it was clearly bottle-shaped, narrow at the summit and wide at the bottom.

To get out unaided was impossible, even if they had physical strength to cling to a few roots; scarcely any animal but a bear could climb a wall that sloped outwards.

No animal but a bear!

Pete had used these words, and as he did so, both glanced eagerly and hurriedly around.

The ground was actually strewed with bones, while in a corner was a human skeleton, that, doubtless, of some unfortunate wretch who, like themselves, had fallen into the huge natural trap, many of which are to be found, of similar shape, on the American continent.

"This is a bar's den," said Pete, lighting his torch, and piling up the dry bones, pulling away some roots from the sides of the horrid cavern, and making a blaze and smoke that nearly choked them.

At that instant a low moan fell on their ears, and the two boys, the instant before limping, and scarcely able to crawl about, stood upright as a dart, and, leaning shoulder to shoulder, peered across the fire to where the cavernous hole retreated somewhat.

There, reluctantly aroused from his winter den, was a black bear (*Ursus Americanus*), which was sitting up on end, and glaring at the fire. Presently, with a slow and lazy movement, he again fell upon his fore-feet, and came sniffing and smelling around, always, however, away from the fire, upon which the boys, with beating hearts, piled up bones, sticks, and roots. They never allowed the bear to see them, for they moved backwards as the unwieldy and sleepy brute advanced.

Pete all the while whispered to Jack, who felt that, under any circumstances, their last day was come, and therefore it mattered little how it was ended. He accordingly, profiting by a momentary halt of Bruin, who again squatted on his hind legs to peer across the fire, had lit another torch, which next moment, by the instruction of the more experienced lad—he had heard his father and Indians tell the story—he flared right in the bear's face.

The foolish chap, instead of resenting the act, when the torch flared in his eyes, sat bolt upright, in a most comical attitude, and covered his eyes with his clumsy paws.

"Put it close," said Pete, in an agonized whisper, as he cocked his rifle, loaded with two balls.

Jack, shaking like an aspen-leaf, did so, and saw on

the animal's breast a spot where the hair grows in a sort of a round; once put a bullet in there, and Bruin falls like a Pawnee tent when the props are cut away.

Hideous was the din which followed; and when the noise and smoke subsided, the boys found themselves close up against the wall, but, instead of being torn to pieces by the bear, only sore and stiff from bruises. Pete, in the agony of that moment, had lived a life, and, knowing the perilous stake he played for, he had taken slow, steady, and sure aim: the bear was dead.

The cavern was now examined for some other outlet, but there was none; so the boys agreed to skin the bear, anoint their bruises with the fat, and, having cut a steak or two and supped, to sleep until they were refreshed. With this view, sticks, roots, and bones were piled on, after which both sat astride of the warm carcass, ready to begin.

"Hillo!" said a thin voice from the upper regions.

"Hurra!" shouted the boys, jumping up.

"*C'est bon!*" growled the well-known voice of the Canadian. "Ah! waitee one leetle beet, you bad boys, till I only get at you; von't I trash you nicely. It's all rite, Monsieur Antoine. Givee me the *cordon*. Juss poot dat fire out, and no chokee me."

"It must be a good strong one," replied Jack.

They now ceased their labours, and scattered the fire. For awhile the smoke obscured everything, but when the embers glowed, a light appeared in the neck-like mouth of the bottle cavern, and the boys saw, by the pine-torch, the haggard, pale, and anxious faces of the two hunters.

"Eef I leaf you all night, only serve you right," said the Canadian, growling. "Dere, tie yourselfe bofe to dat rope."

A stout, thick, sturdy, and compact rope now descended.

Pete winked wickedly at Jack, who grinned across his whole face, and then, without a word, the bear was fastened to the cord, and the signal given.

"Vell!" grunted the Canadian, "I never shall belief as de poys vas so heavy. Pull avay, mine fren'! Ve'll gif it to 'em ven ve gets 'em up. Pull avay! Gif him a turn rount dat tree. Got for tam—it is one *ours*——"

A shout of laughter from the boys, and then down came the rope. This time it was hoisted up without a word, so eager were the two elders to learn the boys' terrible story. Full two minutes elapsed ere anybody could speak, and then the brave youths, half suffocated with embraces, grimy with smoke and blood, told the story of their adventure.

"Te fire saved you, poys," said the Canadian, whose eyes were moist with tears. "De stupid *bête*, he no come near one torch. Vell, dis is de debble of an *aventure*."

Though father and friend had scarcely yet recovered from the suffering of mind and fatigue of body they had endured, yet were they singularly anxious to be stirring. They thought of those who were watching in the camp. Still, it was resolved to return in triumph, and, with this view, a stout staff being cut, the bear was hoisted upon the shoulders of the men; the boys, elated, but sore, marching in front.

We need not say that they were joyously and rapturously received, while care was taken, during the remaining period devoted to hunting, that no more such perils were endured, the boys being kept strictly in sight.

CHAPTER XVIII.

THE LAUNCH OF THE SNOW SHIP.

AND now all are once more snugly ensconced in the hut, or shanty, of the old squatter, and have been for a day or two, during which time a heavy snow-storm has rendered out-door exercise impossible. But to this none object, for all are busy preparing for an excursion which, to the Hatfields, has the merit of utter novelty. They are about to start across the lake in a Snow Ship.

It is time that we described the nature of this vessel, which is peculiar, we believe, to the Canadian lakes, though something similar has been used on polar journeys. As soon as snow and frost set in, all ordinary navigation ceases upon those vast inland seas, which thus, during the four winter months, are only available to sledges and snow-shoes. In time of war, however, they have sometimes been crossed by soldiers in Indian file, the first few thus making a hard path.

But human ingenuity is endless, and so it came about that a cute Scotchman invented what are locally called ice-boats, but which, built as we shall presently describe, we have dignified by the more important name of " Snow Ship." They are not very common, as their management requires an extreme degree of skill and coolness. They are a sort of barge, or pinnace, cutter-rigged for the most part, and built of the toughest wood the colony can produce. Under the keel there is a raised runner of polished iron, at its edges quite as sharp as a skate, and made for a similar purpose—to plough the ice or snow of the lakes. In all other respects these crafts are like sea-going vessels, being urged forward by sails and steered by helm. It is almost incredible to what speed they can attain, far beyond that of any vessel cleaving the water, and, to use the words of one who knew them well, "not much inferior to an express train." The only drawback is their extreme danger from breaking of the ice, upsets, and sudden squalls. But of this, more as we proceed.

It was arranged that as soon as the storm abated, advantage should be taken of the steady breeze to try the experiment. The wind, probably, would not be too high, while it was further settled that, with a view to double surety, the sleigh should accompany them. All were to go; Antoine and his family in the Snow Ship, the others in the sleigh,—the Hatfields being extremely anxious to witness the working of this singular craft.

The third morning broke clear and bright. The snow had ceased, leaving a vast white mantle upon the earth, which, a severe frost having set in soon after midnight, was crisp and hard, while in places the wind had bared the ice itself. All were now on foot, suitably clothed for the occasion in blanket suits and robes, with fur gloves and flap-eared caps of racoon skin, and were endeavouring to keep themselves warm by that most efficacious caloric producer—exercise. The men took their way to the dock, where lay the mystic craft which had kept Ralph, Harry, and Jack awake half the previous night, while the women prepared the provisions which were to be their mainstay during the voyage.

The dock was, in summer, a pleasant little cove, entirely shaded by trees, on the shores of which had been erected a boat-house, with a snow-proof roof and strong doors. These opened, the craft lay full in view. It was an elegantly-shaped pinnace, with a flush deck, and no bulwarks save a line of plank about three inches high all round. In the stern was a space in which four could stand, the whole of the rest of the boat being cabin and hold, sufficient for eight or ten persons, when seated, as the flat bottom and roof were only four feet apart. An iron chimney with a turning top indicated the presence of that most essential article—a stove.

With hearty good-will the pinnace was now sent flying down the polished wooden flooring of its house, until it rested on the snow, when, no wind being perceptible in that densely-sheltered spot, all hands were in another moment impelling it along the crisp surface of a huge drift, until it lay abreast of the settlement.

The ladies had not been idle, for the horses were harnessed, the sleigh loaded and left in charge of Jack and Pete, who lolled in the fur-clad seat, while the small barrels of flour, pork, and other provisions needed for a journey, were brought down to be put in the hold of their wonderful craft.

The mast was speedily stepped, the bowsprit run out, the topmast hoisted, and then the sails were bent, which at once presented her in such a favourable point of view as to elicit loud applause from the Hatfields. M. Antoine now went to fasten up the house, leaving his wife standing on the bank, while the girls and the young men saw to the loading of the craft.

The Misses Antoine clambered into the hold to receive the goods which Ralph and Harry would hand to them; and Batiste got all ready for hoisting the sails, when, as ill luck would have it, there came a sudden puff of wind which sent the jib flapping violently out. The leading horse of the sleigh shied, stood up, and then went away at a headlong pace, dragging his companion, nothing loth, after him.

The sleigh equipage had run away.

The Canadian made as if he would have run after them, but he instantly perceived the folly of any such attempt, as he saw the light vehicle whirled by at furious speed, its young charioteers tugging with might and main at the reins, but whether simply to guide the wild and terrified animals, or to endeavour to restrain them, he could not tell.

"The boat!" cried Madame Antoine, in an agonized tone.

Batiste wasted no time in words; but, signing to the youths what to do, he began hoisting the sails, and in two minutes, way was felt upon the craft, when, rushing to the helm, while the boys and girls trimmed the sails, he began guiding the Snow Ship upon its course. One glance showed him that the horses were still in sight, the sleigh uninjured, the boys safe, but going at a rate fearful to contemplate; nothing more was needed to rouse him to action, the trail being marked and clear.

As none in the Snow Ship thought more of the affair than as a race in which the merits of a boat against horses would be tried, or at most accompanied by the dangers of a spill on the snow, all were intent on the craft in which lay their hopes of gaining upon the runaways. Ralph and Harry were breathless with excitement as, feeling the full force of the wind upon topsail, mainsail, and jib, the pinnace whirled along, ploughing up the snow, and sending aloft myriads of bright and sparkling particles, or rushing with redoubled swiftness over the dark surface of the ice, that looked like shining sheets of metal.

They had never felt anything like it before. Without the rocking and pitching of sea-going vessels, without the jolting of waggons, and even sleighs, without the swaying motion of spring carriages, it sped along so softly, easily, and pleasantly as to resemble nothing more closely than floating in the air; nor would they have thought, but for the way in which trees and shore sped by, that they were equalling in speed the fastest steamers which were, in a few years, to dot those broad waters.

Ralph, the first thrill of excitement over, crept along the deck to the mast, whence he could command a good view of the country in advance. The horses, probably from some instinct of shelter, were running close in shore, being thus protected by the trees from the wind; while the Snow Ship, with the opposite view, was kept several hundred yards further out. The runaway steeds still kept their course, showing no sign of diminished speed, which was the more perplexing, as the wind soon indicated a tendency to be feeble and unsteady.

Now, as a fiercer puff than ordinary swelled out their sails, the Snow Ship, regardless of obstacles, ploughed the seams of snow, or skirled over the glassy ice, and clearly gained upon the horses, which, in all probability, must soon slacken their speed, and thus be again placed under control. But scarcely had the pinnace got thorough way on her, when there came a lull, or such light and transitory puffs as barely sufficed to keep her in motion.

Before they could again move with any hope of success, the sleigh was a faint speck in the distance.

"Light de fire," said Batiste, gloomily, as he looked round at the heavens; "p'raps ve camp dis night."

His advice was felt to be good; for, despite all their clothes, they could scarcely prevent their blood from stagnating, the cold being bitter in the extreme, their breath freezing in icicles on their fur and woollen wrappings. In another minute or two all hands going below, except Batiste, there issued from the chimney a thin wreath of smoke which proclaimed the welcome presence of a fire.

The cabin, in all but height, was comfortable, the beam of the pinnace being considerable. The stove was a small iron one, from which radiated, when its sides were hot, an unwholesomely dry heat, which was counteracted by a large bowl on the summit being kept full of water. This was movable, and could be replaced by an iron pot or kettle when meals were under weigh.

As soon as the fire was thoroughly lighted, all crowded up to Batiste to request him to go in and warm himself, while Ralph and Harry guided the boat, but the Canadian shook his head. His naturally grim face was stern in the extreme, his eyes gleamed with an unnatural fire, an expression of settled gloom was upon him, and he refused to leave his post.

He explained that a new complication had arisen. The horses, he could tell—for he had approached the trail near enough to decide this—had ceased their mad career, and were completely under control. This was indicated by the steadiness of their footsteps, and the several occasions on which they had been carefully guided round various obstacles that presented themselves. The boys, therefore, were running a race, which, as they had some provisions, they might prolong until night time, when the wearied steeds would halt of themselves. Now came the danger. They had no means of making a fire; and, as sleep was an inevitable necessity, they would seek repose in the sleigh, in which case the chances were they might be frozen to death. All this was said with a gravity which went to the heart of every one. Still the brave Canadian would not despair; but all the time, putting the helm in turns in the hands of Ralph and Harry, he taught them how to manage the boat.

CHAPTER XIX.

A STORM ON THE LAKE.

NIGHT was on them ere they expected it, and with it a decrease of wind, though still enough remained to enable them to glide along the smooth and white surface with a ghost-like motion. Batiste now confessed to the lads that even his iron frame was overcome, and that he required sleep, if only for an hour; he had previously made all rest for an hour or two, so that, with many an earnest piece of advice, he went to rest near the opening into the cabin, the anxious girls burrowing, as it were, in the bows.

Harry and Ralph now remained in charge of the singular machine, which its inventor elevated to the dignity of a ship, and a proud and happy moment it was for them, despite the impatience they felt to be up with the runaways. There was something inexpressibly beautiful in thus skimming over the soft surface of the snow, under the twinkling silvery stars, past the white phantom-like trees, with their dark gulf-like openings. It was both the poetry and the sublimity of motion.

The boys were used to it now, and guided their iron barque cheerily over the lake, one in turns warming himself by stamping on the deck near the mast. This continued for some time, the gusts being more or less fitful. They kept outward, as far from the still clear trail as possible, with the sails hauled close aft, taking advantage of every puff of the feeble breeze. Suddenly a death-like stillness was upon them, the wind ceased utterly; and the sails, pendant from their yards fixed as boards, proclaimed that Nature slept.

As nothing could be done until the wind resumed its sway, they furled the mainsail, and crept below. The cabin door, for greater warmth, was made to slide inwards. Pushing it back as gently as possible, they crawled past Batiste, and proceeded to warm themselves and partake of a morsel of biscuit, a stale barrel of which was all they had on board.

A quarter of an hour later all slept.

It was about four in the morning when Batiste rose, and found the boys beside him, and the boat motionless. Leaping to his feet, he pushed open the door, waking Ralph and Harry by so doing, who followed him into the open air. A wondrous change had come over the scene. Not a breath of air was stirring, but snow had been falling for some time, and now whitened the air with its myriad flakes, as they slowly and gracefully fell to the ground.

Suddenly, a low sough, a whisper, as it were, from the north, came moaning through the trees; and Batiste, reaching forward, took in the jib, and hauled down the topsail.

"Von *tempête*, vat you say, snow-squeak?" said the Canadian.

"Squall," replied Ralph, laughing. "It is coming, I fancy, but it hasn't frightened the wolves."

And he pointed to a dozen black spots behind the Canadian's back as he had been standing, which were crawling arduously and painfully through the snow, forming, as they did so, a half circle.

"Hein!" said the Canadian in a low whisper, "bring

up de fusils; and den, boys, you shall see vat you shall see. Dis infant, he nevare know'd de *loup* crawl in the snow before. You, Ralph, shoot dat big debble close by, I take de tree to de lef', and den God give us de vind."

All fired, with steady aim, despite the flickering of the snow-flakes; and, as they did so, with a furious yell —the horrid sounding war-whoop—up rose twenty Indians, who, casting off their flimsy disguise, came with fearful strides towards the boat.

But the wind sighed no longer; with a rush and a roar it struck them, as by the directions of Batiste the mainsail and jib were hauled out, and the pinnace was once more set in motion, but not with its usual rapidity, so imbedded was it in the soft element. But in another minute the boat was free, the snow was swept from its decks, the snow-flakes wheeled past with a wild dash, and the graceful *Bertha*, as she was called, was scudding before the wind.

With hideous cries of rage and fury the savages came after, rushing over the snow with terrific rapidity.

"Gib she de jeeb," said Batiste, quietly, though every moment the pinnace threatened to heel over and upset.

Now began a race, such as no man in a temperate clime ever saw. The Canadian put the boat nearly before the wind, that being the safest course, and one which evidently suited the craft, for she sped at such a rate as filled the boys with amazement, realizing almost the fabled swiftness of the arrow's flight. On! on! she rushed into the blending, drifting snow, with the hissing gale aft, nothing visible but her own decks; all else, above, below, and around, an utter void. The Indians were out of sight the instant the pinnace attained its full pace; but boy, and man, and girl knew that, go whither they might, they would follow, and that all hope of escape lay in putting a vast tract of country between themselves and the savages.

But what of Jack and Pete?

None dared hardly think of them, though all were fully determined to return to the search as soon as they had succeeded in throwing the savages off their trail. This could only be done by perseverance. Ralph, with everything but his eyes buried in furs, despite the rattling pace at which they sped, stood in front of the mast, to which he clung, as a watch. Fortunately, as the wind rose, the snow gradually abated, and at length ceased, enabling them to gaze around over the vast plain.

There, afar off, were the Indians coming on, with that infernal perseverance which is the characteristic of their race.

But to them no heed was given. They were now out in a part of the inland sea, where other dangers existed of a very different character. The lake was deep, where they were now being driven; and the ice in these places is seldom thick enough to bear even a sleigh, as they soon discovered. As yet their pace had not been relaxed; but it soon became evident that something must be done, for they could both feel and hear the danger.

The ice groaned and bent under them, like an elastic plank.

Ralph proposed that they should lie to until daylight, or until the heavier part of the squall was over. He knew that every day, every hour, every minute, in fact, unless the wind shifted more southerly, the ice would be consolidated, and therefore safer. But Batiste pointed out two extreme dangers. In the first place, if they took in sail, they would probably be captured by the enraged Indians; while, if they happened to halt on a spot where the ice was seamed and cracked, and water came up, they would be frozen fast for the whole winter.

There was nothing for it, therefore, but to advance, which they accordingly did, and another snow-squall came down upon them ere the former had left them half an hour. This time it was so thick and dense, as to fall like a heavy blanket on the deck, while it concealed everything for many yards before them.

Suddenly, as a wild weird shriek of the blast seemed to send hundreds of demons past them in the air, the pinnace shivered, as if it had struck a rock, heeled over a moment, casting everybody to the ground; and then uprose on the night air, first an awful groan, then a hideous crashing sound, the report as of a hundred muskets; and, lastly, a heavy booming, as of distant cannon. Clambering to his feet, and clasping his arms round the mast, Ralph gazed wildly around, and saw everywhere spouts of water, open fissures, upheaving masses of snow-clad ice, whirling, uprising like walls, and then falling with a splash that sent the sparkling water high into the circumambient air.

"Great God!" cried Ralph, "where are they all?"

He was alone on the deck, though next instant he saw Harry clambering in; while the girls, stunned by the shock, appeared, confused and trembling, from the cabin. Batiste was nowhere to be seen; and, though they all shouted until they were hoarse, no answering sound greeted their anxious ears, and their minds were filled with the fearful apprehension that he had been pitched headlong from the stern by the concussion, and had fallen into the water.

But why were they perfectly stationary, while all around was in motion?

They were hard and fast aground on dry land, about an inch or two above the ordinary level of the water.

CHAPTER XX.

FROZEN IN.

NOTHING can be conceived more dreary than the position of these two boys and two girls thus wrecked, in such weather, upon a shoal or sandbank, the hold of a boat their only tenement, without food, and with scarcely any firewood. But they were not of those who despair; so, taking in the sails, which caused the mast to bend before the storm, they went below to hold council as to what was to be done.

Barely enough biscuit for two meals remained, and as all were weary and exhausted, a mess was made with snow water, when a long and desultory conversation took place, which necessarily ended in nothing; for until day revealed to them their true position, nothing could be done. At length, though the hearts of all were bursting with anxiety as to their friends, and wildly beating on account of the uncertainty of their own fate, nature asserted its magic power, and slumber was decided on. Ralph peered out, saw that the wind, which had veered to the south, brought sleet with the snow, and that, as far as the eye could reach in every direction, nothing was to be discovered but broken water. Satisfied that for the moment all was safe, he closed the slide, and they prepared for slumber and repose.

Health of body always ensures sound sleep when the

mind is at ease; but so powerful is the effect of mental suffering that both health of body and peace of mind are required to give perfect repose. Wearied as they were, therefore, our young people were on foot as soon as the sun rose over the eastern shore, and shed its benignant and beneficent light on all nature, tropical and polar, giving to everyone his needful allowance.

The shipwrecked young people now discovered the real state of affairs. They were on the eastern spur of a small island, scantily wooded, chiefly by willows and cotton woods, with rose and wild raspberry bushes intermixed. Round this for many hundred yards the waters extended, turbid and swift; and there was evidently a strong current, as might be seen from the rapidity with which lumps of ice were carried past.

Far away, at a distance not easily to be calculated, they could see that the ice was still firm, and unless some great change took place, their only hope of safety lay in reaching a spot where their feet could find solid walking ground. But as not one of them had any idea how this was to be done, they preferred, in the first instance, providing for those immediate necessities which would enable them to prolong life—namely, food and fuel.

Leaving the girls to prepare, with the last of their biscuit, a scanty and insufficient meal, Ralph and Harry took their tomahawk-axes, and floundering to where a cotton wood rose on high, they began chopping and chipping boughs and trunk until they had collected two good loads. All this time their eyes were cast around in search of anything eatable: but in vain. Not a bird, not a beast, nor the track of one, could be distinguished anywhere.

Loaded with wood they returned to the pinnace,

placed the larger pieces outside, taking in only enough for the day's use below. All now sat down to their scanty meal, and began revolving in their minds,—first, the chances of escaping at all, and then, how to keep alive until either the freezing of the waters enabled them to fly over the lake, or till succour reached them.

Strangely enough, not one of them ever thought for a moment that any fatal accident had happened to Batiste. They had too much faith in his talent and good fortune to suppose anything of the kind; a dozen things being suggested, but death never being alluded to. Talking and devising as best they might, their tasteless breakfast was soon over, and then a minute examination of the hold was made, resulting in nothing but the discovery of some planks, fish-hooks, and lines.

"If we could catch fish," said Harry, brightening up, "we might live."

Ralph shook his head.

"I have frequently caught fish under ice," replied Bertha.

"But not without bait," said the young man, sadly—at which expression of opinion all countenances fell. "What are these boards and this pole for?" he added.

"To roof over the after-part of the pinnace," replied Bertha. "When the cold sets in again it will give us breathing room; we can watch, too, abroad, without much exposure to the air."

Mechanically, because it gave him something to do, Ralph, being careful to use his mittens, drew forth the planks, when Harry and he, guided by the girls, soon erected them, thus providing a dry cabin six or seven feet high, which promised to add considerably to their comforts, could life only be prolonged. It must be recollected that in these cold countries food is more essential by far than in warmer ones. It is required oftener, and in larger quantities. My excellent friend, and yours, Captain Mayne Reid, speaks of Hudson Bay voyagers being allowed eight pounds of solid meat a-day, and finding it scarcely enough; but what of that, when Esquimaux savages will swallow twenty pounds of blubber in a day, and on a heavy march we—the Texan volunteers—consumed in a warm and humid climate ten pounds of venison per diem, without bread or vegetables.

In the position in which the wrecked young people were placed, food, and food immediately, was an imperative necessity, and with this knowledge it was that the boys, leaving their female friends to keep up the fire, sallied forth to search the island. Without a hope of using them to any purpose, they slung their guns over their shoulders, and removing a board, crawled on to the deck, and thence to the small wooded island, which presented to the eye the singular aspect of trees and bushes growing out of snow.

Taking the southern side on this occasion, the youths moved silently along, without much hope,—indeed with none; for they had both come to the same conclusion, which was that no animal of any kind would venture out towards the shore, when the distant woods were there for them to nestle in. The truth is, both felt an earnest desire to converse apart from the society of their younger and more tender companions.

Reaching the extreme western end of the island they halted, and cast a wary glance around. The current to which we have already alluded sweeping past both sides of the island in a westerly direction, met here, and this was the object of their silent studies. They both saw that it swept hence in one steady stream to the solid ice, which was about three hundred yards from where they now stood, and that every fragment of ice drifted in a straight line until it struck the fixed ice.

"A fellow might swim," said Harry.

"He might," replied Ralph, "but he would be frozen to death. He could not move unless naked, and, if he tried, he would never live to put his clothes on. But a raft might be poled over in ten minutes."

"Let us do it—the cotton tree and those planks would make one in half an hour."

"How far are we from land, Harry?" said Ralph, putting his arm affectionately on his brother's shoulder; "and how far could those girls walk? No! one alone must try the experiment. I am strongest; I must venture, while you guard over the dear girls."

"It is, perhaps, best—but how shall we live until your return? The island has not even a bird."

"True!" said Ralph, gloomily. "I fear we must all die together. God be merciful unto us!"

Scarcely had the words passed his lips when they were startled by a series of sharp cries, followed by the utterance of their own names in a shrill and terrified voice, which set them running as fast as the snow allowed them in the direction of the boat, nearing which they heard a great splashing and noise, and then saw Bertha and her sister holding on to a stout fishing-line, from the other end of which something was making violent attempts to escape. In an instant the young men had relieved them of their task, and then drew ashore a magnificent sturgeon, the largest fish known in those waters, which abound in salmon, trout, pike, mullets, and eels.

Loud were the congratulatory words of the young men, particularly when they found that the bait used was nothing but a piece of red flannel taken from some mysterious garment. The sturgeon will bite at almost anything, but especially at anything red or shiny, like the bowl of a metal spoon. All the party now confessed to intense hunger, and the sturgeon being cut up, a portion was prepared for immediate use, while the rest was hung up to freeze.

This fortunate take induced Ralph to postpone his dangerous attempt, and so the day passed, alternately watching, fishing this time without success, and bringing in more wood, as their main comfort consisted in keeping the inside of their pinnace at a proper heat, which at night could only be done by closing the slide. The smallest hole would admit more cold air than they could endure. The pinnace had been carefully caulked, but the outer roof of planks was too thin and full of cracks to be bearable.

At nightfall all wrapped themselves in their robes; the two girls lying close behind the stove in the bow end, and the two youths in front of it, about midships, sought that repose which is so much needed in a cold, dry, and bracing climate. About midnight Ralph woke up with the cold, replenished the fire, and went out. A northerly wind was blowing, bleak and chill, over the lake; the water no longer rippled, its surface was covered by a thin sheet of ice. Had it been strong enough to bear them, Ralph would have called all hands to launch the boat, and trusted their fortunes once more to the ice, but it was as brittle as glass.

Warily examining the horizon, Ralph saw that heavy snow would follow this shift of the wind. He sighed deeply; but as anything was better than inaction, he tried to cheer up at the mere prospect of moving; but there was a leaden weight upon his mind, which he could not shake off—a sense of something evil at hand, for which the naturally cheerful young man could by no means account. Slowly, sadly, he returned to his place, piled on wood, made the fire crackle and blaze, and then lay down, not to sleep, but to lie awake—*cold and shivering.*

When morning broke, every particle of water had disappeared, and all but Ralph, who was seriously ill, proceeded to break the ice with a view to fishing. This being done, Bertha left Harry and her sister at work, and said she would stroll about the island. The real truth was, that the poor girl was in a regular trance of fear about Ralph, upon whom, since the hour that he had saved her life, she had fixed her affections with an ardour transcending even that of a sister. She knew that he was ill,—ill from anxiety and distress of mind, but ill also from want of food—fish alone being utterly incapable of supporting life in one accustomed to more nutritious food. There was, besides, a tinge of a fever which she well knew, and from which her whole family had been "down" more than once.

Advancing towards the western end of the island, she halted by the cotton trees, where the growth ceased for a moment, and was then renewed in the shape of a thicket of pines. The snow lay very superficially on the island, being, from its slightly raised position, swept by the wind, so that Bertha easily scraped it away, until the sparse grass of that naked and sterile spot was exposed to view. But the girl's eye sparkled with delight as it fell upon a leaf she knew well, the root of which she proceeded to dig up, until she had some dozen as a reward for her labour.

At this moment a slight noise made her look up, and she at once saw something move on the side of the nearest pine. It was evidently an animal, and, with her heart in her mouth, she remained perfectly still. It had very long fur, its body was short and thick, something resembling that of the beaver, while the head was like that of the rabbit. It was coming down the tree, very slowly, head downwards, its tail being, to a certain extent, prehensile, and preventing it from falling. Bertha slowly drew off her fur cape, and the moment the animal touched the ground she flew at it. Thus first noticing its hereditary enemy man, the beast uttered a shrill, sharp cry, and then putting its head between its forelegs, it thrust forth its armour of quills, about two inches long, prepared to defend itself, as it might have done against a dog or small animal. But Bertha now knew her prize was the *Histrix dorsato*, a porcupine, and casting her cloak over it, she rolled it dexterously in it, and then with one sharp blow against the tree killed it, well aware that the Indians esteem it as agreeable and wholesome food.

Satisfied with her prize, though utterly unable to account for its presence, she returned to the pinnace. The fish, it seemed, would not bite that day, so leaving the line out with a float to keep it up, and making it fast to the boat, all went in beside the fire. Ralph was neither asleep nor awake, but rousing himself from a kind of lethargy, he asked for water. Bertha gently bade him wait, and scraping two of her dearly prized roots, she cut them into small pieces and put them into a quart of water, which she then boiled. In half an hour she had a pot of what the French call *tisane*, which she administered to her patient with all the tenderness of a Nightingale, and all the decision of a sister of charity.

Then, while Ralph, refreshed and cool, went off into a doze, she proceeded to pluck and skin the hedgehog, which, in its turn, was soon placed upon the fire, and proved to these hungry souls not only palatable but most delicious.

CHAPTER XXI.

FEVER ON BOARD.

That night the hold of the Snow Ship presented a scene which, if taken with spirit, would have made the fortune of a great painter. All seemed to sleep but one. The beds of fur-skins and buffalo robes lay against the sides of the pinnace; in the centre was the stove. Behind that could be seen the form of young Miss Antoine, her face only visible, so wrapped was she in furs. On each side, with their heads to the foreground of the picture, lay the two boys, or rather young men,—Harry in a stupidly heavy sleep, Ralph only kept from rising by the hands of Bertha. Resting on her knees, a rude lamp in the centre illumining her face, she, while keeping down the patient, cast her streaming eyes to heaven in prayer.

Ralph, at nightfall, had become delirious; and, while Bertha was busy preparing his night's *tisane*, he had tried to rise and go out. He talked wildly and incoherently, of father and mother, of Jack and Pete, of his dear Bertha, who was slowly dying of hunger.

"There are bears, there are wolves, there are deer—she shall not die, I will go forth and hunt. The winter is gone—I feel the summer heat. Ah! what is this? some Indian savage who holds me in chains—avaunt! avaunt, I say—I will none of you."

But, thanks to his weakness, Bertha kept him down, and gave him drink,—drink that soothed him, that seemed to conquer the fever awhile, and compel drowsiness.

Bertha, with that devotion and forgetfulness of self which characterize her sex, now seated herself beside the sufferer, all thought of sleep banished from her mind. Scarcely had she done so, when a dull moan, followed by a deep sigh, showed her that she had another patient in the person of her sister. Long before morning Harry also was taken ill.

What the heroic girl endured, what trials she went through during that terrible night, she never revealed; but it made a woman, and a brave little woman of her before her time. Out into the air for water; in again preparing the drink; now covering up and controlling one patient, now another, she never hesitated a moment to do the duty that had devolved upon her by reason of her strength, for which she most earnestly thanked God, as well as for the opportune discovery she had made of the root, by means of which she hoped to save them all.

Towards daylight Bertha saw her patients still and slumbering heavily; so with a thoughtful regard, more for them than for her own pleasure, she yielded to nature's power and snatched a moment's rest in the embrace of sleep. When she awoke they were all three sitting up, having reached this position with difficulty.

"Lie down directly, you naughty people!" she said, springing up, "I can't take just a doze but you must be trying to get up."

"We are very ill, Bertha, and you are an angel," said Ralph.

"You have been very ill—fever, delirium, and all that; but you are all better. What will you have for breakfast—fish, or porcupine soup?"

"I could eat a bit of fish," said Ralph, while the others nodded; "but it's all gone."

"Well, there's another on the hook. I heard him

splashing when I went out for water," and with a pitcher and axe Bertha went forth.

The cold was now intense, every particle of water had disappeared, and snow clothed even the ice in its chaste and cold mantle. But Bertha knew that where they had already so often broken the ice there would be a chance, so she swept away the snow with her feet, and with her axe soon opened a hole, where the fish-line entered the water. She was not mistaken: a sturgeon was on the hook just dead. This she hauled up, filled her pitcher, and returned to her patients.

What with *tisane*, broiled fish, and porcupine soup, they got through that and the next day very well; but, on the morning of the third day, from being frozen up, there was not a scrap of food, and the ice was, with difficulty, broken. There had in every case been several fresh paroxysms of fever, but now the disease appeared conquered, the patients, in every instance, expressing themselves weak but *very hungry—and Bertha had nothing to give them.*

When they found the true state of things, the sufferers closed their eyes in silent prayer, and when they opened them again every countenance had upon it that heroic expression of submission to the will of God, that sublime, calm look of resignation which has been ever characteristic of the brave going to certain death. Bertha herself shook with suppressed agitation. She saw the agony they had endured, she knew the glorious resolve of their hearts.

"No! no! there is a just Providence above," she whispered to herself; "they shall not die."

And rising, she took Ralph's double-barrelled gun, as well as Harry's rifle, hung a glittering tomahawk by her side, put on her snow-shoes, and went out. These snow-shoes were simply two pieces of wood, like bows, the ends of which were made to meet, while at the centre they were little more than a foot apart. Across were laid other sticks, the bones of fish, the whole lashed by sinews, of which there was a plentiful supply on board. With these there is no danger of sinking in the snow.

"Are you about to leave us?" said her sister, with all the querulousness of sickness, while Harry watched her wistfully.

"Hush!" cried Ralph, severely, "do not malign the angel who has saved our lives. I would, indeed, if we must die, that she *would* leave us."

"Never," said the noble girl; "I will save you, or come back to die."

And, without a word or look of reproach, she went forth, after trimming their lamp, which was a kind of rude saucer with a tow wick, fed by grease from a pot kept always on board; nor did she forget to place a pannikin of drink close to every head.

The sick who remained were too weak for much talking, though every now and then a few words were exchanged as to the desperate mission the brave girl had undertaken. All joined in her prayer, but not one present entertained the slightest hope of success. What game could she hope to find on that white and desolate plain!

Suddenly, borne upon the wind, there came something like a moan, low and indistinct, but it speedily rose to a howl, which all knew to be that of wolves. A thrill of horror passed through every bosom at the thought of Bertha being exposed to the fearful assaults of a ravenous pack of beasts so hungry and so remorseless; and by a common motion all began crawling to the outlet.

Meanwhile the young girl, her heart beating wildly, had gone forth determined, even if she had to walk to the mainland, to bring back something in the shape of food. With this view she had slily taken a small tarbogin, and, selecting a distant point as a guide, she started resolutely for the land, trusting to her trail, and to the boat's mast as a landmark for her return. Pocket compasses, so useful and interesting, were not then known.

She had not gone a hundred yards when she, too, heard the cry of the wolves, at first like a moan on the frozen waters, then the full howl of a tremendous pack. They were coming directly her way, and, from her knowledge of woodcraft, she knew they must be in chase of a deer, as what else would bring them out upon that terrible plain?

Now, Bertha, who was brought up in the wilds, being born on the island of Manitoulin, acted in a very different way from what a girl of the woods would have done. It was quite clear to her that a deer had been driven to the edge of the water, when, sore pressed, and tempted by the smooth but treacherous expanse, it had plunged upon the snow, and taken to running in a tolerably straight direction. Wearied with the heavy trudging in the coagulated water, it now steered for the wooded clump, with some vague hope of escape.

Bertha, brave girl, was right. There it came, dashing, floundering along the snow, moving in a circular way that would bring it directly to the island. Now, good shot as Bertha was, nothing could have been easier than to have shot the deer from the boat; but this would only have been acting the part of provider to the wolves, which, an instant after, would have torn the reeking beast to atoms, and lapped up its life-blood.

Bertha meant to kill the deer, and to have it in spite

of the wolves, or perish. If she failed, hunger—the worst, the most agonizing of deaths—stared her in the face.

She was about a hundred feet from the boat; but, drawing the tarbogin back to within twenty feet, she concealed herself behind it, clutching her rifle in her hand, while the heavily loaded double-barrel was leaned against the small sleigh. Then, with such a heartfelt prayer for success as no hunter perhaps ever before sent to Heaven, she waited.

Her heart beat wildly, but not from fear; though the dismal howl of the wolves, which we have already described, might have sent a chill to the soul of the most lion-like of men: her heart throbbed with intense anxiety for those whose thread of life hung upon the three shots that were in her gun. But her suspense was not to be of long duration, for here they are.

The deer is but little in the van, not twenty yards, coming straight for the clump. The girl's nerves, strung to the highest pitch, enable her to take steady, and, it is to be hoped, deadly aim; for he is bringing the wind with him, not fifteen paces off, when a crack is heard, a light curling smoke rises, the deer flounders, plunges, and falls dead at her feet, as much from exhaustion as from the bullet.

Up! up! my brave, good girl; for fifty blood-thirsty throats are howling; fifty red, ragged tongues are lolling out; fifty pair of awful eyes are gleaming upon you, and fifty sets of pointed teeth are ready to devour you. Standing erect, and trusting to the native dread of man which even her little figure may inspire, she pours two barrels into the midst of the astonished and amazed hordes. Three savage brutes fall, while several limp away. The "dog of the woods," as the Indians call him—they tamed him to hunt before they knew of real dogs—is naturally cowardly, but in packs he is, like many other beings more human in shape, vastly brave. The whole troop, fifty in number, halted at sight of Bertha, and when she fired they sneaked away, to return, however, in an instant, all falling upon the killed and wounded, and devouring them.

Casting her guns on the tarbogin, Bertha tore at the quivering deer, and by superhuman exertions placed it beside the weapons, one of which—the double-barrelled —she hastily re-loaded, each barrel receiving half-a-dozen balls and an extra charge of powder. She then quickly lashed it to the sleigh, to prevent the recoil, and began dragging her prize towards the boat.

No sooner, however, did she move, than a dozen gaunt and furious wolves, the largest of the ferocious pack, dashed in her direction. Bertha watched them, and saw that in less than two minutes they would be upon her. They came up, two in front, three close behind, the rest in a confused heap. Kneeling down, she took aim at their open throats, and simultaneously, the explosion of the two barrels and a dozen wild and ferocious yells rose into the air.

Bertha now ran for it, her feeble strength being quite equal to moving the sleigh at a rapid pace, and drew up close to the stern of the boat. But a second band of wolves were up to her, and two fastened on the dangling head of the deer. Bright is the gleam of her tomahawk axe, of good Sheffield steel, and with a nervous hand does she strike the first monster, braining him on the instant; fast and furious are the blows that now assail the raging beasts, which rush to the unequal conflict, only sparing her for the pasture she provided them with.

But this cannot last; Bertha is out of breath, and the hungry brutes, their voracious appetites but whetted by the blood or reeking flesh they have devoured, press on, and one powerful and gigantic animal fixes his long teeth in the arm that wields the axe. A cry of pain bursts from the lips of Bertha, as her left hand plunges into her belt, and a pistol is levelled at the monster, which falls back—dead. But myriads of eyes seem to gleam upon her; a thousand tongues loll forth, and the whole brutal crew prepare for a rush at the deer and its defender, when the boards of the quarter-deck are lifted, and three ghastly faces appear—faces that look more like those of corpses than of living beings.

But every hand clutches a weapon, and two guns and one pair of pistols poured in among the hideous crew, announce a rescue; and the blood-thirsty gang retire to seat themselves at no great distance on their hams.

"Reload, if you can," said brave Bertha; "the deer must be brought in."

Heedless of her wound, heedless of the devouring jaws of the *Canis lupus*—Bertha cuts off the head of the deer, which she can then just lift and cast into the interior of the Snow Ship. Then she bounds in, after securing her weapons, and the planks once reclosed and secured, they are safe. Bold and brave Bertha is thanked by faint and feeble voices, as the invalids crawl slowly back to their beds, from which they had risen, only, as it were, by a miracle.

But all her courage has vanished for a moment, and a hysterical flood of tears relieves her pent-up feelings. Wayward are the ways of woman, who, bold as the most undaunted martyr in the hour of real danger, will faint when the peril is past.

Stretching forth her hand, Bertha opened a small locker, sacred to her father, which contained small flasks of brandy, rum, and whisky. Taking a small glass of the first, Bertha drank it down, with a very wry face.

"That's my first drink of spirits," she said, with a smile, "and it ain't nice, but my children may have a drop after their hard work; and moving to the fire, she mixed a little with boiling water, and handed a glass to each.

"Now, have patience," she said, laughing, "and see if I don't soon bring you all round."

With this she began to cut out very choice parts, which she shredded or minced into cold water, with salt, in this way preparing, in about ten minutes, a pint of broth for each of her invalids, which they drank with a relish and gratitude only known to those who have suffered the awful pangs of hunger—pangs which, when once felt, are never forgotten. I speak from doleful experience.

Bidding them all lie quiet while she prepared a second and more substantial meal, in the shape of a broil, Bertha, despite the terrific chorus of howls without, like a hundred dogs snapping and snarling over one bone, told the Hatfields many stories of wolves: how, when taken in a trap, they will crouch down, awaiting their fate, and with no intention of resisting the trapper; how they will attack sheep, small dogs, but never man.

"I had, when eleven years old, a pet lamb," she said, "of which I was very fond, and which I kept in a small inclosure near a fountain. One day, going down to the well for water, with a pitcher on my head, I saw what seemed to me a great dog worrying my poor sheep. It was indeed walking off with it in its mouth. I caught up a stray stick, and putting down my pitcher, I struck the ugly beast several times, upon which it dropped my favourite, and turned upon me with a most wicked snarl. I saw at once when he faced me, by his pricked ears, high cheek-bones, long bushy tail, and gaunt figure, that it was a wolf; but as he seemed anxious to get at my pet again, it crouching close to me, I struck him several times over the head, beating him about the ears, and fairly driving him away. But what I believe frightened him most was my shrieking, which I kept up all the time, until poor Pete came and shot him."

A dead silence followed the mention of this name. In their terrible hour of tribulation and danger they had momentarily forgotten their previous miseries.

"Bertha, you are an angel!" cried Ralph; "let us only regain our strength and all will be well. Pete shall be found."

Aouth has one blessing—that of rapidly recovering from illness. The two meals and a small modicum of sleep enabled the invalids to sit up without much exertion, all sign of their illness having vanished, save debility and thirst. All asked for a drink.

"*There is no water,*" said Bertha.

All fell back aghast.

CHAPTER XXII.

AN UNEXPECTED REUNION.

EVERYBODY knows the fearful trials endured in tropical climates from thirst. Though the suffering be nothing like the same in temperate zones, yet everywhere, the wide world over, the want of water is imperatively felt. Not man only, but every living thing, whether animal or vegetable, perishes for want of that, which in abundance we despise.

The whole party were for a moment appalled at the

announcement made to them in those few words, and yet only for a moment.

"A lump of ice, a little snow," said Ralph, "would amply supply us."

Bertha made no remark, but, seizing a tin kettle and an axe, she rose to go forth, as usual the provider and good genius of the party, when there came, clear and distinct to all their ears, the renewed yell of the ravenous wolves, howling around the Snow Ship for their prey.

"You must not go alone," continued Ralph; "the hungry brutes would tear you to pieces. If you can carry the tin, I will accompany you."

Because of the mental sufferings he had secretly endured, Ralph, since his illness, looked ten years older than before;—his mien and countenance were so aged, and his strength had so deserted him, that it was only by an amount of courage and resolution almost incredible that he contrived to clutch his gun and load it.

Bertha watched him with a tender and careful interest; but perceiving, after a while, that he was better able to move than she expected, she had recourse again to her father's store of spirits.

Now, Ralph required no Dutch courage to reanimate him, but the fiery fluid passing through his veins, gave him a fictitious strength, which at the moment was useful. He followed Bertha from the cabin to that part of the boat usually left open and uncovered in fine weather—namely, the stern sheets.

To their mutual amazement, the savage wolves, rendered furious by the terrible promptings of hunger, were endeavouring to tear down the wooden barrier which alone separated them from their prey. They flew at the frail planks with their teeth and paws, and not without success. One pine board, weaker or not so well placed as the others, had yielded to their frantic efforts.

A whole row of horrid jaws, thrust through the opening, met their astounded gaze.

But Ralph was quite prepared for this. Not one by one, but together, did he fire his two barrels, and, while the small vessel was filled with smoke, the air resounded with the howlings of the infuriated animals, increased by the horrid cries of those which, not yet dead, were being torn to pieces and eaten by their fellows.

"I do not see what is to be done," said Ralph, in a voice of sadness, as he proceeded once more to load his gun; "they are too many."

"Give them another broadside," cried the brave little heroine.

Ralph did so, and the result was that the savage animals, whose appetites were beginning to be satiated by feeding on their own kind, withdrew to a respectful distance, and allowed Bertha to pull out another plank and leap into the open air.

We have already said that the crew of the peculiar vessel we have endeavoured to describe, had collected a considerable amount of fuel, the portion of which not required for immediate consumption was placed outside. The young people had made a heap of layers of stout sticks, on which they had erected a pile of pine knots and small wood.

Bertha's eye fell upon this at once, and an idea suggested itself.

"Make haste and fetch me a brand from the fire," she said.

Ralph, though not exactly understanding why she asked for it, went in, and soon brought out a blazing pitch pine torch, which he handed to the girl. It had been the peculiar idea of the fugitives to select this very kind of fuel, so that the pile was in part composed of pine knots and cones, into the very midst of which Bertha thrust the flaming torch.

There was a momentary struggle between the frost and snow and that great power which vivifies the earth, and then, the cold yielding, the pile blazed on high a perfect beacon, scaring the wolves to a respectful distance, where they continued their hideous chorus of howls.

Bertha, meanwhile, had not been idle; watching her opportunity, she had easily chopped lumps of ice from the vicinity of the fire, which caused the solid mass to split, and these she bestowed in the kettle, which was then handed up to Ralph, who clutched it with the little strength he had left.

Just as she had succeeded in doing so, a low faint moan seemed to sweep across the vast waste of congealed water, and then a breeze came swiftly in their direction. If they could but hoist their sails, they might proceed upon their journey, especially as it was a northerly wind, which would render the ice secure.

The subject was debated warmly that evening, and it was finally decided that, God willing, they should resume their journey the next morning, when the whole party would be somewhat invigorated by another night's repose and sleep. This matter settled, all lay down to win that slumber which was so necessary to their debilitated frames.

Again all was silent; again nothing was to be heard but the breathing of the sleepers in that small cabin; but all slept not. It was not the howling of the hungry wolves, pawing and scraping around the cage which contained their human prey, that prevented this desirable consummation. Undefined alarm, terror of she knew not what, anxiety of the most poignant character with regard to the boys, kept Bertha awake. Vainly she tried to think of pleasanter things—of home, of the happy hour when all should be again united, and when the perils that now environed them should be spoken of with a smile.

She could not sleep.

Desirous of trying the soporific effect of cold, Bertha went into the after cabin, and, despite the patient wolves, removing a plank, she looked out into the night. The sight was magnificent. The wind was high, and scattered far and wide the snowy flakes, until the air was laden with milky particles. The sky was cloudless, while a full moon sailed across the blue expanse of ether, flooding hills, distant forests, and the wide waste of ice with its silvery frost.

But what comes yonder, under the moon, stalking in the stilly night?

Not stalking either, but running straight in their direction. Bertha veils her eyes with both her hands, and gazes wistfully at it. But the flood of light is such that she cannot distinguish its form.

Nearer and nearer, until, with a wildly beating heart, Bertha clutches her gun.

It is a man, and he is clothed in the **winter garb** of the trapper.

"Up, up!" she cries; "here is Batiste."

In another moment, after a shot at the wolves, the faithful old trapper was with them, while all were giving vent to their frantic delight at again seeing him, whose absence they had felt so much.

"Did you make von big fire to guide me?" inquired Batiste at last.

"No," cried Bertha, with a smile, as she explained how it happened.

"Vell, it vas lucky and it vas unlucky—for de same smoke as make me know you here, tell de Indians de same. Ve must go."

All were too well convinced of the hunter's logic, to waste time in argument. Taking a kind of harpoon from the cabin, the trapper went forth and began removing the ice from round about the runners on which the Snow Ship ran. The wolves, from some mysterious motive, had disappeared—a circumstance at the time unnoticed.

As soon as Batiste had successfully performed his task, it was easy to push the boat, which lay on a slope, on to the level ice, when, after some difficulty, the sails were hoisted, and once more the strange conveyance was under weigh, but it proceeded at a very moderate speed, the wind being light and vascillating.

CHAPTER XXIII.

A RENCONTRE.

WHEN Batiste was pitched off the Snow Ship, after the sudden breaking of the ice, he was cast upon a loose floe, which, though at first agitated by the winds and waves, presently settled down into a tolerably safe raft. By this time, however, the mast of the boat was scarcely visible, while every moment he was being carried to the northward and eastward. Finding that for the present he must be separated from his companions, he resigned himself to his fate, only intent on securing himself from the dangers of his peculiar navigation, and from the Indians, who had doubtless witnessed the catastrophe.

It was no easy matter, on a raft of so slippery a character, to maintain himself without being thrown into the water, as every now and then, from contact with other lumps or floes of ice, he was whirled round or struck backwards. The only satisfactory plan was to kneel and use the butt end of his gun as a kind of oar.

Presently he noticed that his raft stood still, upon which, cautiously rising, he found that he had once more reached a spot where the ice was able to bear his weight. But nowhere on the horizon could he catch the faintest glimpse of the Snow Ship.

Batiste was too experienced in everything connected not only with woodcraft, but also with the navigation of the lake, not to be fully aware that as long as the southern breeze lasted, the open water would cut off all communication between himself and his friends. His mind was, therefore, at once made up,—he would camp in the woods, and wait until the lake was again frozen over.

With this resolve, though his heart was rent with anxiety as to the fate of his young charges, the cheery old hunter shouldered his rifle, and struck out for the dark line of forest, which could be distinguished at no great distance.

The spot selected by Batiste was a wooded spit of land, that projected about half a mile into the lake, and the point of which was so thickly, and even densely wooded, that he had to cut himself a passage with his short, glittering axe, ere he reached the foot of a kind of cliff which, rising perpendicularly, was untouched by snow. When we say perpendicularly, we scarcely do justice to the fact; as the summit of the earthen bank hung very much over the base.

This at once decided Batiste, who in twenty minutes

had rigged for himself a temporary hut of the most primitive kind. A number of young trees and large boughs were cut down and placed leaning against the cliff, so as to leave a space of about three feet wide by five feet high. Against the outside of this some earth and snow were thrown, and the wigwam was complete.

Not quite complete, however; as a rude kind of hurdle had to be constructed, by way of a door, without which the cold could not have been kept out.

The most simple and natural proceeding would have been to make a fire; but the old French trapper was too experienced a hand to commit himself in a hurry. He knew that his old enemies, the Indians, who had inflicted many an honourable scar upon him in the late wars, were prowling about, and would rejoice in taking the scalp of one whose rifle was so dreaded.

To light a fire would have been to bait a trap for his own destruction.

At all events, Batiste exercised, on the present occasion, all the wary caution which appertains to those who have lived from their boyhood in the mighty woods, and become familiar with every art and device whereby to circumvent or overcome an enemy—or, if need be, to escape from them.

Taking his way once more to the extreme point of the promontory, he looked wistfully out into the night, which was black and rather tempestuous. His surprise, and at the same time his gratification, was great, when, at less than half a mile distance, on a similar spit to that which he now occupied, he saw a large fire, and around it were seated about thirty Indian warriors.

"*Diable!*" muttered Batiste; and with that characteristic ejaculation he retired to his slab hut to muse and sleep.

To muse first as to the wisdom of his own movements. In the first place, it was quite clear that the Redskins had camped under some huge trees, to await the same change in the weather which he anticipated : it was certain, therefore, that they would not leave the neighbourhood for the present. Hence a fire was out of the question, and still less could he indulge in a shot. How, then, was he to live during the hours, days, perhaps weeks, that he might be confined to his present shelter by the southern wind?

There was no resource for it but to trap—with which determination he went off into a sound and pleasant slumber.

No one who has not himself known the Indian race, can form any conception of the patience with which they will carry out any favourite project. The warriors, who had chased the Snow Ship, had never before seen a canoe that would float over ice; and their curiosity—an Indian feeling—was excited to the last degree. They were, therefore, resolved to capture it at any cost of time and labour.

This Batiste surmised when, on the following morning, he found the Redskin camp in exactly the same position which it had occupied the previous night. This was, to say the least of it, a very serious and awkward business; for though Batiste had, in his youth, gained the reputation of being the keenest Indian fighter on the whole of the Indian frontier, yet he was but mortal, and in a contest with thirty savage warriors, armed to the teeth, he must expect to be defeated.

His only plan, therefore, was to remain completely concealed.

How was he to live? He had nothing in his pouch, for though men of his stamp are rarely ill-provided, yet, on the present occasion, all had been taken by surprise. There was abundance of game in the woods, but to fire a shot would be fatal.

It is, however, not easy to defeat an old and experienced backwoodsman. So Batiste proceeded to make traps both for the birds of the air and the beasts of the forest, with wood cut from trees within the thicket, and with twine which he always carried in his pocket.

Before night he had caught a hare and two pigeons, which, however, proved but a sorry meal, since he was obliged to eat them raw. Still, this kind of food was nutritious and life-supporting, and Batiste was thankful for it. Having thus provided against ordinary contingencies, he took up his position in such a place as to command a view of the Indian camp, and then he quietly indulged in his favourite luxury—a pipe.

Now, this was incautious on the part of the wary old man; for the eyesight of Redskins is wondrously keen, while no one can more readily apply the proverb, that "where smoke is there must be fire." He, however, was not ready to believe that this would betray him, so he puffed away with the assiduity of an old Dutchman.

Days passed; and the trapper began to feel so fearful an agony of suspense with regard to his young friends, that he was half inclined to risk the dangerous road and cross the ice, though the absence of all movement on the part of the Indians indicated that it was not yet safe. This decided him to wait a little longer, in fact, until that very evening on which Bertha found that she was without water.

The loveliness of the night made Batiste wakeful; and he stood under a pine tree, taking his last pipe before retiring to rest. He stood on the opposite side to that which overlooked the camp occupied by the Indians. He was in the deep shade cast by three dismal looking trees, so that he could see without being seen.

Suddenly his quick eye detected something in motion, in the direction of his trap, about thirty yards distant.

He did not move, but stood motionless as a statue. Next instant he could see, shining in the moonlight, a pair of glaring eyeballs, followed by the head, and then by the whole body of an armed and painted savage, who was examining the trap with some curiosity.

Batiste clutched his rifle, and was about to take aim, when his better nature prevailed, and he waited, in the hope that the Indian might depart. The miraculously quick vision of the savage, however, was too much for him.

"Ugh!" said he, in his deep guttural tone, and then added, as he advanced, "bojoo brudder!"

"Keep back—Batiste no frère to de loping savage, vat vould kill his friend—go thy way, and quick, or I shoot."

The Indian started. He seemed to know the voice. For a moment he stood erect, and star-gazing, as it were, at vacancy, but all the while having his eyes searchingly fixed upon the tree.

He was, though ugly, a splendid specimen of an Indian—tall, erect, and sinewy; with limbs that would not have disgraced an Apollo. He was quite six feet high, and though but a young warrior, he was no mean competitor to contend against. He stood with the muzzle end of his gun in his hand, the butt end rested on the ground, as if irresolute how to act. Batiste broke the long silence by addressing him in the native Indian dialect.

"Go thy way, brave, and backward too. I know why you are scouting here, and, but that I was a man without a cross, I would have shot you through the brain like a dog. But I do no needless murder."

"A great white chief gives good advice to his son—but why should the hatchet be dug up between the paleface and his red friend?"

"Why did the crafty vulture of the Sioux attempt to catch my boat?"

Tutored as he was in the acts of the savage race to which he belonged, the young Sioux warrior started. He had, it is true, been one of those who had chased the Snow Ship; but how could the solitary hunter know this unless he were one of the crew, and if one of the crew, how was it he was there?

"My white brother speaks in riddles—but the hour is late, will not my brother come to the tents of my people?"

"No," said the other, sternly, "I will not—for there is blood between us—go!"

The Indian bowed with a lofty courtesy, that well became his graceful carriage, and as if trusting wholly to the generosity of the paleface, he turned his back, and leisurely entered the forest. Not so the cunning trapper, who next instant whisked behind a tree, and was amply rewarded for his caution, by seeing a gun-barrel protrude from amid the clump of bushes, where the Redskin had disappeared.

"*Sacré traitre,*" muttered the old trapper, and he instantly fired a foot below the barrel pointed at him.

The two shots were simultaneous, but while that of the Canadian sped with deadly aim, the other was expended in the air—the wily and treacherous savage falling forward towards the lake downwards, as he fired.

"Poor fellow!" exclaimed the Canadian, sorrowfully, "but he brought it on himself. I must be off, or the ravenous wolves will be upon me—ah! what is that yonder?"

Suddenly he saw far out on the wide and level plain, a column of smoke, with a faint, lurid light at the bottom.

"They are making signals," he whispered to himself; "but the signals will be seen by more than one."

The trapper knew very well that the two shots, fired simultaneously, would bring the whole body of Redskins down upon him in less than ten minutes; he had, therefore, no time to lose; but clutching his rifle, and turning his back upon the wretched Indian, he started over the white and glossy plain at a long loping trot, that was not a bad similitude of that of the Indians themselves.

He looked not once behind, but, putting forth all his strength, he pushed forward over the ice, guided first by the dark column of smoke, and then by the thin tapering mast of the Snow Ship. The result we know.

CHAPTER XXIV.

THE SNOW SHIP DESERTED.

THE boat was, while Batiste told his story, rushing hither and thither over the icy plain, something after the manner of a skater, the wind being still changeable, while the snow fell in those heavy flakes which betoken a long-continued storm. The Canadian consulted the horizon with a wary eye, but as yet not a sign was to be detected of the pursuing Indians, who, however, if at no very great distance, could easily follow the trail of the Snow Ship, some considerable fall being required to obliterate marks so clear and distinct.

The trapper reflected deeply. Under his charge were two girls and two boys, for whom he felt the affection of a father. Should the Indians come up, he had quite decided what course he would pursue, as a defence of the craft, when assailed by so many warriors, was out of the question. He was, however, still in hopes that he might be able to outwit the pursuers. All he asked for was wind.

The breeze seemed at times to second his wishes, but as the snow-storm increased it became evident that a total lull was imminent.

"The cold is getting terrible," said Ralph; "we must make up a fresh fire."

"No," replied Batiste, looking out upon the mighty plain, only a small portion of which he could now see, "we must leave the boat to its fate, or perish. Wrap yourselves up warmly, my children, clutch your weapons, and follow me."

As he spoke he once more lowered the sail, and then the mast, his companions obeying his orders with that blind fidelity which, under the circumstances, was wisdom. Then each one loading himself and herself with necessaries, they followed him on to the ice. The Canadian appeared to require no guide, striking out, as if by instinct, across the dreary waste.

His design soon became evident, for they had not proceeded for more than ten minutes, when they saw looming in the distance a dense forest of pines, growing so close together, and so loaded with snow, as to present a most singular appearance. Under the dark arches thus peculiarly formed, there was but a small coating of snow. This, however, did not influence Batiste, who hurried his charges along until they reached a small lake.

"It is one chance, and that is all," said Batiste, with a deep sigh.

And as he spoke, he darted across the snow-clad surface of the pond—it was little more—reckless of the trail which he left. The direction in which he headed was a hill, very steep and rugged, with brushwood and undergrowth of every kind upon its sides.

As soon as they had reached the foot of the mountain, Batiste led them behind a little thicket, and thus disclosed a small hole or crevice, through which they passed into a cavern, one of the many secret *caches* known to the old and experienced hunter.

Men who devote their lives to the chase never think of carrying with them the whole of the stock which they capture in a season. Their plan is to hunt one district well, camping in the woods for perhaps a fortnight, at the expiration of which they have a goodly pile, as no hunter remains long in a neighbourhood unless game is abundant.

As soon as the trapper makes up his mind to remove from the scene of his labours, he proceeds to *caché* his goods, which he does generally in one way. He selects a spot of ground where the green turf is smooth and even. This he proceeds to remove with his hunting-knife, in four pieces of about a foot square. Having completed this part of his task, the trapper places his blanket on the ground beside the spot, and then digs a pit, placing every atom of earth on the blanket, and as soon as a load is ready, he carries the whole to a distance, scattering the contents to the four winds, or casting it into a stream, as circumstances allow.

As soon as the hole is deep enough, the cautious hunter puts in all his spoils of the chase, scatters earth over them, and then replaces the turf, in general so artistically that few but experienced sportsmen are able to detect the handiwork of man. In some instances a fire is made over the spot, but in general faith, is put in the simple plan described; and should no curious eye fall upon the spot for a day or two, rain or the heavy dews do their work, and the grass grows firmly and well-rooted as before.

Hundreds of such *cachés* exist; some now unknown, even to those who made them, while many have passed away from memory by the death of the owners.

In one of his summer hunts, Batiste had fallen upon the present cave, which, when the lake was free from ice, could only be approached by swimming.

It was a natural cave, about ten feet high by as many wide, with a narrow entrance, and was guarded from view by the thicket, which grew up to within a foot of the opening.

But this was no barrier now; for if their trail were once discovered, the Indians would walk straight up to the cavern. Batiste, like most men of his class, had a motive in all he did. He had thrown the Snow Ship as a sop to wolves. He knew well that the Redskins would ransack this thoroughly before they continued on their way, and in the interval the falling snow might obliterate their tracks.

Down it came, the flakes falling with provoking slowness, but still slowly and surely erasing the marks of their footsteps. Batiste watched the progress of the storm with intense interest; for unless they put the Redskins entirely off the scent, there remained to them no hope, save in the last appeal to arms—a mode of action which, as it would surely end in the massacre of the party, the Canadian had no intention of having recourse to.

Down, down came the milk-white floss, loading rock, and bow, and tree, with its snowy mantle, but not enough for the impatience of Batiste, who, with knit brow and clenched fists, peered through the half-naked boughs. His eyes were rivetted on the terrible evidence of their presence.

So fixed was his gaze, and so accustomed was his eye to the impression of the snow-shoes, that it was some minutes after the trail was utterly obliterated before he was aware of the fact. Then it seemed providential, for, lifting his gaze to a higher horizon, he saw on the skirts of the forest the whole party of the Redskins fully accoutred for war, and bent upon tracing their progress.

But the powerful hand of nature had swept it away for ever.

Batiste could see the angry look of astonishment—could hear the savage execrations to which the baffled Indians gave vent, for they were not quite a hundred yards from the spot where the fugitives lay concealed.

" One cough, one sneeze, one whisper louder dan mine, and we is lost ! "

He had retreated into the cavern, where the young people were crouching up close together for warmth, to whisper these words. Next minute he was again at his post. The Indians had not yet moved, but scarcely had he resumed his ambuscade when he saw the enemy divide into three bands, one of which turned to the right, the other to the left, with the intention of walking round the pond, or lake.

The third band, eight in number, struck across the lake in the direction of the cavern where the palefaces were concealed. Batiste, with one deep sigh, laid down his gun, and, standing in an attitude of submission, prepared to surrender without striking a blow.

On came the Indians, so silently and yet so quickly, as to look like shadows in the gloom of the snow-storm. Their heads were thrown slightly forward, in an attitude of acute attention, their black sullen eyes constantly flitted from one point to the other, never resting for a second on any single object. All trailed their rifles in their left hand, while their right rested on the handle of their terrible tomahawks.

They were within twenty yards of the cavern, and the Canadian, anxious to prevent bloodshed, was about to step forward, when his purpose was suddenly arrested by a voice which came, almost directly, from above where he stood.

"My young men waste their time on the lake: a skunk could not hide," said one, in the authoritative tones of a chief. "The palefaces are in the woods skulking; but the eye of Onema is keen—he will find them."

The band of Redskins on the lake at once obeyed the orders of the head warrior, rushing tumultuously towards the shore, and disappearing beneath the gloomy and sombre arches of the tall pine forest. Batiste drew a long sigh of relief, and then retreated into the *caché* to announce to his young charges what was comparatively good news.

The Redskins were evidently utterly at fault, as they could hear them hallooing one to the other in the woods, now far, now near, until at length, after gradually receding, their voices were lost altogether. Still, they were not safe, as a second and more searching examination was sure to follow, when the fissure might at any moment be discovered.

There was, however, no help for it. They must for a while remain secreted, and put their faith in the very simplicity of the *caché* they had selected, as, despite the rapid falling of the snow, it would take some time to efface their trail did they seek to return to their vessel, on board of which all now heartily wished themselves.

Jack knew him to be right, but looked forward rather gloomily to the idea of passing a day in that hole without any prospect, and with the blast roaring through the huge pines, like distant echoes of the artillery of heaven. It was grand, it was magnificent, but it was terribly monotonous. Jack expressed his opinion to Pete, who coolly remarked that he was a young bear, and had all his sorrows to come.

This made Jack laugh, and in revenge he challenged Pete to tell him some story of bear-hunts, in which his father and Batiste had been concerned. This just suited Pete, who was enormously fond of talking, like most jolly fellows, and so the day passed, eating, drinking, and lying down, until once more they considered it time to go to rest.

The next morning was warmer far; the wind had more southing in it, and, though the snow was soft and sloppy, they determined to make the attempt. They carried as much ham in rashers as they could, and as much whisky as their bottles would hold, trusting to the snow for water. Each, moreover, had made free with a bear-skin, after which the *caché* had been filled up, everything returned, and the earth rendered as hard and as level as possible.

They ascended from the bottom of the hole, crawling; and, when they reached the summit, they put on their clumsy snow-shoes, and began their journey along the crest of the hill. For some time they continued in utter silence, so arduous and terrible was the walking, which they had hardly commenced ere they were sorry. At every step they either glided or slipped, sometimes tumbling, until they were so exhausted, so done-up and weary, that they stood still, and felt ready to lie down and give way to their feelings in a good cry, as many boys, and brave ones, too, have often done.

"Them snow-shoes," said Pete, "is dreadful walking. They fairly cuts me in two. I says, give in and go back."

"I'm too tired," said Jack; "couldn't walk another mile at present."

"If I tell the truth," answered Pete, "that's about the size here."

And, with a dexterity worthy of a man, he slid down a small declivity to where a fallen trunk afforded a seat. Jack followed tolerably well; and then, after panting for breath for a minute or two, they held counsel together. Both were unanimously of opinion, that while the south wind kept the snow in its present state it would be wise for them to attempt a return to the old retreat; but this appeared impossible without a good rest.

The fallen tree was one of a dense thicket with undergrowth; and beneath this they crept, and, wrapping themselves in their bearskin cloaks, they sought rest and sleep.

When they awoke it was night; and, though the south wind still blew, there was an evening frost, which made them start up and resolve to return the way they had come, there to abide until the weather changed, and the snow should become permanently solid. They were in deep distress about their friends; for, though joy seldom kills, yet grief, with its canker-worm, often does.

The mother, naturally, was the one spoken of with the deepest expressions of anxiety

They were still stiff from the horrible journey of the morning; but, by degrees, the exercise and their burdens warmed them, so that by the time they were half-way they were once more brisk enough, and finally gained their first *asile*, as the Canadians call them, in quite high and hearty spirits. It seemed something like home under the circumstances; and, when a fire and supper appeared, they lay by the fire and laughed with pleasure.

They were detained two whole days, when, on the third morning, the weather suddenly changed, and they were, within an hour after sunrise, assured of a good road. They had now but one ham left. This they cut up into slices, wrapped them into their bear robes, and then, boldly shouldering their guns, they began their journey anew.

The wind was so keen and piercing on the top of the ridge, that they thought it wiser to descend a little to the southward, to be protected from the gale; and, this delicate point once settled, they started, keeping their eyes fixed upon the crest of the hill as a guide. Pete knew how careful one ought to be in the woods, and therefore he never for a moment relaxed his vigilance, while Jack followed carefully in his footsteps. It was pleasant enough walking, as the snow now appeared dry and floury, so that they advanced at a rapid pace for hours, when a snow-storm of considerable duration compelled a retreat to some trees, which, standing almost wall-like in their proximity, fairly screened them.

This lasted about an hour, at the expiration of which time, though the fall had ceased, the sky continued dark and lowering.

"Well, I guess I'm puzzled," said Pete, with a rather rueful expression of countenance.

"Not lost?" said Jack, who never forgot his experience in that line.

"I hopes not, Jack, but I'm very much afraid we've missed the top of the ridge, somehow. The wind in my face has nearly sent me to sleep. There's nare a track of the way we came."

Now, as it often happens under similar circumstances, when the boys began to compare their experiences and memories, they differed widely. One recollected a willow, the other a cotton-wood tree, until at last they were fully aware that they could not both be wrong, and so they could not be lost.

Then began one of those tiresome tramps in the pine forest, which try the energies and cunning of most men. But the boys bore up wonderfully, and probably had they persevered, they might have gone right; but they soon lost confidence in any one route, and tried another, until, when night came, they had scarcely any idea of the direction of the compass.

And then they slept close to one another, with one rug over, and one rug under them, and with a fire on each side.

They would, under the circumstances, have rather liked being found by the Indians.

The next day was the same, and again the next; until at last their food was all gone, and they had no hope. No game had come within their reach, though once they thought so, when they found an old Indian crone watching their trail. They immediately ran after her, imploring her to lead them to her village—but she, alarmed at their gestures, concealed herself so cunningly, and then disappeared, that they soon thought she must have been a vision.

And all this time no game.

At length, one day, when, after chewing boughs, and trying barks, they were utterly in despair, they came upon a fine moose buck, scratching in the snow. Both stood still, and both, leaning their guns on the boughs of trees, took such steady and deliberate aim as men do, who know that life or death rests upon the shot.

Both hit him, and he bounded away over the snow, followed by the hunters.

They knew by his pace that he was wounded, and so, keeping up their strength by a last drop of whisky, on they went; but oh, how slowly, it was pitiable to see! They could scarcely draw their snow-shoes along, and yet, such is the heavenly attribute of hope, they still went on.

Several weary miles were traversed ere they sighted their prize, and it was down upon the ground, out of sight, with wolves in shoals upon him. With a cry of anguish the youths fired at the savage brutes, which at once took to their heels and fled—a rare instance of cowardice when they are in flocks. The reason was soon evident—of the moose deer there remained but the bones.

The poor boys sank in the snow in utter despair, but Pete was soon up, and, with a determination and energy indicative of the hunter's character, he compelled himself to make a fire, with the intention of broiling the bones for the sake of such little nutriment as they contained.

This done, and one or two mouthfuls feebly snatched, the deadly sleep of such climates seized upon them, and they gave way. In five minutes more they would have perished, but, with a joyous shout, that was soon changed to a cry of distress, up rushed Batiste, the brothers, and the sisters.

CHAPTER XXIX.

THE SNOW SHIP AGAIN.

THE whole party were at first under the impression that life was extinct, and that the two brave boys were gone for ever. Batiste, however, hastily kneeling down, and placing his hand upon their hearts, soon became convinced that a certain amount of vitality remained. His first act was to pour a mouthful of spirits down their throats, and then to chafe their hands and faces, rubbing with snow such parts as appeared frost-bitten—the common practice of experienced hunters.

The lads soon opened their eyes, and gazed for a moment wildly at their friends, totally unable to speak, but expressing in their eyes the deep gratitude and affection which they felt.

"Now, poys," said Batiste, "we must take them to de camp, and fill their estomacs with something to eat. Can you walk?"

They tried to rise, but the effort was too great for them. The old hunter scratched his head, and then, lifting Jack in his arms, left Pete to be carried by the others. In this way they were taken more than half a mile to the camp, where the party had passed the night in a deep hollow, so over-shadowed by trees, as to admit of a fire being made without fear of its betraying their presence.

Being careful not to put the sufferers too near the fire, they were comfortably disposed, and by a moderate admixture of brandy and food, they were soon brought to such a state of convalescence as to be able to tell their story, to which the others listened with rapt attention.

Now came the question as to what they were to do. The weather was very severe, and the boys were as yet unfit to walk, so that at all events they resolved to pass one more night in the same spot, as it was sheltered and comparatively warm. The rest of the day was spent in mutual explanations; but when evening set in, all were glad to seek that repose which their necessities and the excitement they had passed through, so much demanded.

It was somewhat late next morning, ere they were all ready to move, but when they did awake, it was with intense satisfaction that the elder brothers noted the improvement in Pete and Jack, who appeared quite renovated. The snow had now ceased falling, so that a short journey was practicable that day, and a short journey the hunter determined it should be, lest over-fatigue should throw the invalids back again.

His object was to make speedily for the Snow Ship, which alone could enable them to reach home. There was, however, one consideration of great importance. Should there be no wind, he determined to make for Manitoulin Island, abandoning the ark to the mercy of the Indians.

Every precaution was taken to avoid ambuscade, as from necessity they were compelled to pass at no very great distance from the Indian village. Batiste, however, selected secluded dells, valleys, and wooded bottoms, where the Indians were least likely to be concealed.

In this way, before night they were once more near the borders of the vast lake, which spread before them its white and placid mantle, unruffled by a breath of wind. The atmosphere was quite clear, so that they imagined that in the distance they could see the Snow Ship, almost wholly concealed by the snow which had fallen since they abandoned it to its fate.

A very serious consideration now arose. If they could see the Snow Ship, so could the Indians, if indeed they were on the look-out for it, instead of following on the trail of the fugitives. Nothing more probable might have occurred, than that the Redskins were in possession of their vessel, and that in its hold lay a treacherous ambush.

As, in a perfect hole in the ground, they lit their fire, much speculation was indulged in on this point. They were all well aware both of Indian artifices, and also of the untiring patience with which they will carry out any plan upon which they have set their hearts.

It now became a question whether they should not creep along the banks, secreting themselves at night, and travelling by short stages in the day, instead of venturing upon such a risk as an ambush on board the Snow Ship would prove. No decision had been come to when the hour for sleep had arrived, Batiste being fairly puzzled, and unable to make up his mind what to do.

The young people were soon in a sound sleep, but Batiste could not close his eyes. He was racked by doubt and sinister pesentiments. The feud between the Indians and themselves was, he knew, mortal, and capture might result in death to the whole party.

However, something must be done; so, suddenly rising and clutching his gun, the hunter strode away from the sleepers, determined at any risk to discover the truth with regard to their boat, which lay out upon the lake, still and motionless, but probably with very dangerous customers in the hold.

Now Batiste showed his great skill as a hunter and bush fighter. The moment he was about to leave the shadow of the trees, he stooped low, well aware that if the boat were in possession of the enemy, his only hope was to keep so low as not to be easily detected by any watchful eye.

The task was equally arduous and slow, but the Canadian was not a man to be easily deterred from anything he once undertook. He kept his eye steadily fixed on the beacon before him, and at last he had the satisfaction of seeing that he was rapidly nearing it.

And still it remained to all appearance utterly still and motionless.

He was nearly an hour making his journey, but at

length he paused within about twenty yards of it. The dead silence seemed ominous, and Batiste examined the boat with a keen and curious eye. It appeared wholly abandoned to its fate, and yet, somehow, the Canadian had his suspicions. The deck, it was true, was covered with snow, but it seemed to Batiste that the entrance at the back was clear. This was almost a confirmation of his worst suspicions.

Determined, however, to make sure, and well aware that the Indians would wish to take him alive, he resolved to advance boldly.

Casting his rifle in the hollow of his arm, and treading with the lightness of a dancer, he soon was able to verify his suspicions. The Indians had been there, for there were regular steps to the stern sheets.

But the stout oaken door to the cabin was closed. Batiste began to suspect the truth. A light flashed upon his face, as, with a bounding heart and a cautious step, he entered the boat and peered through a chink. He could see nothing, but he could distinctly hear the heavy breathing of several sleepers, evidently, as he suspected, in a state of intoxication.

They had found old Antoine's locker, and, unable to withstand the temptation, they had drunk themselves insensible.

Quick as thought, Batiste secured the door by a thick wooden bar, that completely locked it on the outside, and effectually prevented any chance of escape.

This done, he returned without delay to his companions, to whom he announced his extraordinary adventure. Not a moment was lost. The whole party hurried to the bark, in which their hopes of safety now lay, and in about half an hour they were diligently at work, clearing the deck of snow, after which, the breeze being favourable, they hoisted sail, and once more glided rapidly over the hardly-frozen snow.

Not many minutes elapsed ere the motion seemed to wake the sleepers, who tried at once to rush forth, but were evidently much surprised to find themselves prisoners. A deep guttural conversation followed, after which one of the men asked to speak with a chief.

"I am no chief," said Batiste through the chink, "but I am a hunter, and the oldest of the party. Speak, if you have anything to say."

"The paleface is very cunning, and his fire-water is hot. We have drunk too much, and have been trapped like beavers. It is the fortune of war. But whither would our brother take us? why not rather let us go in peace, and let the hatchet be buried between us?"

"Harkee, Redskin, if you mean treachery, let me tell you here are six guns, which will make pretty short work of you. But I am willing to treat, and if you will come forth one at a time, unarmed, you are free, and your arms shall be thrown to you when you are clear out of this boat, where you never ought to have been."

The Redskins whispered a word or two, and then again spoke aloud.

"A brave has but his word. It is peace. We will leave one by one," said the former spokesman.

Batiste, now seizing a hatchet, bade the others clutch their rifles, while he opened one panel of the door, which just allowed one man to pass; as soon as this was done, a plumed, grim head appeared, and one by one four warriors came forth, mightily crest-fallen. They each went to the end of the vessel, and leaped lightly upon the snow.

When the last man was out, their tomahawks were thrown to them, and, the wind freshening, the two strange parties were speedily separated.

All were now in a fever of excitement to get home, as their protracted absence must have caused great misery. Fortunately, they kept a fair wind, and, never pausing day or night, they arrived on the morrow at the house of Mr. Antoine, where they found Mr. and Mrs. Hatfield; for on the return of the horses, with broken harness and no sleigh, the anxious parents became so frenzied as not to be able to endure the suspense.

Accordingly, they harnessed the animals to a lumber-sleigh, and hurried, without a moment's delay, to seek for tidings of their children. The meeting may be conceived. It was all tears one moment, all smiles the next; but, before parting for the night, a happier circle could not have been found in all Canada. Past miseries made present comforts all the more delightful.

CHAPTER XXX.

A RIDE ON AN OX.

THE rest of the winter was spent in the usual occupations of Canadian farmers; but when the spring came, all were bent upon attending to agricultural occupations, which, however, being similar to those of the previous year, need not here be described. Great improvements were, however, made in the house, which was enlarged and made more comfortable, while three cottages were built for some honest Welsh labourers and their wives, who were hired for the season.

Mr. Hatfield was desirous, that while his sons should

learn farming and forest life thoroughly, they should not neglect those studies which might enable them to take a part in life, when the noblest colony in the world should be more densely peopled, and towns and villages should stand where only forests now existed. This made him secure hired labour, which enabled the boys to divide their days between labour and study.

Early in the spring, their neighbourhood received the welcome accession of two new settlers, one about eight, the other about eleven miles distant. They were both Scotch: able and industrious farmers. In the spirit of hospitality, which is almost universal in new countries, the Hatfields gave to each of the emigrants, on their first arrival, a week's help, which, considering that our heroes had excellent oxen, was of great value.

It chanced that an adventure befel Jack through this, of which in after life he was always very proud, though at the time it was far from a pleasant one. The nearest farmer, a Mr. M'Alister, had occasion to borrow a pair of oxen. Having served the purpose for which they were taken, they were given in charge to Jack to take home. It was rather late when he started, but though the road by the river side was dreary enough in the evening hour, the boy, ever fearless and brave, resolved to start, and as he did so, he saw the deepening shades sink into night without experiencing any real apprehension.

Of course he was not proceeding very rapidly, but there he was, trudging on stealthily, singing cheerfully, as he walked; now urging the animals forward, now leading them, when there came a sound upon the night air that made the brave boy shiver, for he knew it to be the war-cry of the ravenous wolves. At first he hoped that they might be chasing some stray deer, as was their wont, but as the hideous and horrible uproar came nearer and nearer, he knew they were after him, and that he must instantly adopt some means of making his escape.

His road, I have said, was close to the river bank, and he was a ready and active swimmer; but the night was very dark, and he might be carried into the rapids. To be dashed to pieces on the rocks was scarcely less dreadful than to be mangled and devoured by wolves. With a calmness and decision which, when he became a man, served him well, he sent up one brief, hurried prayer to God, and then made up his mind to what seemed the only chance of escape.

Mounting the near ox, he began, by using his goad and by shouting, to excite him to his utmost speed. In almost every case the heavy and unwieldy horned steed would have flung off his rider and left him to his fate, but in this instance the ox, accustomed to be made use of by Jack as a steed, started off with the speed of a race-horse, as if conscious of the young rider's peril.

The other ox, hearing the wolves, and unwilling to part from his companion, followed at a brisk pace. But faster than either, coming closer and closer every moment, the yelling pack came up behind, and letting Jack hear

"Their long, hard gallop, which could tire
The hound's deep hate, and hunter's fire."

Fortunately, however, the ox heard it too, and instinctively dreading the savage brutes, he galloped along without any pause, but still the wolves came nearer and nearer. Jack shouted loudly to keep them off, the oxen almost flying, and their chains rattling as they went.

This was their salvation.

The clanking sound, to which the hideous pack were

unaccustomed, made them hesitate when they came close to the oxen, whilst the latter increased their speed, till at length they came in sight of the farm, when everybody rushed out, unable to understand the frightful clamour, and both astonished and terrified to see Jack riding a race to which that of John Gilpin was as nothing.

The true state of things was speedily seen, when all were too glad to congratulate Jack on his good sense and courage; nor did his family ever again allow him to make such an excursion until the country was more clear and thickly peopled.

CHAPTER XXXI.

THE SCHOONER VOYAGE.

FEW but those who have seen it, can realize to themselves the indescribable beauty of autumn in Canada; especially in the woods, when the light of the rising or the setting sun falls upon them. Every conceivable shade of yellow and red, green and brown, may be found in the forest trees, shrubs, and creeping plants, and vines; every backwoodsman's home can boast of more gorgeous colouring and richer beauties, than any park-surrounded mansions in England.

It is then that the pine, in contrast to other trees, puts forth a richer and fresher foliage, and frequently a tree, still green, will have a single branch covered with red or orange leaves, like a gigantic bouquet of flowers.

It was at this season of the year that the Antoines paid a return visit to the Hatfield family. They came in a canoe, and were to stay some little time. Ralph had contrived this visit, for he wished his mother to see a little more of Bertha. It must be noted as a peculiarity in America, that people marry very young—and very wisely too, when the world is all before them where to choose. It was an understood thing between the young people, that as soon as a hut could be built, and a small farm cleared, they were to be married.

The elders were all agreeable, and a circumstance then suddenly occurred which promised to expedite the affair materially. A relative of Mrs. Hatfield, dying in England, left to each of the boys a thousand pounds, subject to the control of their father, until they reached the age of twenty-one. Mr. Hatfield determined that Ralph's portion should be put at his disposal at once, in order to expedite his farm, while Harry wished his to be reserved for the study of a profession, which he still preferred to a life in the woods.

The money was payable at Montreal, and thither Ralph was to start at once to fetch it, his father having received a power of attorney in the letter of advice. It was intended that the journey should be performed on horseback, but, by great good fortune, before the young man started, a small schooner hove in sight, chartered by an enterprising Canadian, for the sale of stores, and to look up goods for purchase. The owner of this craft earned a large fortune by his ingenuity and his shrewd way of doing business. Having purchased all the Hatfields had to sell, the captain, one Jerome, gladly gave Ralph a passage, and made a further arrangement to bring the young man back.

The young lovers, and all, indeed, parted cheerfully, for though the Huron is at times as dangerous as the sea, all had faith in Providence; and Bertha, who was to remain with the Hatfields, promised to be always on the look-out.

Away, then, the boat started, with a fair wind blowing fresh, and reached the Thames River, the end of the boat's journey, without any event, except that they had some difficulty in finding it. At length, however, they espied a large tree of the swamp-elm species, the only one in sight for miles, and this the skipper declared was his only landmark.

Here Ralph took a transport boat, with which to reach the end of his journey, leaving the schooner to trade and load until his return. His journey was without accident, his business was transacted, his purchases were made, and the money, chiefly in notes, was fastened in a belt round his person. Away, then, for home, and that dear undertaking which was to lead him to happiness, as the reward of industry.

The schooner was just ready; and, full of life and spirits, the whole party started on the return voyage. Getting under weigh, they dropped down the River Thames, which falls into St. Clare, which they crossed, and anchored amongst some low islands at the mouth of the river. Here they were detained three days, waiting for a wind. Ralph's impatience knew no bounds, and while others went ashore duck-shooting, he leaned over the bulwarks watching for a wind.

It came at last, but light and baffling, which made their progress very tedious. To keep out of the strong current they had to creep along shore, so that they were constantly running aground. The second day, however, the wind turning against them, they had to anchor again for twelve hours; when suddenly the long hoped-for chance took place in the shape of half a gale from the south-west, which enabled them, aided by a tow-rope, to pass the rapids, and once more dash out upon the broad bosom of the mighty Huron.

Ralph, who was a favourite of the captain's, walked the quarter-deck with him for some time, well aware, from the increasing sea, that they must prepare for a rough night. No serious alarm was yet felt, for the gale was aft, and would land them home at daybreak. But as the night came on, the storm increased in force, so that by midnight it blew a hurricane. The howling of the wind, the rattling of chains, the roar of the breeze through the ropes was something awful. The skipper now persuaded Ralph to retire to rest, and being weary, he agreed; and, despite the uproar, he slept until daylight.

He then clambered on deck, and looked out for land. None was in sight; but the schooner was scudding before the gale under a close-reefed foresail and jib, the sea running in dark, heavy masses, that threatened to poop their frail bark every moment. Nothing could be seen but mist; while, had there been breakers ahead, they would not have been visible twenty feet off.

"Where are we?" asked Ralph.

"I don't know," replied the captain, in a whisper; "but we must be careful, for at this rate we shall reach the Manitoulins before we are aware of it."

"Why not lay-to?"

"Impossible, in this sea, to wear. We must keep on, and put our faith in Providence."

There was no replying to this, so Ralph took a biscuit and a cup of cold coffee, after which he ensconced himself where he could act as a look-out, and waited. By four o'clock in the evening the storm was at its height, and it certainly blew with awful and terrific violence. They shipped heavy seas—so heavy as to sweep the deck of several barrels of flour, and to compel all to use the utmost caution and discretion.

Night came, and with it night's horrors on the sea. There was no moon, so that it was dark as pitch. Ralph thought those ten long hours would never pass. He had never known time hang so heavily. Every instant he expected to feel the shock, and hear the crash that would consign all to a miserable and instant death. Inwardly and silently he prayed; inwardly and silently he thought of Bertha.

From where he sat, he several times thought he heard the sound of breakers, but the pitchy darkness and the terrific uproar of the wind made it impossible to be certain.

At length day dawned, just as they rushed in amongst islands *two hundred miles from home!* On all sides was land, or piles of rocks. The skipper rushed to the helm, and, to the astonishment of everybody, steered directly for a reef of rock, upon which the sea broke with a thundering sound, throwing up the spray high into the air. All saw that to weather this reef was impossible, and a thrill of horror went to every heart. However, just as certain death appeared before every one, all noticed a narrow spot of smooth water.

Like an arrow from a bow, the gallant schooner hurtled through, but so near the rocks that a biscuit could have been thrown upon them. Next instant they were in a beautiful and spacious harbour, with a smooth, sandy beach.

Three tremendous cheers rewarded the captain for his exploit, and then all freely returned thanks to God for His great mercy. In this romantic bay they were windbound for several days, during which they explored a spot never visited but by the wandering trapper and the prowling savage, and spent their time in shooting and fishing, where, ere many years, will resound the voices of thousands.

The wind was light, at times quite calm, so that they proceeded but slowly, until at last it again headed them, and blew stiffly night after night, compelling them to lay-to. At length, a month later than they expected, they came in sight of the long-looked-for haven. The skipper now announced that until the wind changed he could not enter the harbour.

At the same moment a beacon fire blazed upon the beach, intimating the delight of those on shore to see them at last. This so roused Ralph, that he begged the Captain to try. He good-naturedly agreed, though pointing out the spot where wind and current would meet them.

A heavy sea broke over the bar as they darted through. Ralph was looking out eagerly—for whom we need not say—when a tremendous sea struck the schooner, deluged the deck, and sent him headlong into the boiling waters. It was well for him that he was a powerful swimmer, and could buffet the waves manfully; for the set of the current drove him to the southward, without his reaching the shore until he was at the foot of a cliff a hundred feet high. The first twenty feet of the base of this cliff was composed of stiff clay, and was quite perpendicular, against which the waves dashed with extreme fury.

Land here he must, for his strength was failing him; and, by superhuman exertions, darting through the billows, he suddenly saw the head of a birch-tree hanging down from the cliff, and cast down by the wind, though firmly secured to the bank by large masses of roots and earth.

A huge wave which came roaring behind, now lifted him at least ten feet, when, reaching out his hands, he clutched the branches, and was left by the receding water hanging in mid air. Still, he was not yet saved, as he could obtain no footing. Casting his eyes back, he saw, coming roaring on, a mountain of water, which must inevitably carry him back to certain destruction.

At the very last minute, and just as the remorseless wave touched his feet, a soft hand caught his, and he felt himself lifted up about a foot, when he was able to clutch the tree more firmly, and even to place his foot on the clay, in which position he remained until he felt the water recede, when, lifting up his eyes, he saw facing him the pallid countenance of Bertha.

Next moment he lay panting in her arms, out of the reach of danger.

We will not unveil the secrets of that happy meeting, during which poor Bertha told him he had been mourned as dead, none expecting the schooner to have survived the late fearful gale. When these explanations were over, and when both were able to move, they commenced the ascent of the cliff, down which Bertha had come at the peril of her life. By the exercise of caution, and by the help of young twigs and brushwood, they, however, were at last in safety, and in the arms of their delighted and admiring friends.

CHAPTER XXXII.

A WEDDING.

The accession of wealth which the legacy, so opportunely left to Mr. Hatfield, brought to the family, was, in Canada, very differently estimated to what it would have been in England. It not only enabled the father to stock his own farm with such necessaries as were required, but it enabled him to purchase a plot of land for Ralph, which, in England, would have cost a fortune. The young man, though not intended for a farmer, had, since his arrival in Canada, acquired sufficient knowledge of the business to begin life for himself; and, being desirous of settling, a location was soon found, a few acres cleared, and a log-hut built; and then Ralph, like a sensible man, determined to take unto himself a wife.

His marriage with Bertha was, however, deferred until the following autumn, as the whole summer was required for the necessary preparations, even with the additional labour which they were now enabled to procure by means of the inheritance. Ralph selected as his future home, a wild and lovely spot in the neighbourhood of Rice Lake, where the picturesque and the beautiful are as completely blended as in any place upon the face of the earth. They found a site under some high hills, that, while casting their huge shadows over the estate, also protected them from the north-west wind, which is probably felt as severely there as in any part of the world.

It was a bright and green valley, in which the log-hut was built—a valley with quite a wealth of foliage, which, in the summer-time of the year, is of a deeper and a richer green than is, perhaps, to be found anywhere on the whole continent of America. Then it was one mass of wood, and few could have imagined that it would ere long become a highly cultivated and populous State. Where Ralph selected his residence, and had literally to hew and hack his way in the virgin forest, there are now waving ridges of richly-cultivated land, teeming with crops of buckwheat and Indian corn.

Here, on a sunny summer day—the warm and balmy Indian summer day—were assembled the whole family of the Antoines and of the Hatfields, with Batiste, of course, and such few neighbours as could be collected in that remote district. A missionary clergyman had been induced to attend for the performance of the ceremony, so that nothing was wanting to promote the happiness of the two families, that were now to be united by indissoluble bonds.

Bertha saw her future home for the first time, and, as she looked around, she thought that had it been made for her, it could not have been more lovely, more enchanting. The wild rice-lake at the mouth of the valley—sleeping in sweet repose—the magnificent trees, the lovely, rich, and promising soil, that only needed to be touched to bring forth in rich profusion; all, too, her own—made the hunter's daughter feel a very queen among women.

The ceremony was performed with all due solemnity: the feast, abundant and copious, as all American feasts are, was done justice to, and then the guests departed, leaving the young and happy couple in their own home, attended only by a Scotch girl, a recent emigrant, who, not having obtained employment in the towns, had found her way into this remote district.

There were three labourers on the estate, one experienced chopper, and two new hands; but they lived in huts at some distance from the main habitation.

Thus was a useful citizen gained to Canada; for Ralph, naturally of an ambitious turn of mind, would probably have selected some profession—one which would have necessitated a journey to Europe, but for this early settlement in life. The almost universal prevalence of this system in our colonies is, indeed, the great source of their prosperity and rapid progress.

The Hatfields naturally felt the separation very much, as Ralph had always been the most active member of the family, and latterly his father and mother were in the habit of turning to him for advice. Harry, however, having honestly made up his mind to remain in the country, even if he did learn a profession, at once took his elder brother's place as far as he could. The healthy life he led, the regular and sober habits of the emigrant, had strengthened his frame, and given him a taste for those sports which, at an earlier stage of their establishment in Canada, had been somewhat distasteful to his rather indolent habits.

With increased muscular vigour he soon combined great accuracy of aim, so that, ere a month passed over—dating from the marriage—he was the hunter of the estate, and kept the whole family amply supplied with game.

At first, when he went out shooting, he took his young brother with him, as Jack's tastes were decidedly those of a hunter and trapper; but on some occasions he went alone, and at last, simply giving a hint that he might be detained all night, he started on an expedition which he was determined should outshine anything he had previously accomplished.

His secret design was to shoot a fine deer, and take the choice parts, as a surprise and present to the young couple.

CHAPTER XXXIII.

TREE'D BY WOLVES.

It was early in the day, when Harry, with his rifle on his shoulder, and his haversack slung behind him, turned his back on the old homestead, and disappeared from view beneath the dark arches of the forest.

There is a solemnity in a vast forest, which is singularly impressive to the mind, and Harry, who was of a contemplative character, felt its influence greatly. It was almost his first ramble alone, for a whole day, far from all habitations, and solely dependent on his own resources to find his way, and to protect himself from the dangers and difficulties, which it is so often the fate of the hunter and trapper to encounter.

For nearly the whole day—now very short as winter approached—Harry took his path through such dense forest, with brake and thicket intervening, that he made very little progress. As evening drew in, he was scarcely ten miles on his road, and had not seen any other game than a strong gobbler or two, which he did not think worthy of a shot.

About half an hour before sun-down, however, he reached one of those small lakes, or ponds, which lie sleeping in their green basins among the hills, with a small hill-stream plunging over a dark rock. Such a spot, Harry knew, would be likely to be frequented by deer, as they are apt to visit them at regular intervals to drink.

Nor was he disappointed, for when he crept up to within some twenty yards of the spot, he saw a stately buck stooping to the water's edge. To cock his gun and to fire was the work of little more than a second; the deer leaping high in the air, and starting rapidly up a pine-clad acclivity on the other side of the pond-like lake.

Harry reloaded while in pursuit, keeping his eyes fixed all the time on the wounded beast, which, however, had only strength to run about a hundred yards, when it fell, and was almost dead ere the young hunter's knife put an end to its sufferings. It was a magnificent animal, and promised Harry the satisfaction of taking a really handsome present to his brother.

The spot where the deer had fallen was a pine grove, and here the young hunter at once determined to pass the night, as he could better cut up the animal in the light of day. The night was cold in the extreme, and a fire was absolutely necessary. This, however, was an easy task, as the ground was strewn with pine cones and broken boughs, while every now and then some fallen monarchs of the forest permitted logs to be cut from them.

The buck had fallen at the foot of a stunted pine, the lower branches of which were not above six or seven feet from the ground. These branches were rather naked; but, some little way above them, however, they were leafy and outspreading, forming quite a canopy which, in case of rain, would be useful.

At the foot of this tree Harry lighted a fire, and resolved to sleep. Having made a frugal meal, tired and wearied with his day's work, he sought refuge in slumber; but, as often happens when we most desire to have rest and repose, he could not sleep. Some odd feeling for which he could not account came over him, and at length, by a kind of sudden impulse, he rose to his feet, and began walking up and down in front of the fire.

Hoarse and terrible there came upon his ear the well-known cry of wolves in the distance.

Harry was brave enough—of that calm and steady bravery, which is so generally characteristic of Englishmen; but he knew that with these savage beasts, bravery would avail nothing.

What, then, was to be done?

He looked around for some means of defence. For several minutes he could see no hope of being able to resist the savage forest-hounds, which were full cry upon his track. At length, however, he cast his eyes upon the branches above his head, and by a kind of inspiration, he saw that his only chance of safety was there.

From the top of his haversack he took his lasso—without which he never stirred—and fastening his gun and other traps to one end of it, he rolled the other round his arm, and commenced climbing. In another minute he was seated on a stout branch, with his gun and knapsack upon a fir-tree bough above him.

And still the horrid cry was coming up the slope towards him, while the keen and piercing wind almost penetrated to the very marrow of his bones. It was quite clear, he knew, that a change of weather, was imminent, and ere he had been in the tree ten minutes, his fears were realized. One of those sudden and blinding snow-storms, which so often usher in a Canadian winter, burst upon the forest, whitening the ground, and loading the branches in less time than it takes to describe it.

The fire was extinguished in five minutes, while the deer was out of sight in less time.

But this mattered little. Not even the snow-storm

threw the ferocious wolves off the scent. With a prolonged howl, fearful to hear, and which, once it has fallen on the ear, is never forgotten, they dashed up the tree, and dragging the carcase from beneath its frail covering, they began tearing it to pieces, with a ravenous haste, which clearly indicated a state of semi-starvation.

For some little time the monstrous beasts—they are larger than the largest dog—took no notice of the presence of Harry; but no sooner had they torn every scrap of flesh off the deer's bones, than they looked upwards, and saw the young hunter. With loud and reiterated yells, the whole band began at once leaping up at the young man, and so fierce and long were they, that one or two very nearly succeeded in biting his legs.

Harry saw that he must do something. To shoot them one after another, would, perhaps, have been possible; but in his haste to ascend the tree, he had left his powder-horn and shot-pouch on the ground, so that he had only one shot available, and this he resolved not to throw away until the very last minute.

Still, something must be done, else the wolves would certainly tear him from his post in the tree. He could not climb higher, as the other boughs were not capable of bearing his weight.

And the snow, steadily falling, would soon put the panting beasts upon higher ground, whence to leap.

He had his hunting-knife in his belt, and with this he might for a time ward off the attacks of his enemies, but only for a time, as every minute they became more daring and frantic in their efforts to get at him. Harry was forced to kneel on the bough, that his feet might not be within reach of the wolves. In this posture he suddenly noticed his lasso, and a strange thought came into his head.

The end of the rope was easily fastened to a bough above, and then firmly clutching hold of the bough with one hand, with the other Harry easily slipped a noose round the neck of the largest and most ferocious of the wolves, which next minute was swinging in the air—nearly dead from suffocation.

With one blow of his knife Harry then put the creature out of its misery, after which, as a kind of trophy of victory, he laid the carcase across a bough. The wolves, however, nothing daunted at the fate of their companion, still flew at him, except that for one moment they rushed at the dripping blood, which they lapped up with a relish that was horrible to see.

A second time did the daring young hunter noose one of the animals—a huge old wolf, which, as he kneeled with one foot lower than the other, flew at it, and actually touched his shoe with its long and yellow fangs.

The carcase was disposed of in the same way as the previous one.

The animals had double reason for attacking him. Their fierce appetites were worked up to a pitch of frenzy at the sight of the carcases, which the dripping blood made them mad to get at. But Harry persevered. A third wolf was noosed and killed, the lasso performing the task with ease, when drawn over the bough.

And still the snow whitened the ground, and enabled the wolves to leap nearer and nearer to him.

At this juncture, a warning crack sent a chill, as of death, through the veins of the brave young hunter.

The bough on which he was kneeling, and on which the wolves were laid, was evidently giving way. With one thrust Harry cast the carcases off, and then clutching a bough above him, he examined the fracture. It was not very large, but there was every likelihood that should he attempt to remain much longer in his present position, he would be cast among the wolves and torn to pieces.

However, he was not disheartened. The carcases of the wolves which the survivors were busily devouring, had obtained for him a few minutes' respite. This he made use of, to shift himself on to another bough, which, though not quite so commodious, was a little higher up, and more out of reach of the furious animals.

CHAPTER XXXIV

AN UNEXPECTED MEETING.

AND now a fresh and fearful danger threatened to render all his courage and devotion useless. The fearful sleep from which there is no waking, a sleep engendered by cold, was beginning to hold him in its clutches; a dull irresistible desire to doze, made him close his eyelids, but hitherto, without his going right off. The howling and yelling of the baffled wolves served to rouse him, while his own consciousness of the extreme danger there was in yielding, made him resist the intense desire he felt to sleep.

Fortunately, he had his brandy-flask, and a sip from this now and then served to warm his body, and keep up his strength.

He had taken no note of time, and could scarcely tell whether the contest had lasted one hour or six.

At all events, it was still dark, and the snow, which came in fitful showers, made the darkness greater.

Clambering on his feet, and seizing the trunk of the tree in his arms, Harry tried to warm himself, and arouse his energies by climbing. But he had overrated his strength. He wanted rest, and food, and sleep; yet none of them were to be obtained.

He began to think that there was only one chance for him, and this was to shoot one of the wolves, which when its companions should begin to devour, he would leap from the tree, seize his powder-horn and shot-pouch, and do battle for his life.

He looked down. The savage monsters were still watching him, but, probably tired of their continued efforts to reach him, they were seated on the snow. Harry clutched his gun, and took aim at the largest of the pack. He knew the value of that bullet, and took cautious aim. His life was, probably, dependent upon that one shot. He fired, and the huge beast rolled over, in the agonies of death, to some little distance from the tree.

In an instant the whole pack were upon it, while Harry leaped to the ground, snatched up his ammunition, loaded hastily, ramming half a dozen bullets into the gun, which, next minute, he discharged amid the howling group.

Then he took to his heels and rushed up the slope, trusting to find some place of concealment better suited to his wants than the one he had left. Up, toiling through the freshly-fallen snow, sinking to his knees at every step, and making but slow progress, the brave youth still pressed on, though almost overcome by the dread heaviness which precedes a snow-sleep,—up, up he struggles, until the summit of the hill is reached. Still nothing but bare pines meet his view.

With a heavy sigh Harry began descending the hill, though, such was his weariness, that he felt strongly inclined to throw away his gun—a somewhat heavy rifle. Still, knowing how much might depend on it, he clung to his weapon, until the howling of the wolves, again upon his track, showed him how necessary it was for his defence.

But by this time, life was much less dear to him than it had been; a reckless kind of despair was upon him. He felt as if it were hardly worth while enduring so much to save it; and then, so inconsistent is the human heart, next minute he placed his back against a tree, prepared to defend himself to the last gasp.

As he did so, the grey light of dawn fell upon all nature, and he was enabled to take steady aim at a long distance. This gave him time to load ere the ravenous beasts came up.

But imagine his delight, surprise, and astonishment when, close to him, he heard a cheerful voice addressing him.

"Hein! who is that shoot by mine door? ah! ah! de *loups*. Come in, stranger, to mine *maison—mon Dieu*, it is Monsieur Henri!"

Next instant Harry was clasped to Batiste's heart, and a door was slammed in the face of the hungry pack.

Batiste, ever since the adventures in the Snow Ship, had felt such an affection for the two families, that he had determined to locate near them. With a view, however, to enjoy his own ways and habits, which at times were solitary, he had kept the place of his residence a secret from all. It was a small log hut of the rudest and most homely character, but it was warm and comfortable, and ten minutes after his entrance within its hospitable walls, Harry was sound asleep.

His fatigue and exhaustion were too great to allow him to care for anything but slumber.

The old hunter, who, rising invariably at the first

glimpse of day, had, as usual, thrown open his window, was indeed astonished to see, close to his door, a man pursued by wolves; but his surprise was doubly great to find that it was one of his favourite boys. He saw at once how wearied and exhausted Harry was, and therefore he asked no questions, but allowed the youth to seek repose on his own warm couch of skins. He then quietly and gravely seated himself by his fire, and proceeded to make the young man a pair of snow-shoes, without which it is almost impossible to travel in Canada during the winter.

Then there were weapons to clean, wood to fetch and chop, so that the hours passed rapidly away, and still Harry slept. At length, however, he awoke, a very different man from what he had been when, nearly dead, with bleeding feet, and a heart sinking within him, he had tottered into the trapper's hut.

"Ah, Batiste!" he cried, "you seem to be my providence—the providence of all. How shall we ever repay you?"

"Say no more—not von vord; but just get up and have some *déjeuner*. You vant it, I am sure—den you tell me how de tefil I find you at my *porte* at daylight, with de big *loups* after you."

Harry smiled.

"My adventures have been so extraordinary, that I an almost ashamed to tell them."

"I vonder at nothing—nothing; ve have so many adventure in our family. Eat and drink, and den you vill tell me all about it."

Harry did eat and drink, and did tell all about it; and Batiste, though he felt much for the young man, could not refrain from laughing at his ludicrous device for hanging the wolves.

"And now," said Harry, "how far is it to Ralph's house?"

"Good bit vay—but too late go there to-night. Rest yourself, and to-morrow at day-dawn ve start on our vay. Besides, mine young friend, ve must take a teer with us."

Harry's feet were so sore that he readily acquiesced in the hunter's wishes; and this decision come to, Batiste left him to his own devices, while he started for a part of the wood where he knew the deer always collected at the commencement of winter, and whence he returned two hours after sundown, loaded with as much as he could carry of the carcase of a deer.

This important affair settled, Batiste determined to enjoy a jolly evening; so, after supper, he brewed some grog, lit his pipe, and sat down to converse with his young friend. Batiste, though moderate, was talkative in his cups, and his fund of stories was great. Harry was enlivened and amused for hours. He declared that never at one sitting had he heard so many thrilling stories, such wonderful hairbreadth escapes, as well as hunting adventures.

At a reasonable hour both retired to rest; and at early dawn, with a brisk breeze, the snow lightly frozen, the air clear and exhilarating, they started on their journey in the direction of Ralph's home.

The way was pleasant enough; but Harry, at about mid-day, was delighted to see the smoke of his brother's chimney, and to receive, a few minutes later, a hearty and enthusiastic welcome from himself and his wife. The sight of their happy faces and pleasant home, drove, just then, even the thought of his sufferings from his head; but when alone at night, it was a long time ere he forgot his fearful encounter with the wolves.

CHAPTER XXXV.

A CANADIAN LAKE HUNT.

It has often been said, and cannot be too often repeated, that Canada is the country for the labourer,—not for a gentleman; that is, as far as the backwoods and farming, as a speculation, are concerned. Even Ralph, with his capital, large for a new country, found this, and found it, too, at most inconvenient moments; the great drawback being the want of labour. Lucky was it for himself and his wife, that they had not been accustomed to be waited on by servants; for of all difficulties that exist in Canada, the greatest is that of keeping your domestics about you. Few ever remain more than six months; while, if it suits them, they will go at a moment's notice. Some of the richer colonists in the more settled districts have been known to lose their cook, about an hour before a large party was expected to dinner.

Ralph was anxious, for many reasons, that his young wife should have assistance in the house; while he himself, though offering good wages, could never secure the services of competent farm-labourers for any length of time. Truly, Canada is the paradise of maidservants, mechanics, labourers, and especially of boys and girls from twelve to seventeen, who are willing to work.

But the young colonist was not to be defeated, so he determined to leave his farm in early spring, go down to the coast, and engage, from the emigrant ships themselves, domestics and labourers, who would sign a bond for at least a year; when, if faithful and true, he would set them up in the world as neighbours, soon in all particulars to be his equals. Such is the universal consequence of free trade in land, the monopoly of which alone keeps up oligarchical institutions.

Batiste and Harry had agreed to keep house for Ralph, during his absence, with Ralph's sister-in-law in addition; so that everything was settled in a comfortable and satisfactory manner, except that neither the husband nor the wife liked the parting, which was consented to only as a stern duty to themselves, and to the posterity which might rise around them.

The thaw was just over, when Ralph, aided by his companions, began to busy himself on his farm, previous to his journey to the towns. He seemed glad of an excuse to linger, so that ere he was ready, great and rapid changes in the weather had taken place; first the soft airs of spring stole, balmy and sweet, over the valley; then came the warm and invigorating sun, to stimulate the dormant powers of the vegetable world, though every now and then, a gusty squall from the north would intervene, to check the progress of the fine weather. But the snow had long since disappeared, and everywhere on the clearings could be seen the green wheat-fields, spotted, as usual, with dark and charred stumps, which the year before had supported some of the finest trees of the district, and which Ralph had not, as yet, been able to eradicate.

We need not describe the early spring occupations of a Canadian settler; they have already been fully detailed.

One welcome change, however, took place. It was now doubtful which of the three, Batiste, Ralph, or Harry, cared most for gunning. It was, therefore, with considerable satisfaction, that all saw large flocks of geese passing over the country, hovering now and then as if in search of water, and then flying away in the direction of Rice

Lake. Hasty travellers, tourists who run through this favoured land upon a beaten track, complain that game is scarce, because it is not jammed up in narrow preserves, as in England; but for those who know where to seek it, splendid shooting may be had in Canada.

Ducks abound, and so do woodcocks; of the former, the black duck and wood duck being the most common. The latter is found upon the wooded banks of rivers, and sometimes alights upon trees, where it also builds its nest, though its feet are webbed, almost like those of other water-fowl. There is only one slight difference— no web is attached to the hinder claw. The only birds which remain all the winter, are partridges and snow-birds, and in the west a few turkeys. The partridge is very like a hen-pheasant in size and plumage. When sprung, he flies invariably to a tree, from whence it is impossible to dislodge him; so, if you can see him, which is difficult, you can shoot him sitting. Wild turkeys are tracked in the snow, and stalked, like deer, with rifles. They show excellent sport, but are rare. All other game disappears during the winter. There are hares, like rabbits, and moose, and deer, and bears; but these are rare.

With these few words on the hunting capacities of the colonies, we shall now continue our narrative.

Ralph could not but reflect that, for some time he would be deprived of his favourite amusement, and therefore he offered but feeble opposition to an excursion to the small lake for a day or two's shooting. This settled, the whole party started on horseback. Bertha was to be left at the home farm, no other means of transit being possible. No one, not *au fait* to new colonies, can form an idea of the roads at this time of the year. There are mud-holes and sand tracks. Now, a mud-hole is a serious thing, a thing to be contemplated and consulted about, measured and sounded, before the final, and often fatal plunge is taken; while a sand track, honoured by the name of road, after a thaw or rain, is something truly fearful to travel upon—a mass of shifting slough and liquid dirt.

The journey's end was safely reached, and the elders duly visited, when, to the astonishment of all the party, they learned that a neighbour had come near them in the shape of a squatter, whom, however, none of the family had ever yet visited. Batiste growled somewhat at this invasion of their territory, which, he said, would soon be too thickly populated for him. As all the others were of a different opinion, the trapper suppressed his indignation, and, in half an hour he was the first to laugh at his own prejudices.

Now, it behove the early lords of the soil to be civil to their neighbours; so Batiste, Harry, and Jack being ready, Ralph supplied himself from his mother's stores, with some tea, sugar, candles, and soap, after which they all started through the forest in the direction of the lake, which, reaching before evening, they found tenanted by the new arrival, a sturdy old woodman of about sixty, his wife, three stout goodnatured sons, two daughters, and any number of dogs.

They had built a rough wooden house, and were busy clearing a small portion of the forest.

The strangers received them shyly at first, but when they learned their business and received their presents, all was well, especially when Ralph privately communicated to the father, that if he wished permanently to settle, Mr. Hatfield, who desired neighbours, would gladly lend him money to purchase his lot. The old man stared, laughed, wrung the youth's hand, accepted the offer, and they were fast friends. Help one another is the law of the wilderness.

Some fish from the lake, some duck's and deer's-meat, with tea, were most acceptable; and then to roost, with a determination to rise early. To roost, but, alas! not to sleep much. The night was a night of horror. Perched on the margin of the lake, and being too close to the ricefields, the house swarmed with every creeping, crawling, flying insect that can be conceived; so that the chief part of the time for sleep was spent in itching and scratching. Ralph, above all, was sleepless, obtaining only an occasional doze. Most wistfully did he look out for daylight, and when at length a faint glimpse of dawn was to be seen, before the sun rose, he rushed out of the house into the lake, where, damp and cold as was the atmosphere, he absolutely luxuriated in the idea of ridding himself of his tormentors. Soon after this, the morning was lovely in the extreme, and after a hasty breakfast all started, vowing that that day a stag should fall.

It was now a lovely morn; so clear, so bright, so cool, so fresh. The trees every day wore a brighter and greener mantle, the little forest flowers a richer hue, the birds appeared every morn to sing more joyously, and it seemed as if the deep voice of the frog had an extra gay note. The lake itself was perfectly calm, scarcely a ripple disturbed its pellucid waters, save where here and there a trout leaped at a frolicsome fly. The sun now gilded with his beams all the higher ground and trees, while under the forest arches, twilight seemed yet to linger.

The young men had two canoes, and, being anxious to do honour to their visitors, they gave them up to them, while they themselves coasted the lake. Batiste and

Jack took one, and the two elder brothers the other. The Canadian was too wary to seek for game near the squatter's house, but pushed to the other end of the lake, which the strangers, as yet busy with their location, had not before visited. He took the waters near the shore, and, rounding a bend, he was soon out of sight of all sign of human progress. The scene was wild enough now, nothing being heard but the voice of the forest birds, the song of the brooks that fell here and there into the lake, and the sighing of the wind amid the trees.

They paddled leisurely along, regardless of the wild ducks and waterfowl, upon which they were afraid to fire, for fear of disturbing the deer; examining all the beautiful bays, and peering into their leafy grottoes, and yet not getting in sight of game. The only thing which the experienced eye of Batiste detected, was the trace of bears, which had been climbing the trees, and had indented the bark with their claws. There were snipe, too, and black squirrels, and pigeons—of which more presently—but the main object was deer, so that all else was considered a lure and a snare.

At last, Ralph, who was sweeping the lake with his telescope, informed Batiste, that at some distance he saw several deer in the water, while one was swimming across to the opposite shore, near which they were. The Canadian at once decided to creep across and drive the animal in their direction, requesting the boys to conceal themselves in a little bay, that shot round, and being hid, as it were, by a rocky point, was so completely secluded, that hundreds might have coasted the lake without discovering them.

As the stalking of the deer would take some time, Harry went ashore and began fishing for trout, while

Ralph, in the boat, posted himself behind a rock at the mouth of the bay, to watch the progress of the deer.

Shooting in America and shooting in England are two very different things. With us the love of field-sports is a mixed feeling, consisting partly in a remnant of the original savage, wild beast destroying instinct, and partly in the pride of skill; neither is sufficient alone, for it gives us no pleasure, either to throw up a stone and fire at it, or to kill a bird sitting.

On the other hand, the Americans and Canadians will paddle in a little punt, suited to one person, through the grass and reeds, and perhaps, after waiting half a day, they get a shot at a flock sitting, and kill a dozen or more. They never shoot flying, and hardly ever at a single bird, so that nothing can be more different than their idea of sport and ours. They are pot-hunters, and despise our "honour and glory" practice, as much as we do their going in for results. An American once said to an English sportsman, "I should like to enter into partnership with you, I should! you should kill, and I would eat."

The deer-hunt in which Ralph was now engaged, was very much on the same principle as pot-shooting. It is the common plan in the colonies, for men to be posted in boats some distance apart, to watch the deer, in case they should take to the water, when roused by the dogs; a lame and "cocktail" style of sporting, which we consider shabby in the extreme. For some time, Ralph, who, like everyone else, was becoming used to the customs of the country, waited in silence; admiring the beauty of the scenery, and feeling the excitement of expectation, until, the wind veering to the southward, he was attacked by a whole plague of musquitos, the pest of all uncleared and watery localities.

Having a great horror of them, Ralph fastened the boat to a rush, and undressed; having done which he jumped out of the boat and enjoyed the luxury of a swim. The way he selected was through some reeds, towards a cool and sheltered place, where he could see numerous broods of wild ducks sporting in the water, now diving, and again skimming to the surface, in playful gyrations round the careful mother. Ralph, as he neared them, became so interested as to pause in his course, and look at them from amid the reeds. While he was watching one of these broods, in a little bay about twenty or thirty yards from him, he saw them, at a signal which he distinctly heard the mother give, dart suddenly from sight amid the flags and rushes, while she hastened to conceal herself.

At first the young hunter thought that he had startled them, and was about to continue on his way, when casting his eye upward, he saw at a great height a bald eagle, soaring majestically over the lake. This king amid the birds is the great destroyer of waterfowl, and here in the wilderness, until the approach of man, he was the only enemy they had to encounter. They were, however, fully aware of the danger they incurred from him, and that the price of their security was nothing but unceasing vigilance. Did the mothers allow one of their brood to leave the shelter of the rushes, their instinct told them how little would be the chance of their return.

Presently the robber bird, perched on a tall tree, evidently saw Ralph, who was about to continue his swim, when he heard a loud cry.

"Qveek, Qveek, mine boy! De teer is close upon you."

With a splash and a dash, that showed how deeply he

was interested, Ralph struck out for the canoe, got into it from the rock, on which were his clothes, and seeing that the deer, slightly alarmed, was deviating from its course, he pushed after the animal in the costume of his great ancestor, Adam. Luckily he did not forget his gun, placing which in the bows, he seized the paddle, and darted in pursuit. The deer now clearly saw him, and taking no notice of Batiste, who was coming up behind, it turned back to recross the lake.

The race was a splendid one; the buck swimming very fast, and having a long start, which it made use of to head for where the females of the flock were feeding afar off. But Ralph gained upon him every moment, and soon saw that he might risk a shot. Dropping the paddle, he seized his gun and fired, after quick but steady aim. The animal bounded from the water, and then was still a moment, when, with feebler limbs, it started for the shore nearest to it. To do this it had to pass close to Ralph, who gave it a second shot, which enabled him to go close up to it, and end its misery with the hunter's knife.

Ralph was delighted, and as, luckily, the animal was in shoal water, he easily lifted it into the canoe; after which he prepared for shore. Up to this moment, the excitement of the chase had prevented him from noticing that he was naked; but he was soon brought to his senses by finding that he was a prey to every sort of venomous and torturing insect; and, exposed to a broiling sun, he had the prospect of a long pull back to the rock where he had left his clothes, before he could get any covering. Fortunately, however, a little breeze sprung up from the northward, which soon dispersed his enemies.

This did not enable him, however, to escape the quizzing of his companions, which he was too good-tempered to care about.

A general halt was now declared in the little bay, to prepare dinner, which consisted of a joint from a deer that Batiste had shot farther down the lake, and some delicious broiled trout, of which any quantity could be caught in a few minutes. Forest appetites are not to be judged by town ones, and as it may interest the reader to know how they managed, let us describe this forest meal.

The deer shot by Batiste was a small two-year old, both fat and tender, from which, with great artistic skill, he cut the sirloin. Meanwhile, a clear fire had been made. Two crotched sticks were then set up before the fire, and at a proper distance from it, and from each other; on the forks of these, and at about the height of six feet, was laid another stick. The venison was then suspended by a string from this cross-bar, close enough to the fire to roast, and was kept continually turning, so that all sides got an equal portion of the heat. They used a pint basin for a dripping pan, from which, ever and anon, they basted it with the rich gravy that dripped from it while roasting.

In the interim, some broiled fish and a broiled duck served to stay their appetites, and when the venison was done, birch bark, just peeled from the trees, served as platters and dish for a meal, which no art of Fren,h cookery could have made so palatable.

And this within ten days' sail of crowded England!

CHAPTER XXXVI.

JACK'S CATS.

As soon after a hearty meal, as men in general like to move, the young hunters and their leader resolved to start for the squatter's shanty, the day being more than half spent, and no one caring for further sport just then. They were not in a hurry, so they moved slowly, looking around at the wondrous beauties of nature to be seen on all sides in the densely-wooded forest, which so soon was to give way before human industry—too often before human recklessness and confidence—for when the trees are all gone, who will replant them?

As they advanced they reached a shallow expanse of some acres, where the pond-lilies grew in rich profusion, covering the surface of the lake with their broad round leaves, in the midst of which there sparkled, like silver, a thousand beautiful white flowers. These lily patches are the pasture-grounds of the deer, and all noticed paths leading into the forest, which were trampled, like those leading to a sheepfold.

"Where's your hurry, brothers?" said Jack, in a low voice; "a couple of deer will be welcome to the squatters. We want one for home—the other will be clean ate up to-night."

"Right, *mon garçon*," said Batiste.

The lassitude which usually follows a hearty meal was in part wearing off.

The brothers exchanged looks.

"Well, Harry, what say you?" said Ralph, laughing in the low noiseless way which is learned by intuition in the woods.

"I don't care," lazily chimed in Harry.

This settled the matter, and the canoes were dropped down the lake, Ralph and Harry selecting an island about one hundred and fifty feet from the shore, where they commanded the lily-pond, Batiste and Jack steering in towards a small bay, where, when night approached, they could *caché* under the overhanging bushes on the bank.

The evening was fast approaching, and all seated themselves calmly at their posts, awaiting the moment when the deer should come down to the water to feed.

About ten or twelve yards from Batiste and Jack, there was a tall boulder, about as large as a moderate-sized haystack. It stood about half a dozen feet from the forest, while between it and the water's edge there was a clean expanse of sand, covered by water at the time of early thaws and freshets.

Batiste and his companion were watching the lily patches and the deer paths, taking no notice of this quiet spot.

Suddenly Jack heard something move, which made him look sharply round, when he saw two little black animals of the size of tom-cats, frisking and playing about on the sandy shore.

"Eh, Batiste!" he whispered in a low hushed tone, "where do those cats come from, eh?"

The trapper turned carelessly round, though his eyes were somewhat distended with wonder.

"*Chats!*" he replied, in an equally low tone, "dat is vat a' you call *ours*—you know de leetle bar!"

"Oh!" cried Jack, with glistening eyes, "shouldn't I like to catch 'em, that's all."

"Vell, my sonny," laughed Batiste; "eef you vill keep yourself *tranquille* in ze bote—I vill try—ven I makes de grab, jist you kim up—and you shall see vot you will see."

In an instant Batiste was in the water, which came up to about his waist, and waded directly towards the bears which were frisking about on the sand, "as black as de debbil—Jack's vera fine tom-cat," as he afterwards remarked.

Now Batiste knew well that the mother was not far off, and would by no means take it kind of him for meddling with her babies, but he had made up his mind to have the young bears, and have them he was determined he would.

The little animals soon saw Batiste, but did not seem in the least afraid, sitting up on their haunches, swaying to and fro, and looking up at him as he stepped ashore, as coolly and impudently as if they had been his own children. Next instant, with a dexterity worthy of his reputation, he made a grab at them, caught one in each hand, and, turning round, found Jack close to him with the canoe.

Tossing them in, Batiste followed, giving the boat a good shove out ere he put his second foot on board.

Jack had caught the two little creatures by the neck, when, for such tiny wild beasts, they set up a terrible cry.

Batiste carefully examined his rifle, ere he spoke a word.

"Pinch dere ears, Jack, pinch dere ears, and make him sqveke," he then said; "make a' 'em cry hout."

Jack laughingly complied, catching hold of the poor animals by the ears, and pinching them, when their cries and contortions became so ludicrous, that the boy himself laughed outright.

"Hush, mine garçon, dis is dangerous vork; is your little double gun loaded—ah?" asked Batiste, in a cautious tone of inquiry.

"Yes," was Jack's quiet reply, the struggling bears taking up his attention.

"Dat is right—is de paddle close to you?" continued the trapper.

"Yes."

"You no speak—do as I bid you, and we shall have some fun."

At this moment there was a dire crashing and crackling among the bushes, a loud puffing and growling, which betokened that the old she-bear was coming at last.

The canoe was about thirty yards from the shore, when she came in sight, sniffing the ground, and calling to her young in her peculiar way.

"Pinch him again," said the hunter, never taking his eye off the shore.

Jack not only pinched one of the bears, but held him up to view; when, attracted by the cry, the bear not only saw her black little baby, but the human enemies that had carried it off.

With a fearful roar, that portended no good, she "put into the water," to swim to the rescue, impelled by that maternal affection which is so strong and enduring, while the young are helpless and require a mother's care, devotion, and attention.

"Kip de debbils from jumping in de water," whispered Batiste, who took up his paddle, knelt, laid the rifle handy, and sent the canoe right into deep water, where the bear would be at a disadvantage.

Then, when the bear was not more than twenty feet from him, he took aim, and—

The powder flashed in the pan.

"Mine Gott!" said the angry and bewildered trapper, "I never load my gun. Batiste is mad!"

On came the bear, so swiftly that it seemed as if she would, in another moment, reach and capsize the canoe—an easy task for one of her great size and strength.

With a mortified air (the trapper never remembered to have done such a thing before) Batiste snatched up Jack's gun, examined the priming—he had loaded it himself, he recollected, and took aim.

The great she-bear, puffing and growling, was within a yard of the boat. The Canadian, with all the coolness of a practised veteran in sport, fired both barrels directly at her head, and then, clutching the paddle, gave way with all his strength.

The bear, though the water, which was tinged with blood, revealed what the ball and charge of duck-shot had done, still followed with awful cries, re-echoed by the little ones, which struggled furiously in the grasp of the youth.

"Shall I shoot?" whispered the voice of Ralph, close at hand.

"No! I, and my poy, vill settle de moser of Jack's tom-cats. Don't speak a vord."

And, with his eye fixed on the bear, the hunter proceeded to load his rifle with studious care, examining the priming and flint with extreme minuteness.

Still, as they paddled away, poor Bruin, being furious at the loss of her cubs, and at the cruel wound inflicted by the double-barrelled gun, swam rapidly after them; and the Canadian knew that if he were now to miss, things would look serious, as no animal is more dangerous than a she-bear under such circumstances.

Batiste gradually slackened his pace, threw down the paddle, and clutched his rifle, determined this time not to be behind his reputation.

The ball struck the animal in the skull, entered the

brain, and, without a struggle, she turned over in the water, dead.

A loud hurra proclaimed the victory, and in a few minutes the whole party were on the little island with their trophies; the cubs were secured by means of silk handkerchiefs, which our young Englishmen always carried; while the old bear was skinned, and cut up; the inhabitants of Canada having no prejudices against the animal, such as influenced old Arctic discoverers. Indeed, bear hams in America are esteemed a general delicacy, and paid for highly.

"Dat makes one vere fine day's hunting," observed Batiste, while engaged in his task—none of the others cared about butchering the bear—"ve kill von—two deer—ve kill von she-bear, and ve catch de leetle tom-cats, as black as de deeble!—ha! ha!"

"Yes," said Ralph, "but what is the use of them?"

"Vat is de use of Jack's tom-cats!" cried Batiste, laughing; "vy much, begose eef Jack he no keep 'em, vy you sell 'em in Montreal, for thirty dollar each him tom-cat."

"If they are mine," said Jack, gravely, "I shall keep them."

"Keep two bears," replied Ralph; "why who is to take care of such great beasts? They will want a cage as big as a wigwam."

"No, mine frent—de leetle bear is as gentle and playful as von kittens—eef you feed him vell—and gif him no raw meat; dat is no meat vid de blood—he quite tame."

"We shall see what mother says," observed Harry, with a grim smile.

"Oh, if that's all, I'm right," said Jack, with a meaning laugh.

"An' now my frents, I vish to know, vile ve is about it, vy ve should not kill de old tom bear; dese animaux is not good; dey kill de cochon, dey eat de corn, dey play de Ole Scratch."

All were agreeable, while they were about it, to uproot the whole brood; upon which decision being come to, preparations were at once made for that purpose. The whole of their plunder was removed to the other side of the island; and then all four, having loaded their rifles, entered the canoes, as before, and made for land.

Each canoe had a cub, as a decoy.

It was now night—dark night—yet at a moderate distance, objects could be easily detected and recognized.

The boats made slowly for the small cove, where the *antre,* or den of the animals appeared to be. When they were both within thirty feet, the canoes were checked, and the little unfortunates, which had fallen asleep, were roused from their slumbers, in order to make them squall; which, being hungry and savage, they did with a vengeance, "crying out to their dad that he was wanted," as Jack facetiously observed.

This manœuvre had to be repeated once or twice, when a distant roar was heard, a dashing through the woods, and, guided by the shrill cries and growls, the old bear was soon upon the shore, angry, and evidently as full of fight as a mad dog. First, he sniffed at the *antre* behind the boulder, and not finding the female, he stood still and roared again, a wailing, half-angry, half-revengeful kind of roar. The remorseless sportsmen once more pulled the ears of the little cubs vigorously, upon which the old fellow plunged into the water, when he received a volley from three rifles and one double-barrelled gun.

With such an awful yell as the Redskins of old might have set up in that mighty forest, the powerful beast again sought the shore, to toss, and leap, and tear, and bite himself, as the loss of blood from his many wounds ended his life.

"*C'est un brave,*" observed Batiste, and the animal's requiem was said briefly but truly.

It was now determined to camp where they were, and no better shelter presenting itself than the very *antre*, or nest, of the bears themselves, it was strewed with fern and grass; the game fetched, a glorious supper enjoyed; and then, after sundry stories of "bars," and other animals, the whole party turned in for the night, leaving a huge fire outside. The two "tom-cats" slept cosily, nestling up to Jack, who found them tame enough; and above them the trees stretching out their long arms, formed an arch, through the vacant spaces of which the stars peered down; while before them were the bright waters, on which the moonbeams played, as the night breeze sent the mimic waves rippling in long billows.

The surprise and pleasure of the squatters at the destruction of the bear was great, while their gratitude for a timely supply of food was almost greater, as they were very short of powder.

CHAPTER XXXVII.

THE BALD EAGLE.

The next morning was clear and bright. A pleasant wind from the northward and westward had driven away the musquitoes, though not the other vermin; so that a breakfast before sunrise, and a bath in the clear waters of the lake, were very pleasant and agreeable. This day,

Josiah, the younger son of the squatter, was to join them, in a dug-out of his own construction. It was simply a hollowed pine log, and was a capital craft for duck shooting, drawing but little water, and being noiselessly worked. Besides, as the paddler sits facing the bow, he can look before him, drop his paddle, and take to his gun in a moment, when he gets within shot. They are, however, desperately fatiguing to those not accustomed to them, for the paddles are worked entirely by muscle, and not as with oars, by weight in a great measure.

It was agreed that each man should on this occasion, to use the local phrase, start on his own hook. Ralph, therefore, who had his secret views, pursuaded Josiah to accompany Harry, and to lend him his dug-out, that he might try his fortune alone. Josiah, to whom he had given an ample supply of powder and shot, was only too glad to oblige him; and, just as the sun rose, the hunters started, Ralph taking the shore as yet unvisited by them, and the others following in the track of the previous day.

Now Ralph, who was not only of an ambitious turn of mind in the way of sports, and somewhat chivalrous withal, had fixed his eye on game of rather a lofty character, and was privately determined not to return home until success had crowned his efforts.

It was *The Bald Eagle.*

Ralph had given a slight inkling of his intention to Batiste, who merely smiled. Our young hero, however, had provided against the necessity of a night or two in the woods, by procuring a bear-skin cloak, and taking a supply of sea-biscuit, some pepper and salt, and a little tea. With these luxuries, venison, and trout, it would be hard if he could not bivouac for a week.

Though Ralph had not said a single word about it, he had carefully, on the previous day, watched the eagle, and hence he started for the opposite side of the lake, towards the hills. His progress was slow, his course being as close to the shore as possible. His rifle rested on his knee, and though hour after hour, various game presented themselves to his notice, nothing could induce him to disturb the stillness of that mighty solitude, by the echoes of his gun. At last he reached a spot, whence he observed a vast field of grasses, lilies, and water weeds, and where he could plainly see the wild ducks disporting themselves.

He now drew his canoe beneath a large, widespreading tree that overhung the water, and waited, amusing himself, however, with a view to his evening meal, by snaring the speckled trout of that richly fertile lake. As usual, there were small ones near the shore, while the larger ones kept out in the open and deeper water. A small but noisy brook fell into the lake, just above where Ralph was posted, which literally swarmed with the favourite fish of that region.

Ralph had soon caught enough to satisfy himself, and was about to indulge in a pipe, to break the monotony of his watch, when a shrill cry resounded through the forest, something like the laugh of a mad creature, or of a certain class of hyæna. It has been said that these cries are hideous enough to frighten any one who is not used to them; but Ralph was not alarmed, for he had heard them on more than one occasion.

He was not much of a naturalist, but he knew enough about the bird he was in pursuit of, to wish to procure one, even stuffed. The Canadians and other hunters are strongly prejudiced against this animal, denying, in the most emphatic manner, that it is a noble and magnanimous bird—accusing it of being simply an audacious thief and robber, as well as a slayer of all things smaller and weaker than itself. "He is," says a true hunter of the prairies, "altogether a mean, selfish critter, that takes no pleasure in being sociable and friendly like; he's always a huntin' for suthin' to devour, and when he gets a holt on a poor duck or a rabbit, he flies to some all-fired out-of-the-way place, and eats it all to hisself. He never invites nobody to dinner, not he, and is sure to pick a quarrel with every bird he meets."

Ralph had been too much in the society of Batiste and Antoine, not to be somewhat influenced by their prejudices, and now that he had the opportunity, he was anxious to watch the bird and judge for himself. Batiste went so far as to declare, that he never knew it to live even with its mate without quarrelling; but this appeared so thoroughly against all nature, that Ralph would scarcely believe it. But the Canadian, who had been frequenting that lake for upwards of a dozen years, insisted that he had never seen two together on more than two or three occasions, and that then they were always quarrelling and fighting.

Again the cry was repeated, but now in another direction, and Ralph, who saw the wild ducks huddling together in the water-grass, crept behind a grape-vine that fell over the trunk of one of the trees, carefully primed his rifle, and then peered out. At the distance of about three hundred yards, a spit of land projected into the lake, covered by the rich verdure of the forest, and at the extreme end of this was the dead branch of an ancient hemlock, that overlooked the lake.

On this branch was perched the great Bald Eagle, peering down upon the waters in search of suitable prey. These birds, when not particularly disturbed by a desire for food, will sit for hours motionless, or pluming themselves.

Again there was a wild scream and maniac laugh, that made Ralph almost incautiously expose himself, when, suddenly, a dark shadow glanced on the water, and gazing upwards, he beheld another Eagle, sweeping down furiously at the one that sat motionless on the hemlock bough. He missed his aim, however, but the attempt was quite sufficient to rouse the ire of his indignant fellow eagle, who dashed at him with the utmost fury. Up and up they went, round and round, kicking, striking out at, and biting one another with the most intense ferocity, screaming all the while like huge owls. At one moment they seemed to close like wrestlers, when the feathers flew on all sides, descending to the lake like scattered snow-flakes. Hotter and hotter, madder and madder they went on, then higher and higher, one, the attacker, which was the weaker of the two, clearly endeavouring to get away. This the other would not allow. Again, after the futile attempt to end the fight, they closed, this time with such determined fury, that their wings became useless, and with one great flop, like that of a broken parachute, they pounced into the deepest part of the lake, as if to rise no more.

But scarcely had the water circles extended a hundred yards, when up they came, a precious distance one from the other, the weaker one entirely cooled of his fighting humour, and soaring away, until, quite like a speck in the air, Ralph saw him alighting in the forest on the opposite bank. The graver and more powerful eagle went quietly back to his perch, though Ralph, with his glass, could see by the blood on his white feathers, that he was wounded.

Another actor now came upon the scene, and one that made the eagle instantly ruffle his plumes and prepare, as it were, for action. A fish-hawk, during the combat had been soaring aloft, waiting for the fight to be over, and now, as if persuaded that the coast was clear for a while, it came soaring with circular gyrations towards the water, descending gradually as he did so. Presently he made a dive for a trout, and came up with it in his mouth. The fish could not, by its size, have weighed less than two pounds, and the falcon had hard work to rise with it from the water. The bird, however, seemed to think the prize worth trying for, for he did rise with it, and, what appeared curious to Ralph, he seemed bent on rising to an enormous height.

A glance explained this. The Bald Eagle had never taken his eyes off the fish-hawk, and now that his purveyor was successful, and had captured a trout worthy of his royal appetite, he prepared to do battle for it. Meanwhile, the falcon kept on struggling upwards, screaming all the time, in a kind of silly and frantic way, until he could not have been less than six hundred feet from the ground.

The eagle despite his wound, now soared from his perch, with a power of wing and rapidity that the hawk could not hope to contend with. On he came, not hurrying himself, uttering no cry, but ascending higher and higher towards the poor falcon, within fifty feet of which it soon was. Then would Ralph gladly have been near enough to use his rifle, for now he began to think, with a good many others, that the eagle was both a thief and a murderer. He fully expected to see the honest bird torn to pieces. But the falcon had too much sense to await the conflict with his foe—no sooner did he see that flight was out of the question, than he dropped the trout, and soared quietly away, aware that that was all his merciless persecutor required from him.

As the fish fell, the eagle closed his wings, and

dropped almost like a stone; then making a sudden dash, out came his vast pinions, and in his claws was the trout, with which he flew away to his old perch, and proceeded quietly to devour his ill-gotten gains.

This scene satisfied Ralph, who now had no compunction whatever about shooting a bird, for which he had hitherto had some reverence. He saw that for the present the bird was fully occupied; so, fastening his canoe, Ralph clambered cautiously and quietly up the bank, with the intention of creeping near enough to him to knock him safely off his lofty perch. Fortunately for Ralph, the ground on the banks of the lake materially assisted him; there being almost all round that water, a beaten path made by the vast herds of deer which frequented its neighbourhood, until civilization either destroyed them, or sent them to pastures new.

Ralph now felt like one of the solitary warriors, who, with noiseless mocassins, had so often trod that and other parts of the vast American wilds. He stole along with the utmost caution, avoiding dead branches, keeping a tree between himself and the bird, and never halting until he was within clear point blank shot of it. Then he once more examined his priming, so anxious was he to succeed in his self-imposed duty. Never, perhaps, had Ralph felt the true instincts of the wild hunter of the prairies until then, as, leaning against a tree, he sighted his rifle and fired.

Open mouthed, with rifle-butt on the ground, with the barrel clutched convulsively, Ralph watched the result.

A moment sufficed. The ball had struck the outer joint of his wing, and down fell the Bald Eagle into the lake, flapping and turning over until he struck the water.

Clutching his rifle, Ralph darted back to his canoe, which, in two minutes more, he pushed out into the lake

As he approached, he saw that, at all events, in outward appearance, it was a noble bird, though old—his head, and the feathers of his neck and tail were white, while the rest of his plumage was of a dark brown, approaching to black,

No one who has seen in a common menagerie, a drooping, dingy, rough, and unwashed thing, called an eagle, can have any idea of him in his native element, where, like Rob Roy on his green heather, he is truly in appearance a king. As Ralph neared him, he tried to fly, despite his broken pinion, but finding flight useless, he turned at bay. His look was defiant, almost cruel; his eye burned with an intense fierceness, that showed both his courage and his rapacity, and it was only a severe blow with the paddle, that ended his sufferings.

As Ralph drew his noble prey into his canoe, he asked himself, if he had done right, and the only consolatory feeling that came over his mind, was when he saw the wild ducks once more swimming about calmly round the field of lilies. Half an hour later, Ralph pulled to rejoin his friends, who were uproarious at his victory.

*　　　*　　　*　　　*　　　*

We have forborne, in the course of this narrative, to allude to the extraordinary and almost incredible quantity of pigeons which live in and about Canada. We might have told of vast districts white with their guano; but we have waited until the opportunity occurred, fitly to introduce them.

Ralph was, with becoming pride, showing his capture to his father and mother, the latter of whom, under the guidance of Batiste, was to stuff and erect it—when Jack came bounding in to announce the long-expected visit of the pigeons, in their transit from one part of the country to the other—a phenomenon remarked in some European countries, though not to the same extent which characterizes America.

Every one had heard of the astounding numbers of these congregating birds, but though nearly all Canadian travellers have vied with one another, in endeavouring to define and describe their multiplicity; yet how far was any preconceived idea from the truth.

Batiste had long foreseen the day, when these useful adjuncts to the economy of a Canadian housewife's treasury would be forthcoming, and had prepared Mrs. Hatfield accordingly. All the hunters were at once ready, and at the call of young Jack they sallied forth into the open air, each clutching whatever weapon particularly belonged to him.

It was true that the pigeon-roosts of the south had broken up, and that the wild, untamed hordes were coming down in millions to the borders of Lake Huron. The heavens were alive with them, as they flew onwards, near to the ground, in clouds that seemed to threaten to weigh down the earth. Could they have been captured, there would have been a meal for every soul upon the American continent, and to spare. On they came, in one serried mass, following their steady course with a quickness of flight, which was not less wonderful than their incredible and countless numbers.

The birds, during this time of transit, are not easily scared, so that, as they fly low, many persons are able to knock them over in great numbers with long poles; just as in Switzerland they are captured in droves, by means of nets placed across the mouth of valleys which they most frequent. One would have thought, to look up at that huge convoy of birds—at those masses, which no one would have pretended to calculate—that some sudden convulsion of nature had driven the entire feathered creation to unite and coalesce, in order to seek some remote region where they should be unmolested.

Our sportsmen, however, were not troubled with many speculative ideas; simply regarding this strange and singular phenomenon, as a means of procuring pleasant and wholesome food, so that in a few minutes every member of the party was busy discharging murderous volleys, not from rifles, but from fowling-pieces, muskets, and a couple of duck guns which did wonderful execution. At every discharge the pigeons appeared to fly faster, though their numbers were undiminished, and the prairie was covered with dead and wounded birds.

The amazed lookers-on now first saw, that what they had imagined to be the main body, was but the vanguard; for there now pressed forward, a flock such as surprised even Batiste. It extended as far as they could see on either side, one blue, solid mass—an army—fifty armies of wild pigeons.

"*Mon Dieu!*" cried Batiste, "dere is von pigeon pie for de hole vorld. Vell, ve vill have a leetle bit."

And, without any of those sentimental compunctions of conscience, which a great master of narrative has ascribed to one of his favourite characters, he continued blazing away, imitated by his companions, as long as one of the flight remained within reach of small arms. Then, and only then, did he pause, to throw away the gun, and begin to collect in rough baskets, the plunder, which made a wondrous pile.

But there was no waste, for Batiste had, as we have said, prepared Mrs. Hatfield. Every bread-barrel, pork, and other cask, had been carefully cleansed and scoured. The pigeons were accordingly plucked, large and numerous fires were made, and for the rest of the day the whole of the household turned cooks. About thirty or forty pigeons were hung to a hoop, and kept constantly turning round before a clear charcoal fire. At the proper moment, that is when half roasted, they were turned. Then, when sufficiently cooked, into the barrel they went, a little salt being put over every layer. On the top was poured a certain quantity of melted salt butter, then the barrels were headed up, rolled into an underground storehouse, and a wondrous provision was thus made for the winter, when the live pigeons were thousands of miles away.

CHAPTER XXXVIII.

THE CONCLUSION.

LEAVING Harry and Batiste to convoy Bertha and her younger sister Lotty to his home, Ralph started the next day on his way to Quebec, where alone he could obtain the assistance he required. We have no desire to record the details of this journey, which, however, would not be without their interest to the emigrant; let it suffice that the young settler reached the great seaport town of Canada, without adventure worth recording. He was much struck by its beauty, coming, as he did, from the wild forest country. Along the banks of the river, ten miles above the town, he saw one continued street of houses, from which the farms ran backwards in long narrow strips, divided by zigzag fences of unhewn logs, and were about three hundred yards in width, and from one to four miles in length. Behind these, at a distance of twelve miles, you may commence a journey straight to the north pole, without meeting a human habitation.

Ralph hired labourers both for himself and his father, for a term of two years, at the end of which time they were to receive a grant of partially cleared land. Having met with a young man named Dance, an engineer and theoretical farmer, who was desirous of trying his fortunes in the woods, Ralph with his engaged men, all of whom had families, started at once for Montreal, being eager not to loose a moment of the year that was coming. From Montreal he sent forward his emigrant families under charge of his old friend the schooner-captain, while he and his companion took another conveyance, with a view to visit the falls, first taking a run up the Ottawa—now to be the seat of the new capital—a river without much scenery, but celebrated, because of Moore's oft quoted line,—

"Ottawa's tide, the trembling moon," &c.

Another reason for diverging was that Ralph had heard much of the timber trade, and was inclined, if he saw his way clear, to engage in it. People said it was profitable, and led not only to certain fortune, but to the effective clearing of a new district. At Bytown he saw the practical working of the machinery. On the Ottawa there is a fine fall, called the Chaudière, on one side of which there is an inclined plane, constructed for the descent of timber rafts; and while they were there they saw several go down with great rapidity. It seemed pleasant and safe, but they heard that lives were often lost by the breaking of the rafts. But here they also heard, that not only was the timber trade overdone, but that it was always a risky speculation, except to the timber men, who being generally Canadians, half-breeds, and Irish of the lowest description, had actually been in the habit of receiving eighteen or twenty dollars a month, besides their keep at the shanty. These wages were paid to them all at once, at the end of six or eight months of work, when the timber was disposed of; and the money was spent in the towns, in the most reckless and profuse manner, without any benefit to the hard-worked man.

"Adieu to lumbering," thought Ralph; who, without delay, dashed forward—and he 'reached Niagara Falls, which certainly astounded him, but which, he halted not long to see; then, as fast as he could, he rushed off to his old home, where he found his father and mother alone. Leaving his friend to locate on the old farm for a day or two, on, on he hurried to the dear valley where she dwelt, who to him was brighter than all else. He arrived there late in the evening, and as he entered his own door, he was hailed by the wailing cry of a healthy child.

Ralph was a father.

*　　　*　　　*　　　*　　　*

A few days after this, when all had settled down, and the new labourers, who had been divided between himself and his father, began to understand the ways of the country, Ralph was seated by his fireside reading a newspaper, Bertha was rocking the babe in a cradle at her feet, while working at some article of dress. At a distance, near an open window, were Harry and Lotty, gazing out upon the pleasant and agreeable prospect. Outside could be heard the hum of voices, as the labourers dispersed to their several homes for the night.

"I tell you what it is, Bertha," said the young husband, with a little swagger in his manner, "I think I've managed this matter very well."

"What matter, my dear?" asked Bertha, looking up pleasantly into his face.

"Why, I've found first-class, honest, and industrious labourers, too glad to learn their business, and enter fairly on land of their own, with capital and experience, which is much better," began Ralph the sedate.

"You are quite right there, though I must go about a little more, to be able to judge."

"That is just it. But you must not go about until you are quite strong enough, and that won't be for a little while yet. Harry seems inclined to help me—and Lotty will stay with her sister all the winter," he continued.

"I don't know that," said Bertha, with a smile; "do you know, my own dear husband, that I half fancy they are going to be as foolish as—us."

"As foolish as—us," he cried, with open mouth; "what do you mean?"

"Why, going to be married to be sure!" she replied, with a bright laugh.

Ralph looked annoyed, then pleased, and finally he ran to the window, and fairly turned the young couple round, until he could see their faces.

"Do you mean to tell me," he said, with profound gravity, "that you two children are thinking of keeping house already?"

They looked conscious, blushed, and then put a bold front upon it.

"We have quite made up our minds," replied Harry; "you see, Ralph, I began to fancy—all your fault—that there is something so real and true in domestic happiness, that I mean to try it. I shall still study—and if people come round us, in time I may get clients."

"And when is it to come off?" asked Ralph, still quite gravely.

"As soon as we have a house ready," continued the young lawyer.

"Hang it if it shan't be to-morrow!" cried Ralph, clasping both his hands.

"No," said Harry, quietly; "you see Bertha will want Lotty for quite a month. During that time I can choose a location, not ten miles away you know,—just a good sleigh distance in winter, and a stout walk in summer. I've half an idea where it shall be—perhaps nearer."

Ralph shook him heartily by the hand, and never was a quartette more happy than they were that evening, in the full indulgence of their innocent joy.

The next day Harry, Ralph, and Batiste, plunged into the wilderness, in a westerly direction, which course would place him between his father's house and that of his brother. Their way lay under lofty arches of leaves, hanging from straight trunks, which rose sixty, eighty, and some of them a hundred feet without a branch. Many of the pines were really majestic, some being a hundred and fifty feet in height, and a few two hundred.

At length they came to a small open space, from which a faint glimpse of the great lake could be seen, and there Harry threw down his staff, declaring that in that spot he would establish his home.

"A wise and happy choice," said Ralph. "When the country is cleared you will have a fine commanding view, while the little stream we have just crossed will surely bring a village, or other population, near to you."

"And vat de debble vant ye vith de village?" said Batiste, in a half sulky tone.

"My dear Batiste," replied Ralph, "the woods and forests, and uninhabited regions, will last beyond your life; but the day is not far distant, when this will be a populous and fertile district of that great empire, upon which, in its might and glory, the sun never sets, while the roll of its evening drum makes a belt around the world. Such magnificent trees, such a productive soil, such valuable lakes and means of water communication, were never intended solely for a few savages, whose trade is war, who are too idle to toil, and too ignorant to avail themselves of the riches which lie around them. Ere twenty years are past we shall be surrounded by neighbours; the anvil, the forge, the mill, the hammer, and the saw will be heard around; and last, though not least, the tinkle of that church bell, which we take with us wherever we go, and which is, at the same time, the memento and the cause of our wondrous and unexampled success as colonists."

"Amen," said Harry.

"Vere fine," whispered Batiste, "but I no *comprenez!*"

And thus it was that Harry Hatfield chose his location. In due time, land was cleared, a house was built by the aid of all, and then another young couple were added to those who had made their home in the wilderness. Though not exempt from labour and care, they there found a happiness which is denied to too many in the crowded abodes of old corporations.

Having thus brought our principal characters to a point when they can have nothing to desire, we leave them for the present. We hope however, some day to have further record of their proceedings, especially of our pet Jack, and his friend Pete, who subsequently became one of the most expert and celebrated of the Rocky Mountain Trappers.

FINIS.

THE MERCHANT OF YAKOUTSK.

CHAPTER I.

THE YOUNG WIDOW.

YAKOUTSK is one of the principal cities of Siberia, a country, the name of which excites exaggerated ideas of stertility and desolation. Watered by rivers, which in every direction do the work of railways, with richly-wooded mountains and valleys, with green slopes, cultivated fields, soft meadows, gardens, and grassy islands in the great streams, with all the common vegetables in pretty fair abundance, with an endless source of commerce in furs and ivory, Siberia, except in its extreme northern provinces, presents, like most other lands, a very considerable amount of compensations for considerable rigour of climate. Yakoutsk is a completely northern town on the great river Lena, with wide streets and miserable huts, all of wood, in many of which ice is still used in winter for panes of glass. A very eminent traveller tells us, that when he visited it there were 4000 people living in 500 houses; with three stone churches, two wooden ones, and a convent. It had once an antiquity to show—the ancient Ostrog or fortress, built in 1647 by the Cossacks; but more and more every day it threatened to become a ruin, being not of stone, but of wood; and at last it disappeared. Even here progress is observable, and wretched cabins give way gradually to houses, some of which are even elegantly arranged in the interior. It is a great commercial centre: from the Anubra to Behring's Straits, from the banks of the Frozen Sea to Mount Aldana, from Okhotsk and even Kamtchatka, goods are brought hither, consisting chiefly of furs, seals' teeth, and mammoths' tusks, which afford excellent ivory, all of which are sold in the summer to itinerant traders, who give in return powerfully-flavoured tobacco, corn and flour, tea, sugar, strong drinks, Chinese silks and cottons, cloth, iron and copper utensils, and glass.

The inhabitants of the town are chiefly traders, who buy from the Yakouta hunters their furs at a cheap rate, and then sell them in a mysterious kind of fashion to the agents who come from Russia in search of them. During the annual fair they stow up their goods in private rooms; and here the Irkoutsk men must come and find them. These traders are the Russian inhabitants, the native Yakoutas being the only artizans. In this distant colony of the human race, the new-born child of a Russian is given to a Yakouta woman to nurse, and when old enough, he learns to read and write; after which he is brought up to the fur trade, and then his education is finished.

Ivan Ivanovitch was a young man born and bred at Yakoutsk. His parents had given him the usual amount of tuition, and then allowed him for a time to follow the bent of his inclination. Ivan took to the chase. Passionately fond of this amusement, he had at an early age started with the Yakouta trappers, and became learned in the search for sables, ermines, and lynxes; he could pursue the reindeer and elk on skates, and had even gone to the north in quest of seals. Thus, at the age of twenty, he knew the whole active part of his trade, and was aware of all the good hunting-grounds on which the Siberians founded their prosperity. But when he was called on to follow the more quiet and sedentary part of his occupation, he was not one-half so quick. His rough and rude life made town existence distasteful to him, and he evinced all that superb contempt for shop-keeping, which characterizes the nomadic man, whether Red Indian, Arab, Tartar, or Siberian.

But Ivan was told he must make his way in the world. His parents, who died before he attained to manhood, left him a small fortune in rubles and furs, which, if he chose to be industrious and persevering, might pave the way to the highest position in his native town. Acting on the pressing advice of his friends, he gave up his wanderings, and went to reside in the house of his fathers, piled up his skins and ivory, bought new ones, and prepared for the annual fair. The merchants from Irkoutsk, the capital, came, and Ivan, who was sharp and clever, did a good trade. But when his furs and teeth were changed into tea, tobacco, brandy, cloth, &c., he did not feel a whit happier. Ivan longed for the arid hills, and lofty mountains, and pellucid lakes—for the exciting hunt and the night bivouac, when grey-headed Yakoutas would, with their *ganzis*—the Irish dudeen—in their mouths, tell terrible and wonderful stories of ancient days. When eating town fare, his stomach yearned after frozen Yakouta butter, cut up with axes, and for *strouganina*, or frozen fish, with reindeer brains, and other northern delicacies. And then his kind friends told him that he wanted a wife—a possession without which, they assured him, life was dull; adding that in her society he would cease to long for communication with bears and savages.

Ivan believed them, and, following their advice, he launched into society—that is, he went more than usual to the noisy festivities of the town, which form the occupation of the dull season. The good people of Yakoutsk—like all peoples approaching to a savage state, sentimentally called a state of nature, especially in northern climes—considered eating the great business of life. Fabulous legends are told of their enormous capacity for food, approaching to that of the Esquimaux; but however this may be, certain it is that a Yakoutsk festival was always commenced by several hours of laborious eating and drinking of fat and oily food and strong brandy. When the utmost limits of repletion were reached, the patriarchs usually took to pipes, cards, and punch; while the ladies prepared tea, and ate roasted nuts, probably to facilitate digestion. The young men conversed with them, or roasted their nuts for them, while, perhaps, a dandy would perform a Siberian dance to the music of the violin or *gousli*, a kind of guitar. Ivan joined heartily in all this dissipation; he smoked with the old men; he drank their punch; he roasted nuts for the ladies, and told them wonderful stories, which were always readily listened to, except when some new fashion—which several years before had been forgotten in Paris—found its way *viâ* St. Petersburg, Moscow, and Irkoutsk, to the deserts of Siberia. Then he was silent; for the ladies had ample subject of discourse, not forgetting the great tea-table topic—scandal; causing the old men to shake their heads, and declare such things were not when they were young. Ivan, however, had one unfailing subject of popularity with the ladies. Like most Russians who have had occasion to travel much in cold places, he relished a cup of tea, even better than the punch, for he had learned by experience that there was more genuine warmth in the pot than in the bowl. Most Russian officers are known to share his opinion.

Ivan had several times had his attention directed to Maria Vorotinska, a young and rich widow, who was the admiration of all Yakoutsk. Her husband had left her a fortune in knowledge of the fur trade and in rubles, with a comfortable house nicely furnished—in Siberia the very height of human felicity. It was commonly reported that Maria, young as she was, was the best bargainer in the land. She got her skins for less than anybody else, and sold them for a higher price. With these qualifications, she must, it was said, prove a jewel to Ivan, who was not a close buyer nor a hard seller. But Ivan for some time remained perfectly insensible both to these social advantages and to the great beauty of the lady. He met her often, and even roasted more nuts for her than anyone else, which was a strong case of preference; but he did not seem caught in the fair one's toils. He neither ate, nor slept, nor amused himself one whit the less than when he first knew her. One evening, however, as Maria handed him his tea, with a hot cake, Ivan, whether owing to some peculiar smile on her face, or to the domestic idea which the act suggested, seemed certainly very much struck, and next day he formally proposed. Maria laughed, and tossed her head, and spoke a few good-natured words; and then, without either accepting or rejecting him, she hinted something about his youth, his want of devotion to business, and his want of fortune. Ivan, a little warmly, declared himself the best hunter in Yakoutsk, and hence the most practically experienced of any in the trade, and then gave the sum total of his possessions.

"Just one quarter of what good old Vorotinska left me!" replied the prudent Maria.

"But if I liked," replied Ivan, "I could be the richest merchant in Siberia."

"How?" asked Maria, a little curiously, for the mere mention of wealth was to her like the smell of powder to the war-horse.

"Being almost the only Russian who has lived among the Yakoutas, I know the secret of getting furs cheaper and easier than anyone else. Besides, if I chose to take a long journey, I could find ivory in vast heaps. A tradition is current of an ivory-mine in the north, which an old Yakouta told me to be truth."

"Very likely," said Maria, to whom the existence of the fossil ivory of the mammoth in large masses was well known; "but the *promich lenicks*—trading companies—have long since stripped them."

"Not this," cried Ivan: "it is a virgin mine. It is away, away in the Frozen Sea, and requires courage and enduring energy to find it. Two Yakoutas once discovered it. One was killed by the natives; the other escaped, and is now an old man."

"If you could find that," said Maria, "you would be the first man in Siberia, and the Czar himself would honour you."

"And you?" asked Ivan, humbly.

"Ivan Ivanovitch," replied Maria, calmly, "I like you better than any man in Yakoutsk, but I should adore the great ivory merchant."

Ivan was delighted. He was a little puzzled by the character of the lady, who, after marrying an old man for his fortune, seemed equally desirous of reconciling her interest and her affections in a second marriage. But very nice ideas are not those of the half-civilized, for we owe every refinement, both of mind and body, to civilization, which makes of the raw material man—full of undeveloped elements—what cooking makes of the potato-root. Civilization is the hot water and fire which carry off the crudities, and bring forth the good qualities.

However this may be, Ivan nursed his idea. Apart from the sudden passion which had invaded him, he had long allowed this fancy to ferment in his brain. During his wandering evenings, a noted hunter named Sakalar, claiming descent from the supposed Tartar founder of the Yakoutas, had often narrated his perilous journey on sledges across the Frozen Sea, his discovery of an ivory-mine—that is, of a vast deposit of mammoths' tusks, generally found at considerable depth in the earth, but here open to the grasp of all. He spoke of the thing as a folly of his youth, which had cost the life of his dearest friend, and never hinted at a renewed visit. But Ivan was resolved to undertake the perilous adventure, and even to have Sakalar for his guide.

CHAPTER II.

THE YAKOUTA HUNTER.

IVAN slumbered not over his project. Only a few days passed before he was ready to start. He purchased the horses required, and packed up all the varied articles necessary for his journey, and likely to please his Yakouta friend, consisting of tea, rum, brandy, tobacco, gunpowder, and other things of less moment. For himself he took a couple of guns, a pair of pistols, some strong and warm clothes, an iron pot for cooking, a kettle for his tea, with many minor articles, absolutely indispensable in the cold region he was about to visit. All travellers in the north have found that ample food, and such drinks as tea, are the most effectual protection against the climate; while oily and fat meat is also an excellent preservative against cold. But Ivan had no need to provide against this contingency. His Yakouta friend knew the value of train-oil and grease, which are alike the staple luxuries of Siberians, Kamtchatkans, and Esquimaux.

The first part of Ivan's journey was necessarily to the *yourte*, or wigwam of Sakalar, without whom all hope of reaching the goal of his wishes was vain. He had sufficient confidence in himself to venture without a guide towards the plain of Miouré, where his Yakouta friend dwelt. He started at early dawn, without giving warning of his departure to any one save Maria, and entered courageously on the frozen plain which reaches from Yakoutsk to the Polar Sea. The country is here composed of marshes, vast downs, huge forests, and hills covered with snow in the month of September, the time when he began his journey. He had five horses, each tied to the tail of the one before him, while Ivan himself was mounted on the first. He was compelled to ride slowly, casting his eyes every now and then behind, to see that all was right. At night he stretched a bearskin under a bush, lit a huge fire, cooked a savoury mess, and piling clothes over himself, he slept. At dawn he rose, crammed his kettle full of clean snow, put it over the embers, and made himself tea. With this warm beverage to rouse him, he again arranged his little caravan, and proceeded on his way. Nothing more painful than this journey can be conceived. There are scarcely any marks to denote the road, while lakes, formed by recent inundations, arrest the traveller every half-hour, compelling him to take prodigious rounds, which are equally annoying and perplexing.

On the morning of the third day Ivan felt a little puzzled about the road. He knew the general direction from the distant mountains, and he wished to avoid a vast morass. Before him was a frozen stream, and on the other side a hillock. Leaving the others to feed as well as they could, he mounted his best horse and rode across. The ice bent under him as he went, and he accordingly rode gently; but just as he reached the middle, it cracked violently right across, and sank visibly under him. Ivan looked hurriedly around. The ice was everywhere split, and the next minute his horse, plunging violently, fell through. Instead, however, of falling into a stream of cold water, Ivan found himself in a vast and chilly vault, with a small trickling stream in the middle, and at once recollected a not unfrequent phenomenon. The river had been frozen over when high with floods, but afterwards, the water sinking to its ordinary level, the upper crust of ice alone remained. But Ivan had no desire to admire the gloomy, half-lit vault, extending up and down out of sight; accordingly, standing on his horse's back, he clambered upon the surface as best he could, leaving the poor animal below. This done, he ran to the shore, and used the well-remembered Yakouta device for extracting his steed; he broke a hole in the ice near the bank, towards which the sagacious brute at once hurried, and was drawn forth. Having thus fortunately escaped a serious peril, he resumed his search on foot, and about mid-day pursued his journey.

A few hours brought him to the curious plain of the Miouré, where he expected to find the camp of his friend Sakalar. Leaving an almost desert plain, he suddenly stood on the edge of a hollow, circular in form, and six miles across, fertile in the extreme, and dotted with numerous well stocked fish-ponds. The whole, as may plainly be seen, was once a lake. Scattered over the soil were the yourtes of the Yakoutas, while cattle and horses crowded together in vast flocks. Ivan, who knew the place well, rode straight to a yourte or cabin apart from the rest, where usually dwelt Sakalar. It was larger and cleaner than most of them, thanks to the tuition of Ivan, and the subsequent care of a daughter, who, brought up by Ivan's mother, while the young man wandered, had acquired manners a little superior to those of her tribe.

This was really needful, for the Yakoutas, a pastoral people of Tartar origin, are singularly dirty, and even somewhat coarse and unintellectual—like all savage nations, in fact, when judged by any one but the poet or the poetic philosopher, who, on examination, will find that ignorance, poverty, misery, and want of civilization, produce similar results in the prairies of America and the wilds of Siberia, in an Irish cabin, and in the wynds and closes of our populous cities. But the chief defect of the Yakouta is dirt. Otherwise he is rather a favourable specimen of a savage. Since his assiduous connection with the Russians, he has become even rich, having flocks and herds, and at home plenty of koumise to drink, and horse's flesh to eat. He has great endurance, and can bear tremendous cold. He travels in the snow without tent or pelisse; on reaching the camp, he lies down on the snow, with his saddle for a pillow, his horsecloth for a bed, his cloak for a covering, and so he sleeps. His power of fasting is prodigious; and his eyesight is so keen, that a Yakouta one day told an eminent Russian traveller that he had seen a great blue star eat a number of little stars, and then cast them up. The man had seen the eclipses of Jupiter's satellites. Like the Red Indian, he recollects every bush, every stone, every hillock, every pond necessary to find his way, and never loses himself, however great the distance he may have to travel.

His food is boiled beef and horse's flesh, cows' and mares' milk. But his chief delicacy is raw and melted fat, while quantity is always the chief merit of a repast. He mixes, likewise, a mess of fish, flour, milk, fat, and a kind of bark, the latter to augment the volume. Both men and women smoke inordinately, swallowing the vapour, as do many dwellers in civilized lands—a most pernicious and terrible habit. Brandy is their most precious drink, their own koumise having not sufficient strength to satisfy them. In summer they wander about in tents, collecting hay; in winter they dwell in the yourte or hut, which is a wooden frame, of beehive shape, covered with grass, turf, and clay, with windows of clear ice. The very poor dig three feet below the soil; the rich have a wooden floor level with the adjacent ground, while rude benches all round serve as beds, divided one from the other by partitions. The fireplace is in the middle, inclined towards the door. A pipe carries away the smoke.

It was almost dark when Ivan halted before the yourte of Sakalar. It was larger and cleaner than any of those around. It had also numerous outhouses, full of cows, and one or two men who tended these animals were smoking their pipes at the door. Ivan gave his horses to one of them, who knew him, and entered the hut. Sakalar, a tall, thin, hardy man of about fifty, was just about to commence his evening meal. A huge mass of boiled meat, stewed fish, and a sort of soup, were ready; and a young girl about eighteen, neatly dressed, clean and pretty—all owing to her Yakoutsk education—was serving the hunter.

"Spirit of the woods protect me!" shrieked the girl, spilling half of the soup on the floor.

"What wild horse have you seen, Kolina?" cried the hunter, who had been a little scalded; and then seeing Ivan, he added, "A Yakouta welcome to you, my son! My old heart is glad, and I am warm enough to melt an iceberg at the sight of you, Ivan! Kolina, quick! another platter, a fresh mug, the best bottle of brandy, and my red pipe from Moscow!"

No need was there for the hunter to speak. Kolina, alert as a reindeer, had sprung up from the low bench, and quickly brought forth their holiday ware, and even began to prepare a cake—such as Ivan himself had taught her to make—knowing that he liked some sort of bread with his meals.

"And where are you going?" cried Sakalar, when the young man had somewhat appeased his hunger.

"To the North Sea, in search of the great ivory mine!" said Ivan, abruptly.

Kolina started back in terror and surprise, while Sakalar fixed his keen eyes on the youth, with sorrow and curiosity, and almost unequivocally testified his belief that his favourite pupil in the chase was mad. But Ivan rose and bade the serving-men of the rich Yakouta bring in his boxes. He then opened up his store of treasures:—there was tea for Kolina; and for Sakalar rum, brandy, powder, guns, tobacco, knives—all that could tempt a Yakouta. The father and daughter examined them with pleasure for some time, but presently Kolina shook her head.

"Ivan," said Sakalar, "all this is to tempt the poor Yakouta to cross the wilderness of ice. It is much riches, but not enough to make Sakalar mad. The mine is guarded by evil beings: but speak, lad, why would you go there?"

"Let Kolina give me a pipe, and I will tell my story," said Ivan; and filling his glass, the young fur-trader told the story of his love, and his bargain with the prudent widow.

"And this cold-hearted woman," exclaimed Kolina, with emotion, "has sent you to risk your life on the horrible Frozen Sea. A Yakouta girl would have been less selfish. She would have said, 'Stay at home—let me have Ivan; the mammoth teeth may lie for ever on the Frozen Sea!'"

"But the lad will go, and he will be drowned like a dog," said Sakalar, more slowly, after this ebullition of feminine indignation.

"You must go with him, father," continued Kolina, with a compassionate look at Ivan; "and as your child cannot remain alone, Kolina will go too!"

"We will start when the horses have had five days' hay," said Sakalar, gravely—the animals alluded to being only fed when about to go a journey—"and Kolina shall go too, for Ivan will be two years on his way."

Ivan listened in amazement: in the first place, at the sudden decision and warmth of his attached friends, with whom he had dwelt twelve years; then at the time required to perform the journey. He felt considerable doubts as to the widow remaining unmarried such a time, but the explanation of Sakalar satisfied him that it was impossible to perform the journey even in two years. The hunter told him that they must first join the tribes dwelling round Nijnei-Kolimsk (New-Kolimsk) where alone he could get dogs and sledges for his journey across the Frozen Sea. This, with the arrangements, would consume the winter. In the summer nothing could be done. When the winter returned, he must start towards the north pole—a month's journey at least; and if he hit upon the place, he must encamp there for the rest of the winter. That summer would be spent in getting out the ivory, fattening up the dogs, and packing. The third winter would be occupied by the journey home. On hearing this Ivan hesitated; but in describing the journey, the spirit of the old hunter got roused, and before night, he was warm in his desire to see once more the scene of his youthful perils. Kolina solemnly declared she must be of the party; and thus these experienced savages, used to sudden and daring resolves, in one night decided on a journey which, elsewhere, would perhaps have been talked of for half a century before it was undertaken.

Kolina slept little that night. In a compartment near her there was one who had, since her childhood, been the ideal of her future. She had loved Ivan as a playmate—she loved him as a man; and here, he whom she had longed for all the winter, and he whom she had hoped to see once more the next summer, had suddenly come, starting on a perilous journey of years, to win the hand of an avaricious, but young and beautiful widow. Kolina saw all her fairest dreams thus vanish, and the idol of her heart crumble into dust. And yet she felt no ill-will to Ivan, and never changed her resolve to be the faithful companion and attendant of her father and his friend, in their wild journey to the supposed islands in the Frozen Sea.

CHAPTER III.

NIJNEI-KOLIMSK.

THE five days fixed by Sakalar for preparing for the journey, were wholly devoted to the necessary arrangements. There was much to be done, and much to be talked of. They had to travel a long way before they reached even the real starting-point of their adventurous voyage. Sakalar, duly to impress Ivan with the dangers and perils of the search, narrated once more in minute detail all his former sufferings. But nothing daunted the young trader. He was one of those men who, under more favourable circumstances, would have been a Cook, a Parry, or a Franklin, perilling everything to make further discovery in the science of geography.

The five horses of Ivan were exchanged for others more inured to the kind of journey they were about to undertake. There was one for each of the adventurers, and four to carry the luggage, consisting chiefly of articles with which to pay for the hire of dogs and sledges. All were dressed alike—Kolina adopting for the time the habits and appearance of the man. Over their usual clothes they put a jacket of foxes' skins and a fur breast-cover; their legs being covered by hare-skin wrappers. Over these were stockings of soft reindeer leather, and high strong boots of the same material. The knees were protected by knee-caps of fur; and then, over all, was a coat with loose sleeves and a hood of double deer-skin. This was not all. After the chin, nose, ears, and mouth had been guarded by appropriate pieces, forming together a mask, they had received the additional weight of a pointed fur cap. Our three travellers, when they took their departure, looked precisely like three animated bundles of old clothes.

All were well armed with gun, pistol, hatchet, and hunting-knife, while the girdle further supported a pipe and tobacco-pouch. They had not explained whither they were going, but the whole village knew that they must be about to undertake some perilous journey, and accordingly turned out to cheer them as they went, while several ardent admirers of Kolina were loud in their murmurs at her accompanying the expedition. But the wanderers soon left the plain of Miouré behind them, and entered on the delectable roads leading to the Frozen Sea. Half-frozen marshes and quagmires met them at every step; but Sakalar rode first, and the others followed one by one; thus the experienced old hunter, by advancing steadily and without hurry, avoided these dangers. They soon reached a vast plain, three hundred miles across, and utterly deserted by the human race; a desert, composed half of barren rock and half of swampy quagmire, soft above, but at a foot deep it was solid and perpetual ice. Fortunately it now froze hard, and the surface was fit to bear the horses. But for this, the party must have halted, and waited for a severer frost. The rivers were not frozen when large in volume; and the Aldana had to be crossed in the usual flat-bottomed boat kept for travellers. At night they halted, and with a bush and some deer-skins they made a tent. Kolina cooked the supper, and the men searched for some fields of stunted half-frozen grass upon which to let the horses graze. This was the last place where even this kind of food would be found, and for some days their steeds would have to live on a stinted portion of hay.

On they went over the arid plain, which, however, affords nourishment for some trees—now fording rivers, floundering through marshes, and still meeting some wretched apology for grass; when, on the third day, down came the snow in a pelting cloud, and in an instant the whole desert changed to white from sombre grey. The real winter was come. Now all Sakalar's intelligence was required. Almost every obvious sign by which to find his way, had disappeared, and he traversed the plain, wholly guided by distant hills, and by observing the stars at night. This Sakalar did assiduously; and when he had once started under the guidance of the twinkling lights of the heavens, rarely was he many yards out at the next halt; to camp he always chose the side of a hillock, where there was a tree or two, and some half-rotten trunks with bushes to make a huge fire.

It was nearly dawn on the fifth morning after entering the plain, and Ivan and Kolina yet slept. But Sakalar slept not. They had nearly reached the extremity of the horrible desert, but a new danger occupied the thoughts of the hunter. They were now in the track of the wild and savage Tchouktchas, and their fire might have betrayed them. Had Sakalar been alone, he would have slept in the snow without a fire; for he knew the peril of an encounter with the independent Tchouktchas, who have only recently been even nominally brought into subjection to Russia.

The heavy fall of snow of the two previous days rendered the danger greater. Sakalar sat gravely upon a fallen tree—a pipe in his mouth, and his eye fixed on the distant horizon. For some time nothing remarkable caught his gaze; but at last he saw a number of dark objects on the snow, galloping directly towards the camp. Sakalar at once recognized a number of reindeer. It was the Tchouktchas on their sledges, bounding with lightning speed along the frozen surface!

"Up!" cried the hunter; and when his companions were on their feet, he added, "Quick with your guns!

The enemy are upon us! But show a bold front, and let them feel the weight of lead."

Ivan and Kolina quietly took up their post, and awaited the orders of Sakalar. No time was lost, and fortunately, for the savages were already near, and next minute were alighting from their sledges: hand in hand they advanced along the snow, to the number of a dozen. A simultaneous discharge of the heavy-metalled guns of the camp—one of which, that of Sakalar, wounded the foremost man—checked their career, and they fell back to hold a conference. It became evident at once that they had no firearms, which removed almost all idea of danger. Ivan and Kolina now proceeded to load the horses, and when all were ready, the whole party mounted and rode off, followed at a respectful distance by the Siberian Arabs.

The travellers, however, received no further annoyance from them, and camped the next night on the borders of the Toukoulane, at the foot of the mountains of Verkho-Yansk. After the usual repose, they began the severest part of the journey. Rugged rocks, deep ravines, avalanches, snow, and ice, all were in their way. Now they rode along the edge of frightful precipices, on a path so narrow that one false step was death; now they forced their way through gulleys full of snow, where their horses were buried to their girths, and they had to drag them out by main force. Fortunately, the Siberian horse, though small, is sturdy and indefatigable, and can live, during a three months' journey, on faded grass and half-frozen, half-rotten herbage. That evening they camped on the loftiest part of the road, where it winds through still elevated rocks.

The middle of the next day brought them to another plain, not much superior to that through which they had passed, but yet less miserable-looking, and with the additional advantage of having youtes here and there, to shelter the traveller. The cold was now intense; and glad indeed was Ivan of the comforts of his Siberian dress, which at first had appeared so heavy. The odd figures which Kolina and Sakalar presented under it, made him smile at the notion which Maria Vorotinska would have formed of her lover under a garb that doubled his natural size. Several halts took place, and caused great delay, from the slippery state of the ice on the rivers. The unshod horses could not stand. A fire had to be lit; and when sufficient ashes were procured, they had to be spread across in a narrow pathway, and the nags led carefully along this track— one of the many artifices required to combat the rigorous character of the climate. And thus, suffering cold and short commons, and making their way for days through frosty plains, over ice and snow, amid deep ravines and over lofty hills, they at length reached Nijnei-Kolimsk, though not without being almost wholly knocked up, especially Kolina, who was quite unused to such fatigues.

They had now almost reached the borders of the great Frozen Sea. The village is situated about eighteen degrees farther north than London, and is nearly as far north as Boothia Felix, the scene of Captain Ross's four years' sojourn in the ice. It was founded two hundred years ago by a wandering Cossack; though what could have induced people to settle in a place which the sun lights, but never warms, is a mystery; where there is a day that lasts fifty-two English days, and a night that lasts thirty-eight; where there is no spring and no autumn, but a faint semblance of summer for three months, and then winter; where a few dwarf willows and stunted grass form all the vegetation; and where, at a certain distance below the surface, there is frost as old as the "current epoch" of the geologist. But by way of compensation, reindeer and elks, brown and black bears, foxes and squirrels, abound; there are also wolves, and the isatis or polar fox; there are swans, and geese, and ducks, partridges and snipes, and in the rivers abundance of fish. And yet, though the population be now so scanty, and the date of the peopling of Kolimsk is known, there was once a numerous race in these regions, the ruins of whose forts and villages are yet found. The population is about 5000, including the whole district, of whom about 300 are Russians, the descendants of Siberian exiles. They dwell in houses made of wood—thrown up on the shore and collected by years of patience—and of moss and clay. In winter the panes of the windows are of ice, six inches thick; in summer, of skins. The better class of the inhabitants are neatly and even tastefully dressed; and they are clean, too, which is the very highest praise that can be given to half-civilized, as well as to civilized people.

They are a bold, energetic, and industrious race. Every hour of weather fit for out-door work, is spent in fishing and hunting, and preparing food for the winter. In the light sledge, or on skates, with nets and spears, they are labouring at each of these employments in its season. Towards the end of the long winter, just as famine and starvation threaten the whole population, a perfect cloud of swans, and geese, and ducks, and snipes pour in; and man and woman, boy and girl, rush forth to the hunt. The fish come in next, as the ice breaks; and presently the time for the reindeer hunt comes round. Every minute of the summer season is consumed in laying in a stock of all these aliments, for a long and dreary season, when nothing can be caught. The women collect herbs and roots. As the summer is just about to end, the herrings appear in shoals, and a new source of subsistence is opened up. Later still, they fish by opening holes in the newly-formed ice. Nor is Kolimsk without its trade. The chief traffic of the region is at the fair of Ostrovnoye, but Nijnei-Kolimsk has its share. The merchants who come to collect the furs which the adventurous Tchouktchas have acquired, even on the opposite side of Behring's Straits, from the North American Indians, halt here, and sell tea, tobacco, brandy, and other articles.

The long night had set in when Ivan and his companions entered Kolimsk. Well it was that they had reached it, for the cold was becoming frightful in its intensity, and the people of the village were much surprised at the arrival of travellers; but they found ready accommodation, a Cossack widower giving them half his house.

CHAPTER IV

THE FROZEN SEA.

IVAN soon found himself received into the best society of the place. All were glad to welcome the adventurous trader from Yakoutsk; and when he had intimated that his boxes of treasure, his brandy and tea, and rum and tobacco, were to be laid out in the hire of dogs and sledges, he found ample applicants, though, from the very first, all refused to accompany his party as guardians of the dogs. Sakalar, however, who had expected this, was nothing daunted, but, bidding Ivan amuse himself as best he could, he undertook all the preparations. Ivan, however, found as much pleasure in teaching to

Kolina what little he knew, as in frequenting the fashionable circles of Kolimsk. But he could not reject the numerous polite invitations to evening parties and dances which poured upon him. I have said evening parties, for though there was no day, yet still the division of the hours was regularly kept, and parties began at five P.M., to end at ten. There was singing and dancing, and gossip and tea, of which each individual would consume ten or twelve large cups; in fact, despite the primitive state of the inhabitants, and the vicinity to the Polar Sea, these assemblies very much resembled in style those of Paris and London. The costumes, the saloons, and the hours, were different, while the manners were less refined; but the facts were the same.

When the carnival came round, Ivan, who was a little vexed at the exclusion of Kolina from the fashionable Russian society, took care to let her have the usual amusement of sliding down a mountain of ice, which she did to her great satisfaction. He contrived, too, at all times to devote to her his days, while Sakalar wandered about from youte to youte, in search of hints and information for the next winter's journey. Sakalar hired the requisite nartas, or sledges, and the thirty-nine dogs which were to draw them—thirteen to each. Then he bargained for a large stock of frozen and dry fish for the dogs, and other provisions for themselves. But the people were most puzzled by his assiduous efforts to get a man to go with them, who would harness twenty dogs to an extra sledge. To the astonishment of everybody, three young men at last volunteered, and three extra sledges were then procured.

The summer soon came round, and then Ivan and his friends started out at once with the hunters, and did their utmost to be useful. As the natives of Kolimsk went during the chase a long distance towards Cape Sviatoi, the spot where the adventurers were to quit the land and venture on the Frozen Sea, they took care, at the furthest extremity of their hunting trip, to leave a deposit of provisions. They erected a small platform, which they covered with drift wood, and on this they placed the dried fish. Above were laid heavy stones, and every precaution used to ward off the isatis and the glutton. Ivan during the summer added much to his stock of hunting knowledge.

At length the winter came round once more, and the hour so long desired at last arrived. The sledges were ready—six in number—and loaded as heavily as they could bear. But for so many dogs, and for so many days, it was quite certain that they must economize most strictly; while it was equally certain that if no bears fell in their way on the journey, they must starve, if they did not perish otherwise on the terrible Frozen Sea. Each narta, loaded with eight hundredweight of provisions and its driver, was drawn by six pairs of dogs and a leader. They took no wood, trusting implicitly to Providence for this most essential article. They purposed following the shores of the Frozen Sea to Cape Sviatoi, because on the edge of the sea they hoped to find, as usual, plenty of wood, floated to the shore during the brief period when the ice was broken and the vast ocean in part free. One of the sledges was less loaded with provisions than the rest, because it bore a tent, an iron plate for fire on the ice, a lamp, and the few cooking utensils of the party.

Early one morning in the month of November—the long night still lasting—the six sledges took their departure. The adventurers had every day exercised themselves with the dogs for some hours, and were tolerably proficient. Sakalar drove the first team, Kolina the second, and Ivan the third. The Kolimsk men came afterwards. They took their way along the snow towards the mouth of the Tchouktcha river. The first day's journey brought them to the extreme limits of vegetation, after which they entered on a vast and interminable plain of snow, along which the nartas moved rapidly. But the second day, in the afternoon, a storm came on. The snow fell in clouds, the wind blew with a bitterness of cold, as searching to the form of man as the hot blast of the desert, and the dogs appeared inclined to halt. But Sakalar kept on his way towards a hillock in the distance, where the guides spoke of a hut of refuge. But before a dozen yards more could be crossed, the sledge of Kolina was overturned, and a halt became necessary.

Ivan was the first to raise his fair companion from the ground; and then with much difficulty—their hands, despite all the clothes, being half-frozen—they again put the nartas in condition to proceed. Sakalar had not stopped, but was seen in the distance unharnessing his sledge, and then poking about in a huge heap of snow. He was searching for the hut, which had been completely buried in the drift. In a few minutes the whole six were at work, despite the blast, while the dogs were scratching holes for themselves in the soft snow, within which they soon lay snug, with only their noses out of the hole, while over this the sagacious brutes put the tip of their long bushy tails.

At the end of an hour well employed, the hut was freed inside from snow, and a fire of stunted bushes with a few logs was lit in the middle of it. Here the whole party cowered, almost choked with the thick smoke, which, however, was less painful than the blast from the icy sea. The smoke escaped with difficulty, because the roof was still covered with firm snow, and the door was merely a hole to crawl through. At last, however, they got the fire to the state of red embers, and succeeded in obtaining a plentiful supply of tea and food; after which, their limbs being less stiff, they fed the dogs.

While they were attending to the dogs, the storm abated, and was followed immediately by a magnificent aurora borealis. It rose in the north, a sort of semi-arch of light; and then across the heavens, in almost every direction, darted columns of a luminous character. The light was as bright as that of the moon in its full. There were jets of lurid red light in some places, which disappeared and came again; while, there being a dead calm after the storm, the adventurers heard a kind of rustling sound in the distance, faint and almost imperceptible, and yet believed to be the rush of the air in the sphere of the phenomenon. A few minutes more, and all had disappeared.

After a hearty meal, the wanderers launched into the usual topics of conversation in those regions. Sakalar was not a boaster, but the young men from Nijnei-Kolimsk were possessed of the usual characteristics of hunters and fishermen. They told, with considerable vigour and effect, long stories of their adventures, mostly exaggerated—and when not impossible, most improbable—of bears killed in hand to hand combat, of hundreds of deer slain in the crossing of a river, and of multitudinous heaps of fish drawn in one cast of a seine; and then, wrapped in their thick clothes, and every one's feet to the fire, the whole party soon slept. Ivan and Kolina, however, held whispered converse together for a little while; but fatigue soon overcame even them.

The next day they advanced still farther towards the

pole, and on the evening of the third, they camped within a few yards of the great Frozen Sea. There it lay before them, scarcely distinguishable from the land; and as they looked upon it from a lofty eminence, it was hard to believe that it was a sea. There was snow on the sea and snow on the land; there were mountains on both, and huge drifts, and here and there vast *polinas*—a space of soft, watery ice, which resembled the lakes of Siberia. All was bitter cold, sterile, bleak, and chilling to the eye, which vainly sought a relief. The prospect of a journey over this desolate plain, intersected in every direction by ridges of mountain icebergs, full of crevices, with soft and salt ice here and there, was dolorous indeed; and yet the heart of Ivan quaked not. He had now what he sought in view; he knew there was land beyond, and riches, and fame.

A rude tent was erected, with snow piled round the edge to keep it firm. It needed to be strongly pitched, for in these regions the blast is more quick and sudden than in any place perhaps in the known world, pouring down along the fields of ice with terrible force, direct from the unknown caverns of the northern pole. Within the tent, which was of double reindeer skin, a fire was lit; while behind a huge rock, and under cover of the sledges, lay the dogs. As usual, after a hearty meal, and hot tea—drunk perfectly scalding—the party retired to rest. About midnight, all were awoke by a sense of oppression and stifling heat. Sakalar rose, and, by the light of the remaining embers, scrambled to the door. It was choked up by snow. The hunter immediately began to shovel it from the narrow hole through which they entered or left the hut, and then groped his way out. The snow was falling so thick and fast, that the travelling yourte was completely buried; and the wind being directly opposite to the door, the snow had drifted round and concealed the aperture.

The dogs now began to howl fearfully. This was too serious a warning to be disdained. They smelled the savage bear of the icy seas, which, in turn, had been attracted to them by its sense of smell. Scarcely had the sagacious animals given tongue, when Sakalar, through the thick-falling snow, and amid the gloom, saw a dull, heavy mass rolling directly towards the tent. He levelled his gun, and fired, after which he seized a heavy steel wood axe, and stood ready. The animal had at first halted, but next minute he came on growling furiously. Ivan and Kolina now both fired, when the animal turned and ran. But the dogs were now round him, and Sakalar behind them. One tremendous blow of his axe finished the huge beast, and there he lay in the snow. The dogs then abandoned him, refusing to eat fresh bear's meat, though, when frozen, they gladly enough accepted it.

The party again sought rest, after lighting an oil lamp with a thick wick, which, in default of the fire, diffused a tolerable amount of warmth in a small place occupied by six people. But they did not sleep; for though one of the bears was killed, the second of the almost invariable couple was probably near, and the idea of its being in the vicinity was anything but agreeable. These huge quadrupeds have been often known to enter a hut and stifle all its inhabitants. The night was therefore far from refreshing, and at an earlier hour than usual all were on foot. Every morning the same routine was followed:—Hot tea, without sugar or milk, was swallowed to warm the body; then a meal, which took the place of dinner, was cooked, and devoured; then the dogs were fed; and then the sledges, which had been inclined on one side, were placed horizontally. This was always done, to water their keel—to use a nautical phrase; for this water freezing they glided along all the faster. A portion of the now hard-frozen bear was given to the dogs, and the rest placed on the sledges, after the skin had been secured towards making a new covering at night.

This day's journey was half on the land, half on the sea, according as the path served. It was generally very rough, and the sledges made but slow progress. The dogs, too, had coverings put on their feet, and on every other delicate place, which made them less agile. In ordinary cases, on a smooth surface, it is not very difficult to guide a team of dogs, when the leader is a first-rate animal. But this is an essential point, otherwise it is impossible to get along. Every time the dogs hit on the track of a bear, or fox, or other animal, their hunting instincts are developed; away they dart like mad, leaving the line of march, and, in spite of all the efforts of the driver, they begin the chase. But if the front dog be well trained, he dashes on one side in a totally opposite direction, smelling and barking as if he had a new track. If his artifice succeeds, the whole team dart away after him, and, speedily losing the scent, proceed on their journey.

Sakalar, who still kept ahead of the party, when making a wide circuit out at sea about mid-day, at the foot of a steep hill of rather rough ice, found his dogs suddenly increasing their speed, but in the right direction. To this he had no objection, though it was very doubtful what was beyond. However, the dogs darted ahead with terrific rapidity, until they reached the summit of the hill. The ice was here very rough and salt, which impeded the advance of the sledge; but off are the dogs, down a very steep descent, furiously tugging at the sledge halter, till away they fly like lightning. The harness had broken off, and Salakar remained alone on the crest of the hill. He leaped off the nartas, and stood looking at it with the air of a man stunned. The journey seemed checked violently. Next instant, his gun in hand, he followed the dogs right down the hill, dashing away like a madman, in his long hunting skates. But the dogs were out of sight, and Sakalar soon found himself opposed by a huge wall of ice. He looked back; he was wholly out of view of his companions. To reconnoitre, he ascended the wall as best he could, and then looked down into a sort of circular hollow of some extent, where the ice was smooth, and even watery.

He was about to turn away, when his sharp eye detected something moving; and all his love of the chase was at once aroused. He recognized the snow-cave of a huge bear. It was a kind of cavern, caused by the falling together of two pieces of ice, with double issue. Both apertures the bear had succeeded in stopping up, after breaking a hole in the thin ice of the sheltered *polina*, or sheet of soft ice. Here the cunning animal lay in wait. How long he had been lying it was impossible to say; but almost as Sakalar crouched down to watch, a seal came to the surface, and lay against the den of its enemy, to breathe. A heavy paw was passed through the hole, and the sea-cow was killed in an instant. A naturalist would have admired the wit of the ponderous bear, and passed on; but the Siberian hunter knows no such thought, and as the animal issued forth to seize his prey, a heavy ball, launched with unerring aim, laid him low.

CHAPTER V

ON THE ICE.

SAKALAR now turned away in search of his companions, whose aid was required to secure a most useful addition to their store of food; and as he did so he heard a distant and plaintive howl. He hastened in the direction, and in a quarter of an hour came to the mouth of a narrow gut between two icebergs. The stick of the harness had caught in the fissure, and checked the dogs, who were barking with rage. Sakalar caught the bridle, which had been jerked out of his hand, and turned the dogs round. The animals followed his guidance; and he succeeded, after some difficulty, in bringing them to where lay his game. He then secured the bear and seal, both dead and frozen even in this short time, and joined his companions.

For several days the same kind of difficulties had to be overcome, and then they reached the *sayba*, where the provisions had been placed in the summer. It was a large rude box, erected on piles, and the whole stock was found safe. As there was plenty of wood in this place, they halted to rest the dogs and to repack the sledges. The tent was pitched, and they all thought of repose. They were now about wholly to quit the land, and to venture in a north-westerly direction upon the Frozen Sea.

Despite the fire made on the iron plate in the middle of the tent, our adventurers found the cold at this point of their journey most poignant. It was about Christmas; but the exact time of year had little to do with the matter. The wind was northerly and keen; and at night they often had to rise and promote circulation by a good run on the snow. But early on the third day all was ready for a start. The sun was seen that morning on the edge of the horizon for a short while, and promised soon to give them days. Before them were a line of icebergs, seemingly an impenetrable wall; but it was necessary to brave them. The dogs, refreshed by two days of rest, started vigorously, and a plain hill of ice being selected, they succeeded in reaching its summit. Then before them lay a vast and seemingly interminable plain. Along this the sledges ran with great speed; and that day they advanced nearly thirty miles from the land, and camped on the sea in a valley of ice.

It was a singular spot. Vast sugar-loaf hills of ice, as old perhaps as the world, threw their lofty cones to the skies on all sides, while they rested doubtless on the bottom of the ocean. Every fantastic form was there; there seemed in the distance, cities and palaces as white as chalk; pillars and reversed cones, pyramids and mounds of every shape, valleys and lakes; and under the influence of the optical illusions of the locality, green fields and meadows, and tossing seas. Here the whole party rested soundly, and pushed on hard the next day in search of land.

Several tracks of foxes and bears were now seen, but no animals were discovered. The route, however, was changed. Every now and then newly-formed fields of ice were met, which a little while back had been floating. Lumps stuck up in every direction, and made the path difficult. Then they reached a vast polina, where the humid state of the surface told that it was thin, and of recent formation. A stick thrust into it went through. But the adventurers took the only course left to them. The dogs were placed abreast, and then, at a signal, they were launched upon the dangerous surface. They flew rather than ran. It was necessary, for as they went the ice cracked in every direction, but always under the weight of the nartas, which were off before they could be caught by the bubbling waters. As soon as the solid ice was again reached, the whole party halted—deep gratitude to Heaven in their hearts—and camped for the night.

But the weather had changed. What is here called "the warm wind," had blown all day, and at night a hurricane came on. As the adventurers sat smoking after supper, the ice beneath their feet trembled, shook, and then fearful reports bursting on their ears, told them that the sea was cracking in every direction. They had camped on an elevated iceberg of vast dimensions, and were for the moment safe. But around them they heard the rush of waters. The vast Frozen Sea was in one of its moments of fury. In the deeper seas to the north it never freezes firmly—in fact, there is always an open sea, with floating bergs. When a hurricane blows, these clear spaces become terribly agitated. Their tossing waves and mountains of ice act on the solid plains, and break them up at times. This was evidently the case now. About midnight our travellers, whose anguish of mind was terrible, felt the great iceberg afloat. Its oscillations were fearful. Sakalar alone preserved his coolness. The men of Nijnei-Kolimsk raved and tore their hair, crying that they had been brought wilfully to destruction; Kolina knelt, crossed herself, and prayed; while Ivan deeply reproached himself as the cause of so many human beings encountering such awful peril. The rockings of their icy raft were terrible. It was impelled hither and thither by even huger masses. Now it remained on its first level, then its surface presented an angle of nearly forty-five degrees, and it seemed about to turn bottom up. All commended themselves to God, and awaited their fate. Suddenly they were rocked more violently than ever, and were thrown down by the shock. Then all was still.

The hurricane lulled, the wind shifted, snow began to fall, and the prodigious plain of loose ice again lay quiescent. The bitter frost soon cemented its parts once more, and the danger was over. The men of Nijnei-Kolimsk now insisted on an instant return; but Sakalar was firm, and, though their halt had given them little rest, they again started as the sun was seen above the horizon. The road was fearfully bad. All was rough, disjointed, and almost impassable. But the sledges had good whalebone keels, and were made with great care, to resist such difficulties. The dogs were kept moving all day, but when night came they had made little progress. Nevertheless they rested in peace. Nature was calm, and morning found them still asleep. But Sakalar was indefatigable, and as soon as he had boiled a potful of snow, he made tea, and awoke his people.

They were now about to enter a labyrinth of *toroses* or icebergs. There was no plain ground within sight; but no impediment could be attended to. Bears made these their habitual resorts, while the wolf skulked every night round the camp, awaiting their scanty leavings. Every eye was stretched in search of game. But the road itself required immense care, to prevent the sledges from overturning. Towards the afternoon they entered a narrow valley of ice, full of drifted snow, into which the dogs sank, and could scarcely move. At this instant two enormous white bears presented themselves. The dogs sprang forward; but the ground was too heavy for them. The hunters, however, were ready. The bears marched boldly on, as if savage from long fasting. No time was to be lost. Sakalar and Ivan, each singled out his animal. Their heavy ounce balls struck both. The opponent of Sakalar turned and fled, but that of Ivan advanced furiously towards him. Ivan stood his ground, axe in hand, and struck the animal a terrible blow on the muzzle. But as he did so, he stumbled, and the bear was upon him. Kolina shrieked; Sakalar was away after his prize; but the Kolimsk men rushed in. Two fired; the third struck the animal with a spear. The bear abandoned Ivan, and faced his new antagonists. The contest was now unequal, and before half an hour was over the stock of provisions was again augmented, as well as the means of warmth. They had very little wood, and what they had was used sparingly. Once or twice a tree fixed in the ice, gave them additional fuel; but they were obliged to depend chiefly on oil. A small fire was made at night to cook by, but it was allowed to go out. The tent was carefully closed, and the caloric of six people, together with a huge lamp with three wicks, served for the rest of the night.

About the sixth day they struck land. It was a small island, in a bay of which they found plenty of drift wood. Sakalar was delighted. He was on the right track. A joyous halt took place, a splendid fire was made, and the whole party indulged themselves in a glass of rum—a liquor very rarely touched, from its own tendency to increase rather than to diminish cold. A hole was next broken in the ice, and an attempt made to catch some seals. Only one, however, rewarded their efforts; but this, with a supply of wood, filled the empty space made in the sledges by the daily consumption of the dogs. The island, however, was soon found to be infested with bears: no fewer than five, with eleven foxes, were killed;

and then huge fires had to be kept up at night to drive their survivors away.

Their provender thus notably increased, the party started in high spirits; but though they were advancing towards the pole, they were also advancing towards the Deep Sea, and the ice presented innumerable dangers. Deep fissures, lakes, chasms, mountains, all lay in their way; and no game presented itself to their anxious search. Day after day they pushed on—here making long circuits, there driven back, and losing sometimes in one day all they had made in the previous twelve hours. Some fissures were crossed on bridges of ice, which took hours to make, while every day the cold seemed to become more intense. The sun was now visible for hours, and, as usual in these parts, the cold was more severe since his arrival.

At last, after more than twenty days of terrible fatigue, there was seen looming in the distance what was, no doubt, the promised land. The sledges were hurried forward—for they were drawing towards the end of their provisions—and the whole party was at length collected on the summit of a lofty mountain of ice. Before them were the hills of New Siberia; to their right was a prodigious open sea; and at their feet, as far as the eye could reach, there ran a narrow channel of rapid water, through which huge lumps of ice rushed so furiously as to have no time to cement into a solid mass.

The adventurers stood aghast. But Sakalar led the way to the very brink of the channel, and moved quietly along its course, until he found what he was in search of. This was a sheet or floe of ice, large enough to bear the whole party, and yet almost detached from the general field. The sledges were put upon it, and then, by breaking with their axes the narrow tongue which held it, it swayed away into the tempestuous sea. It almost turned round as it started. The sledges and dogs were placed in the middle, while the five men stood at the very edge, to guide it, as well as possible, with their hunting spears.

In a few minutes it was impelled along by the rapid current, but received every now and then a check, when it came in contact with heavier and deeper masses. The Kolimsk men stood transfixed with terror, as they saw themselves borne out towards that vast deep sea which eternally tosses and rages round the Artic Pole; but Sakalar, in a peremptory tone, bade them use their spears. They pushed away heartily; and their strange raft, though not always keeping its equilibrium, was edged away both across and down the stream. At last it began to move more slowly, and Sakalar found himself under the shelter of a huge iceberg, and then impelled up-stream by a backwater current. In a few minutes the much-wished-for shore was reached.

The route was rude and rugged as they approached the land; but all saw before them the end of their labours for the winter, and every one proceeded vigorously. The dogs seemed to smell the land, or at all events, some tracks of game, for they hurried on with spirit. About an hour before the usual time of camping, they were under a vast precipice, turning which, they found themselves in a deep and sheltered valley, with a river at the bottom, frozen between its lofty banks, and covered by deep snow.

"The ivory-mine!" said Sakalar, in a low tone, to Ivan, who thanked him by an expressive look.

CHAPTER VI.

ENCOUNTER WITH TCHOUKTCHAS.

The end of so perilous and novel a journey, which must necessarily, under the most favourable circumstances, have produced more honour than profit, was attained; and yet the success of the adventure was doubtful. The season was still too cold for any search for fossil ivory, and the first serious duty was the erection of a winter residence. Fortunately there was an ample supply of logs of wood, some half rotten, some green, lying under the snow on the shores of the bay into which the river poured, and which had been deposited there by the currents and waves. A regular pile, too, was found, which had been laid up by some of the provident natives of New Siberia, who, like the Exquimaux, live in the snow. Under this was a large supply of frozen fish, which was taken without ceremony, the party being near starvation. Of course Sakalar and Ivan intended to replace the hoard, if possible, in the short summer.

Wood was made the groundwork of the winter hut which was to be erected, but snow and ice formed by far the larger portion of the building materials. So hard and compact did the whole mass become, when finished and lined with bear-skins and other furs, that a huge lamp sufficed for warmth during the day and night, and the cooking was done in a small shed by the side. The dogs were now set to shift for themselves as to cover, and were soon buried in the snow. They were placed on short allowance, now that they had no work to do; for no one yet knew what were the resources of this wild place.

As soon as the more immediate duties connected with

a camp had been completed, the whole party occupied themselves with preparing traps for foxes, and in other hunting details. A hole was broken in the ice in the bay; and this the Kolimsk men watched with assiduity for seals. One or two rewarded their efforts, but no fish were taken. Sakalar and Ivan, after a day or two of repose, started with some carefully-selected dogs in search of game, and soon found that the great white bear took up his quarters even in that northern latitude. They succeeded in killing several, which the dogs dragged home.

About ten days after their arrival in the great island, Sakalar, who was always the first to be moving, roused his comrades around him, just as a party of a dozen strange men appeared in the distance. They were short, stout fellows, with long lances in their hands, and, by their dress, very much resembled the Esquimaux. Their attitude was menacing in the extreme, and by the advice of Sakalar, a general volley was fired over their heads. The invaders halted, looked confusedly around, and then ran away. Firearms retained, therefore, all their pristine qualities with these savages.

"They will return," said Sakalar, moodily; "they did the same when I was here before, and then came back and killed my friend at night. Sakalar escaped."

Counsel was now held, and it was determined, after due deliberation, that strict watch should be kept at all hours, while much was necessarily trusted to the dogs. All day one of the party was on the look-out, while at night the hut had its entrance well barred. Several days, however, were thus passed without molestation, and then Sakalar took the Kolimsk men out to hunt, and left Ivan and Kolina together. The young man had learned the value of his half-savage friend; her devotion to her father and the party generally, was unbounded. She murmured neither at privations nor at sufferings, and kept up the courage of Ivan, by painting in glowing terms all his brilliant future. She seemed to have laid aside her personal feelings, and to look on him only as one doing battle with fortune, in the hope of earning the hand of the rich widow of Yakoutsk. But Ivan was much disposed to gloomy fits; he supposed himself forgotten and slighted, and looked on the time of his probation as interminable. While in this mood, one day, he was roused from his fit, by a challenge from Kolina to go and see if the seals had come up to breathe at the hole which every morning was freshly broken in the ice. Ivan assented, and away they went gaily down to the bay. No seals were there, and after a short stay they returned towards the hut, recalled by the distant howling of the dogs. But as they came near, they could see no sign of men or animals, though the sensible brutes still whined under the shelter of their snow heaps. Ivan, much surprised, raised the curtain of the door, his gun in hand, expecting to find that some animal was inside. The lamp was out, and the hut in total darkness. Before Ivan could recover his upright position, four men leaped upon him, and he was a prisoner.

Kolina drew back, and cocked her gun; but the natives, satisfied with their present prey, formed round Ivan in a compact body, tied his hands, and bade him walk. Their looks were sufficiently wild and menacing to make him move, especially as he recognized them as belonging to the warlike party of the Tchouktchas—a tribe of Siberians, who wander about the Polar Seas in search of game; who cross Behring's Straits in skin-boats, and are probably the only persons who, by their temporary sojourn in New Siberia, have caused some to suppose that it is inhabited. Kolina stood uncertain what to do, but in a few minutes she roused four of the dogs, and followed. Ivan bawled to her to go back; but the girl paid no attention to his request, determined, as it seemed, to know his fate.

The savages hurried Ivan along as rapidly as they could, and soon entered a deep and narrow ravine, which, about the middle, parted into two. The narrowest path was selected, and the dwelling of the natives was soon reached. It was a cavern, the narrow entrance of which they crawled through; Ivan followed the leader, and soon found himself in a large and wonderful cave. It was by nature divided into several compartments, and contained a party of twenty men, as many or more women, and numerous children. It was warmed in two ways—by wood fires and grease lamps, and by a bubbling semi-sulphurous spring, that rushed up through a narrow hole, and then fell away into a deep well, that carried its warm waters to mingle with the icy sea. The acrid smoke escaped by holes in the roof. Ivan, his arms and legs bound, was thrust into a separate compartment, filled with furs, and formed by a projection of the rock and the skin-boats, which this primitive race employed to cross the most stormy seas. He was almost stunned: he lay for a while without thought or motion. Gradually he recovered, and gazed around: all was night, save above, where, by a narrow orifice, he saw the smoke, which hung in clouds around the roof, escaping. He expected death. He knew the savage race he was among, who hated interference with their hunting-grounds, and whose fish he and his party had taken. What, therefore, was his surprise when, from the summit of the roof, he heard a gentle voice whispering his own name in soft accents. His ears must, he thought, deceive him. The hubbub close at hand was terrible. A dispute was going on. Men, women, and children, all joined, and yet he had heard the word "Ivan." "Kolina," he replied, in equally low but clear tones. As he spoke, a knife rolled near him; but he could not touch it. Then a dark form filled the orifice about a dozen feet above his head, and something moved down among projecting stones, and then Kolina stood by him. In an instant Ivan was free, and an axe in his hand. The exit was before them. Steps were cut in the rock, to ascend to the upper entrance, near which Ivan had been placed without fear, because tied. But a rush was heard, and the friends had only time to throw themselves deeper into the cave, when four men rushed in, knife in hand, to immolate the victim. Such had been the decision come to, after the debate.

Their lamps revealed the escape of the fugitive. A wild cry drew all the men together, and then up they scampered along the rugged projections, and the barking of the dogs as they fled, showed that the savages were in hot and eager chase. Ivan and Kolina lost no time. They advanced boldly, knife and hatchet in hand, sprang amid the terrified women, darted across their horrid cavern, and before one of them had recovered from her fright, they were in the open air. On they ran in the gloom for some distance, when they suddenly heard voices muttering. Down they sank behind the first large stone, concealing themselves in the snow as well as they could. The party moved slowly on towards them.

"I can trace their tracks still," said Sakalar, in a low, deep tone. "On while they are alive, or at least for vengeance!"

"Friends!" cried Ivan.

"Father!" said Kolina, and in an instant the whole party were united. Five words were enough to determine Sakalar. They all rushed back in a body, entered the cavern, and found themselves masters of it without a struggle: the women and children attempted no resistance. As soon as they were placed in a corner, under the guard of the Kolimsk men, a council was held. Sakalar, as the most experienced, decided what was to be done. He knew the value of threats: one of the women was released, and bade go tell the men what had occurred. She was to add the offer of a treaty of peace, to which, if both parties agreed, the women were to be given up on the one side, and the hut and its contents on the other. But the victors announced their intention of taking four of the best-looking boys as hostages, to be returned whenever they were convinced of the good faith of the Tchouktchas. The envoy soon returned, agreeing to everything. Sakalar had not gone near the hut, fearing an ambuscade. The four boys were at once selected, and the belligerents separated.

Sakalar made the little fellows run before, and thus the hut was regained. An inner cabin was at once erected for the prisoners, and the dogs were placed over them as spies. But as the boys understood Sakalar to mean that the dogs were to eat them if they stirred, they remained still enough, and made no attempt to run away.

A hasty meal was now cooked, and after its conclusion, Ivan related the events of the day, warmly dilating on the devotion and courage of Kolina, who, with the keenness of a Yakouta, had found out his prison by the smoke, and had seen him on the ground, despite the gloom. Sakalar then explained how, on his return, he had been terribly alarmed, and had followed the trail on the snow. After mutual congratulations, the whole party went to sleep.

Early the next morning, the mothers came humbly with provisions for their children. They received some trifling presents, and were sent away in delight. About mid-day the whole tribe presented themselves unarmed, within a short distance of the hut, and offered to traffic. They brought a great quantity of fish, which they wanted to exchange for tobacco. Sakalar, who spoke their language freely, first gave them a roll, letting them understand it was in payment of the fish taken without leave. This at once dissipated all feelings of hostility, and solid peace was insured. So satisfied was Sakalar of their sincerity, that he at once released the captives.

From that day the two parties were one, and all thoughts of war were completely at an end. A vast deal of bloodshed had been prevented by a few concessions on both sides. The same result might, indeed, have been come to, by killing half of each little tribe; but it is doubtful if the peace would afterwards have been as satisfactory to the survivors.

CHAPTER VII.

THE SUMMER AND AUTUMN.

OCCUPIED with the chase, with bartering, and with conversing with their new friends, the summer gradually came round. The snow melted, the hills became a series of cascades, and in every direction water poured towards the sea. But the hut remained solid and firm, a little earth only being cast over the snow. Flocks of ducks and geese soon appeared, a slight vegetation was visible, and the sea was in motion. But one object now principally attracted all eyes. Vast heaps of fossil ivory were exposed to view on the banks of the stream, and were laid bare more and more every year by the torrents of spring. A few days sufficed to collect a heap greater than they could take away on the sledges in a dozen journeys. Ivan gazed at his treasure in mute despair. Were it all at Yakoutsk, he would be the richest merchant in Siberia; but to take it thither seemed impossible. However, in stepped the adventurous Tchouktchas. They offered, for a stipulated sum in tobacco and other valuables, to land a large portion of the ivory at a certain spot on the shores of Siberia, by means of their boats. Ivan, though again surprised at the daring of these wild men, accepted their proposal, and engaged to give them his whole stock. The matter was thus settled, and our adventurers and their new friends dispersed to their summer avocations.

These consisted in fishing and hunting, and repairing boats and sledges. The canoes of the Tchouktchas were wholly made of skins and whalebone, and bits of wood; but they were large, and capable of sustaining great weight. Their owners proposed to start as soon as the ice was wholly broken up, and to brave all the dangers of so fearful a navigation. They were used to impel themselves along in every open space, and to take shelter on icebergs from danger. When one of these icy mountains went in the right direction, they stuck to it; but at other times they paddled away amid dangers, of which they seemed wholly unconscious.

A month was taken up in fishing, in drying the fish, or in putting it into holes where there was eternal frost;

An immense stock of seals' flesh, of oil and fat, was laid in; and then one morning, with a warm wind behind, the Tchouktchas took their departure, and the small party of adventurers remained alone. Their hut was now broken up, the sledges put in order, the tent erected, and all made ready for their second journey. The sledges were not only repaired, but enlarged, to bear the heaviest possible load at starting. Overloading for a few days was not minded, as the provisions would soon decrease. Still, not half so much could be taken as they wished, and yet Ivan had nearly a ton of ivory, and thirty tons was the greatest produce of any one year, in all Siberia.

But the sledges were ready long before the sea was frozen. The interval was spent in continued hunting, to prevent any consumption of the travelling store. Long before it was over, all were heartily tired of a day nearly as long as two English months, and hailed with pleasure the sight of the first white fox. Soon ducks and geese began to disappear, the fish sank away, and were rare, the bears came roaring round the camp, and then the scanty vegetation and the arid rocks were covered with a thin coat of snow. The winter at once set in with intense rigour; the sea ceased to toss and heave; the icebergs and fields of ice moved more and more slowly; and at last ocean and land were blended into one—the night of a month was come, and the sun was seen no more.

The dogs were now roused up, having been well fed during the summer; the sledges were harnessed, and the instant the sea was firm enough to sustain them, the party started. Sakalar's intention was to try forced marches in a straight line. Fortune favoured them. The frost was unusually severe, and the ice thicker and more solid than it had been the previous year. Not a single accident occurred to them for some days. At first they did not move exactly in the same direction as that in which they had come, making more towards the east; but they soon found traces of their previous winter's journey, proving that a whole plain of ice had been forced away at least fifty miles during the thaw. This was Sakalar's explanation, but the men of Kolimsk persisted in stating that they were going wrong. A dispute ensued, which threatened to break up the party. But Ivan declared that he would pay no one who abandoned the guidance of Sakalar; so the three men obeyed.

The road was now again rugged and difficult; firing was getting scarce, the dogs were devouring the fish with rapidity, and only half the ocean journey was over. On they pushed, however, with desperate energy; every eye once more keenly on the look-out for game. But this time a stray fox alone rewarded their exertions. No man spoke. Every one drove his team in sullen silence, for all were on short allowance, and all were hungry. They sat upon what was to them more valuable than gold, and yet they had not what was necessary for subsistence. The dogs were urged every day to the utmost of their strength. But so much space had been taken up by the ivory, that at last there remained neither food nor fuel. None knew at what distance they were from the shore, and their position seemed desperate. There were even whispers of killing some of the dogs; and Sakalar and Ivan were loudly upbraided for their avarice, which had brought the party to such straits.

"See!" said the old hunter suddenly, and with a delighted smile, pointing towards the south.

The whole party looked eagerly. A thick column of smoke rose in the air, at no very considerable distance, curling up in dark wreaths, and then dispersing in light vapour. This signal was agreed upon with the Tchouktchas, who were to camp where there was plenty of wood, and thus guide them in the right direction by a continued beacon.

Every hand was raised to urge on the dogs towards this point. The hungry and weary animals pulled, but unwillingly. They were impelled forward, however, by every art; and at last, from the summit of a hill of ice, they saw the shore and the blaze of the fire. The wind was towards them, and the atmosphere was heavy. The dogs smelled the distant camp, and darted forward almost recklessly. The adventurers kept themselves in readiness to leap, in case of being overturned. But the will of the animals was greater than their power, and they sank near the Tchouktcha huts, panting and exhausted.

Their allies of the spring were true to their plighted faith, and gave them food, of which both man and beast stood in the most pressing need. Dogs and men ate greedily, and then all sought repose. The Tchouktchas had performed their journey with wonderful success and rapidity, and had found time to lay in a pretty fair stock of fish. This they freely shared with Ivan and his party, and were delighted when he abandoned to them his whole stock of tobacco and rum, and part of his tea. Two days were spent in the mutual interchange of good offices, in repose, and in letting the dogs recover from their prostration. But no more time could be spared. There were many days' journey yet before them, and certainly there were not provisions enough for the time.

The Tchouktchas, too, had been absent four years in their wanderings, and were eager to get home once more to the land of the reindeer, and to their friends. They were, perhaps, the greatest travellers of a tribe noted for its faculty of locomotion. And so, with warm expressions of esteem and friendship on both sides, the two parties separated—the men of the east making their way on foot towards the Straits of Behring.

CHAPTER VIII.

THE VOYAGE HOME.

UNDER considerable disadvantages did Sakalar, Ivan, and their friends prepare for the conclusion of their journey. their provisions were very scanty, and their only hope of replenishing their stores, was on the banks of the Vchivaya River, which being in some places pretty rapid, might not be frozen over. Sakalar and his friends determined to strike out in a straight line. Part of the ivory had to be concealed and abandoned, to be fetched another time; but as their stock of provisions was so small, they were able to take the principal portion. After some debate, it had been resolved to make in a direct line for the Vchivaya River, and thence to Nijnei-Kolimsk. The road was of a most difficult, and, in parts, unknown character; but it was imperative to move in as straight a direction as possible. Time was the great enemy they had to contend with, because their provisions were sufficient for only a limited period.

The country was at first level enough, and the dogs, after their rest, made very satisfactory progress. At night they had reached the commencement of a hilly region, while in the distance could already be seen rather lofty mountains.

According to a plan decided upon from the first, the human members of the party were at once placed on short allowance, while the dogs received as much food as could reasonably be given. At early dawn the tent was struck, and the dogs were impelled along the banks of a small river completely frozen. Indeed, after a short distance, it was taken as the smoothest path. But at the end of a dozen miles they found themselves in a narrow gorge between two hills, and at the foot of a once foaming cataract, now hard frozen. It was necessary to retreat some miles, and gain the land once more. The only path which was now found practicable was along the bottom of some pretty steep rocks. But the track got narrower and narrower, until the dogs were drawing them along the edge of a terrific precipice, with not four feet of holding. All alighted, and led the dogs, for a false step was death. Fortunately the pathway became no narrower, and in one place it widened out, and made a sort of hollow. Here a bitter blast, almost strong enough to cast them from their feet, checked further progress; and on that naked spot, under a projecting mass of stone, and without fire, the whole party halted. Men and dogs huddled together for warmth, and all dined on raw and frozen fish. A few hours of sleep, however, were snatched; and then, as the storm abated, they again advanced. The descent was soon reached, and led into a vast plain without tree or bush. A range of snow-clad hills lay before them, and the only practicable pathway was through a narrow gully between two mountains. But all hearts were gladdened by the welcome sight of some *argali*, or Siberian sheep, on the slope of a hill. These animals are the only winter game, bears and wolves excepted. Kolina was left with the dogs, and the rest started after the animals, which were pawing in the thin snow for some moss or half-frozen herbs. Every caution was used to approach them against the wind, and a general volley soon sent them scampering away to the mountain-tops, leaving three behind.

But Ivan saw that he had wounded another, and away he went in chase of it. The animal ascended a hill, and then halted. But seeing a man coming quickly in pursuit it turned and fled down the opposite side. Ivan was instantly after him. The descent was steep, but the hunter only saw the argali, and darted down. He slided rather than ran with fearful rapidity, and passed the sheep by not checking himself soon enough. A tremendous gulf was before him, and his eye caught an instant glimpse of a deep distant valley. Then he saw no more until he found himself lying still. On the very brink of the precipice he had sunk into a deep snow-bank formed by some projecting rock, and had only thus been saved from instant death. Deeply grateful, Ivan crept cautiously up the hill-side, though not without his prize, and rejoined his companions.

The road now offered innumerable difficulties. It was rough and uneven—now hard, now soft. They made but slow progress for the next three days, while their provisions began to draw to an end. They had still at least a dozen days' journey before them. All agreed that they were now in the very worst plight in which they had yet been. On the evening when they dined on their last meal of mutton and fish, they were at the foot of a lofty hill, which they determined to ascend while strength was left. The dogs were urged up the steep ascent, and after two hours' toil they reached the summit. It was a table-land, bleak and miserable, and the wind was too severe to permit camping. On they pushed, therefore, and camped a little way down its side.

The next morning the dogs had no food, while the

men had nothing but large draughts of warm tea; but it was impossible to stop. Away they hurried, after deciding that, if nothing turned up by the next morning, two or three of the dogs must be killed to save the rest of the party. Little was the ground they got over with hungry beasts and starving men, and all were glad to halt near a few dried larches. Men and dogs eyed each other suspiciously. The animals, sixty-four in number, had they not been educated to fear man, would soon have settled the matter. But there they lay, panting and faint—to start up suddenly with a fearful howl. A bear was on them. Sakalar fired, and then in rushed the dogs savage and fierce. It was worse than useless; it was dangerous for the human beings of the party to seek to share this windfall. It was enough that the dogs had found something to appease their hunger.

Sakalar, however, knew that his faint and weary companions could not move the next day, if tea alone were their sustenance that night. He accordingly put in practice one of the devices of his woodcraft. The youngest of the larches was cut down, and the coarse outside bark taken off. Then every atom of the soft bark was peeled off the tree, and being broken into small pieces, was cast into the iron pot, already full of boiling water. The quantity was great, and made a thick substance. Round this the whole party collected, eager for the moment when they could fall to. But Sakalar was cool and methodical even in that terrible hour. He took a spoon, and quietly skimmed the pot, to take away the resin that rose to the surface. Then gradually the bark melted away, and presently the pot was filled with a thick paste, that looked not unlike glue. All gladly ate, and found it nutritive, pleasant, and warm. They felt satisfied when the meal was over, and were glad to observe that the dogs returned to the camp, completely satisfied also, which, under the circumstances, was matter for great congratulation.

In the morning, after another mess of larch-bark soup, and after a little tea, the adventurers again continued their journey. They were now in an arid, bleak, and terrible plain of vast extent. Not a tree, not a shrub, not an elevation was to be seen. Starvation was again staring them in the face, and no man knew when this dreadful plain would end. That night the whole party cowered in their tent, without fire, content to chew a few tea-leaves preserved from the last meal. Serious thoughts were now entertained of abandoning their wealth in that wild region. But as no one pressed the matter, the sledges were harnessed again next morning, and the dogs driven on. But man and beast were at the last gasp, and not ten miles were traversed that day, when they came to a large river, on the borders of which were some trees. Being wild and rapid, the river was not frozen, and there was still hope. The seine was drawn from a sledge, and taken into the water. It was fastened from one side to another of a narrow gut, and there left. It was of no avail examining it until morning, for the fish only came out at night.

There was not a man of the party who had his exact senses about him; while the poor dogs lay panting on the snow, their tongues hanging out, and their eyes glaring with almost savage fury. The trees round the bank were large and dry, and not one had an atom of soft bark upon it. The only resource they had was to drink huge draughts of tea, and then seek sleep. Sakalar set the example, and the Kolimsk men, to whom such scenes were not new, followed his advice; but Ivan walked up and down before the tent. A huge fire had been made, which was amply fed by the wood of the river bank, and it blazed on high, showing in bold relief the features of the scene. Ivan gazed vacantly at everything; but he saw not the dark and glancing river—he saw not the bleak plain of snow—his eyes looked not on the romantic picture of the tent and its bivouac-fire: his thoughts were on one thing alone. He it was who had brought them to that pass, and on his head rested all the misery endured by man and beast, and, worst of all, by the good and devoted Kolina.

There she sat, too, on the ground, wrapped in her warm clothes, her eyes fixed on the crackling logs. Of what was she thinking? Whatever occupied her mind, it was soon chased away by the sudden speech of Ivan. "Kolina," said he, in a tone which borrowed a little of intensity from the state of mind in which hunger had placed all of them, "canst thou ever forgive me?"

"What?" replied the young girl, softly.

"My having brought you here to die, far away from your native hills?"

"Kolina cares little for herself," said the Yakouta maiden, rising and speaking perhaps a little wildly; "let her father escape, and she is willing to lie near the tombs of the old people on the borders of the icy sea."

"But Ivan had hoped to see for Kolina many bright happy days; for Ivan would have made her father rich, and Kolina would have been the richest unmarried girl in the plain of Miouré!"

"And would riches make Kolina happy?" she said, sadly.

"Young girl of the Yakouta, hearken to me! Let Ivan live or die this hour: Ivan is a fool. He left home and comfort, to cross the icy seas in search of wealth, and to gain happiness; but if he had only had eyes he would have stopped at Miouré. There he saw a girl, lively as the heaven-fire in the north, good, generous, kind; and she was an old friend, and might have loved Ivan; but the man of Yakoutsk was blind, and told her of his passion for a selfish widow, and the Yakouta maiden never thought of Ivan but as a brother!"

"What means Ivan?" asked Kolina, trembling with emotion.

"Ivan has long meant, when he should come to the yourte of Sakalar, to lay his wealth at his feet, and beg of his old friend to give him his child; but Ivan now fears that he may die, and wishes to know what would have been the answer of Kolina?"

"But Maria Vorotinska?" urged the girl, who seemed dreaming.

"Has long been forgotten. How could I not love my old playmate and friend! Kolina—Kolina, listen to Ivan! Forget his love for the widow of Yakoutsk, and Ivan will stay in the plain of Vchivaya, and die."

"Kolina is very proud," whispered the girl, sitting down on a log near the fire, and speaking in a low tone; "and Kolina thinks yet that the friend of her father has forgotten himself. But if he be not wild, if the sufferings of the journey have not made him say that which is not, Kolina would be very happy."

"Be plain, girl of Mioure—maiden of the Yakouta tribe! and play not with the heart of a man. Can Kolina take Ivan as her husband?"

A frank and happy reply gave the Yakoutsk merchant all the satisfaction he could wish; and then followed several hours of those sweet and delightful explanations, which never end between young lovers, when first they have acknowledged their mutual affection. They had hitherto concealed so much, that there was much to tell!

and Ivan and Kolina, who for nearly three years had lived together, with a bar between their deep but concealed affection, seemed to have no end of words. Ivan had begun to find his feelings change, from the very hour when Sakalar's daughter volunteered to accompany him, but it was only in the cave of New Siberia that his heart had been completely won.

So short, and quiet, and sweet were the hours, that the time of rest passed by without thought of sleep. Suddenly, however, they were roused to a sense of their situation, and leaving their wearied and exhausted companions still asleep, they moved with doubt and dread to the water's side. Life was now doubly dear to both, and their fancy painted the coming forth of an empty net as the termination of all hope. But the net came heavily and slowly to land. It was full of fish. They were on the well-stocked Vchivaya. More than three hundred fish, small and great, were drawn on shore; and then they recast the net.

"Up, man and beast!" thundered Ivan, as, after selecting two dozen of the finest, he abandoned the rest to the dogs.

The animals, faint and weary, greedily seized on the food given them, while Sakalar and the Kolimsk men could scarcely believe their senses. The hot coals were at once brought into requisition, and the party were soon regaling themselves on a splendid meal of tea and broiled fish. I should alarm my readers did I record the quantities eaten. An hour later, every individual was a changed being, but most of all, the lovers. Despite their want of rest, they looked fresher than any of the party. It was determined to camp at least twenty-four hours more in that spot; and the Kolimsk men declared that as the river must be the Vchivaya, they could draw the seine all day, for the river was deep, its waters warmer than others, and its abundance of fish such as to border on the fabulous. They went accordingly down to the side of the stream, and then the happy Kolina gave free vent to her joy. She burst out into a song of her native land, and gave way to some demonstrations of delight, the result of her earlier education, which astonished Sakalar. But when he heard that during that dreadful night he had found a son, Sakalar himself well nigh lost his reason. The old man loved Ivan almost as much as his own child, and when he saw the youth in his yourte, on his hunting trips, he had formed some project of the kind now brought about; but the confessions of Ivan on his last visit to Miouré, had driven all such thoughts away.

"Art in earnest, Ivan?" said he, after a pause of some duration.

"In earnest!" exclaimed Ivan, laughing; "why I fancy the young men of Miouré will find me so, if they seek to question my right to Kolina."

Kolina smiled and looked happy; and the old hunter heartily blessed his children, adding, that the proudest, dearest hope of his heart was now within probable realization.

The predictions of the Kolimsk men were realized. The river gave them as much fish as they needed for their journey home; and as Sakalar now knew his way, there was little fear for the future. An ample stock was piled on the sledges, the dogs had unlimited feeding for two days, and then away they sped towards an upper part of the river, which, being broad and shallow, was no doubt frozen on the surface. They found it as they expected, and even discovered that the river was gradually freezing all the way down. But caring little for this now, on they went, and after considerable fatigue, and some delay, they arrived at Kolimsk, to the utter astonishment of all the inhabitants, who had long given them up for lost.

Great rejoicings took place. The friends of the three Kolimsk men gave a grand festival, wherein the rum, tobacco, and tea, which had been left at the place as payment for their journey, played a conspicuous part. Then, as it was necessary to remain here some time, while the ivory was brought from the deposit near the sea, Ivan and Kolina were married. Neither of them seemed to credit the circumstance, even when fast tied by the Russian Church. It had come so suddenly, so unexpectedly on both, that their heads could not quite make the affair out. But they were married in down right earnest, and Kolina was a proud and happy woman. The enormous mass of ivory brought to Kolimsk excited the attention of a distinguished exile, who drew up a statement in Ivan's name, and prepared it for transmission to the White Czar, as the emperor is called in these parts.

When summer came, the young couple, with Sakalar and a caravan of merchants, started for Yakoutsk, Ivan being by far the richest and most important member of the party. After a single day's halt at Miouré, on they went to the town, and made their triumphal entry in September. Ivan found Maria Vorotinska a wife and mother, and his vanity was not much wounded by the falsehood. The *ci-devant* widow was a little astonished at Ivan's return, and particularly at his treasure of ivory; but she received his wife with politeness, a little tempered by her sense of her own superiority to a savage, as she designated Kolina to her friends in a whisper. But Kolina was so gentle, so pretty, so good, so cheerful, so happy, that she found her party at once, and the two ladies became rival leaders of the fashion.

This lasted until the next year, when a messenger from the capital brought a letter to Ivan from the emperor himself, thanking him for his narrative, sending him a rich present, his warm approval, and the office of first civil magistrate in the city of Yakoutsk. This turned the scales wholly on one side, and Maria bowed low to Kolina. But Kolina had no feelings of the *parvenu*, and she was always a general favourite. Ivan accepted with pride his sovereign's favour, and by dint of assiduity, soon learned to be a useful magistrate. He always remained a good husband, a good father, and a good son, for he made the heart of old Sakalar glad. He never regretted his journey; he always declared that to it he owed wealth and happiness, a high position in society, and an admirable wife. Great rejoicings took place many years after, in Yakoutsk, at the marriage of the son of Maria, united to the daughter of Ivan, and from the first until the last, none of the parties concerned ever had reason to mourn over the perilous journey in search of the Ivory-Mine.

For the information of the non-scientific, it may be necessary to mention, that the ivory alluded to in the preceding tale, is derived from the tusks of the mammoth, or fossil elephant of the geologist. The remains of this gigantic quadruped are found all over the northern hemisphere, from the 40th to the 75th degree of latitude; but most abundantly in the region which lies between the mountains of Central Asia and the shores and islands of the Frozen Sea. So profusely do they exist in this region that the tusks have, for more than a century, constituted an important article of traffic—furnishing a large proportion of the ivory required by the carver and turner. The remains lie embedded in the upper tertiary clays and gravels; and these, by exposure to river-currents, to the waves of the sea, and other erosive agencies, are frequently swept away during the thaws of summer, leaving tusks and bones, in masses, and, occasionally, even entire skeletons, in a wonderful state of preservation. The most perfect specimen yet obtained, and from the study of which the zoologist has been enabled to arrive at an accurate knowledge of the structure and habits of the mammoth, is that discovered by a Tungusian fisherman near the mouth of the river Lena, in the summer of 1799. Being in the habit of collecting tusks among the *débris* of the gravel cliffs (for it is generally at a considerable elevation in the cliffs and river banks that the remains occur), he observed a strange, shapeless mass projecting from an ice-bank, some fifty or sixty feet above the river; during next summer's thaw he saw the same object rather more disengaged from amongst the ice; in 1801 he could distinctly perceive the tusk and flank of an immense animal; and in 1803, in consequence of an earlier and more powerful thaw, the huge carcase became entirely disengaged, and fell on the sand-bank beneath. In the spring of the following year the fisherman cut off the tusks, which he sold for 50 roubles (£7 10s.); and two years afterwards, our countryman, Mr. Adams, visited the spot, and gives the following account of this extraordinary phenomenon:—"At this time I found the mammoth still in the same place, but altogether mutilated. The discoverer was content with his profit for the tusks and the Yakoutski of the neighbourhood had cut off the flesh, with which they fed their dogs; during the scarcity, and beasts, such as white bears, wolves, wolverines, and foxes, also fed upon it, and the traces of their footsteps were seen around. The skeleton, almost entirely cleared of its flesh, remained whole, with the exception of a foreleg. The head was covered with a dry skin; one of the ears, well preserved, was furnished with a tuft of hair. All these parts have necessarily been injured in transporting them a distance of 7330 miles (to the imperial museum of St. Petersburgh), but the eyes have been preserved, and the pupil of one can still be distinguished. The mammoth was a male, with a long mane on the neck. The tail and proboscis were not preserved. The skin, of which I possess three-fourths, is of a dark grey-colour, covered with reddish wool and black hairs; but the dampness of the spot where it had lain so long, had in some degree destroyed the hair. The entire carcase, of which I collected the bones on the spot, was nine feet four inches high, and sixteen feet four inches long, without including the tusks, which measured nine feet six inches along the curve. The distance from the base or root of the tusk to the point is three feet seven inches. The two tusks together weighed three hundred and sixty pounds, English weight, and the head alone four hundred and fourteen pounds. The skin was of such weight, that it required ten persons to transport it to the shore; and after having cleared the ground, upwards of thirty-six pounds of hair were collected, which the white bears had trodden while devouring the flesh."

Since then, other carcases of elephants have been discovered in a greater or less degree of preservation; as also the remains of rhinoceroses, mastodons, and allied pachyderms—the mammoth, more abundantly, in the old world, the mastodon in the new. In every case these animals differ from existing species; are of more gigantic dimensions; and, judging from their natural coverings of thick-set curly-crisped wool and strong hair, upwards of a foot in length, they were fitted to live, if not in a boreal, at least in a coldly-temperate region. Indeed, there is proof positive of the then milder climate of these regions, in the discovery of pine and birch-trunks, where no vegetation now flourishes; and further, in the fact that fragments of pine leaves, birch twigs, and other northern plants, have been detected between the grinders, and within the stomachs of these animals. We have thus evidence that, at the close of the tertiary, and shortly after the commencement of the current epoch, the northern hemisphere enjoyed a much milder climate. That it was the abode of huge pachyderms now extinct; that a different distribution of sea and land prevailed; and that, on a new distribution of sea and land, accompanied, also, by a different relative level, these animals died away, leaving their remains to be embedded in the clays, gravels, and other alluvial deposits; where, under the antiseptic influence of an almost eternal frost, many of them have been preserved as entire as at the fatal moment when they sank under the rigours of external conditions, no longer fitted for their existence. It has been attempted by some to prove the adaptability of these animals to the present conditions of the northern hemisphere; but so untenable in every phase is this opinion, that it would be sheer waste of time and space to attempt its refutation. That they may have migrated northward and southward with the seasons, is more than probable, though it has been stated that the remains diminish in size the farther north they are found; but that numerous herds of such huge animals should have existed in these regions at all, and that for thousands of years, pre-supposes an exuberant arboreal vegetation, and the necessary degree of climate for its growth and development. It has been mentioned that the mastodon and mammoth seem to have attained their meridian towards the close of the tertiary epoch, and that a few may have lived even into the current era; but it is more probable that the commencement of existing conditions was the proximate cause of their extinction, and that not a solitary specimen ever lived to be the cotemporary of man.

P. B. St. J.

THE END.

THE MAYNE REID LIBRARY.

In Foolscap 8vo, handsomely printed on toned paper, cloth gilt, price 3s. 6d. per Volume, with numerous Illustrations by HARRISON WEIR, W. HARVEY, HUARD, &c.

LOST LENORE;
Or, THE ADVENTURES OF A ROLLING STONE.

THE WILD HUNTRESS.

THE WHITE GAUNTLET.

THE MAROON;
Or, PLANTER LIFE IN JAMAICA.

THE TIGER HUNTER;
Or, A HERO IN SPITE OF HIMSELF.

THE SCALP HUNTERS;
Or, ROMANTIC ADVENTURES IN NORTHERN MEXICO.

THE RIFLE RANGERS;
Or, ADVENTURES IN SOUTHERN MEXICO.

THE HALF-BLOOD;
Or, OCEOLA, THE SEMINOLE.

THE WOOD RANGERS.

THE WHITE CHIEF:
A LEGEND OF NORTHERN MEXICO.

THE HUNTERS' FEAST;
Or, CONVERSATIONS AROUND THE CAMP FIRE.

THE CLIFF CLIMBERS;
Or, THE LONE HOME ON THE HIMALAYAS.

London: CHARLES H. CLARKE, 13, Paternoster Row.

Sold by all BOOKSELLERS and at all RAILWAY STATIONS.

CAPT. MAYNE REID'S
CELEBRATED NOVELS.

In Foolscap 8vo, price 2s. each, fancy boards.

LOST LENORE.

THE WILD HUNTRESS.

THE WHITE GAUNTLET.

THE RIFLE RANGERS.

THE CLIFF CLIMBERS.

THE SCALP HUNTERS.

THE MAROON.

THE HUNTERS' FEAST.

THE HALF-BLOOD.

THE WHITE CHIEF.

THE WOOD RANGERS.

THE TIGER HUNTER

London: CHARLES H. CLARKE, 13, Paternoster Row.

Sold by all BOOKSELLERS and at all RAILWAY STATIONS,

www.ingramcontent.com/pod-product-compliance
Lightning Source LLC
Chambersburg PA
CBHW022045230426
43672CB00008B/1075